MW01073394

The Letter to Philemon

The New International Commentary on the New Testament

General Editors

Ned B. Stonehouse
(1946–1962)

F. F. Bruce
(1962–1990)

Gordon D. Fee
(1990–2012)

Joel B. Green
(2013–)

The Letter to PHILEMON

Scot McKnight

William B. Eerdmans Publishing Company
Grand Rapids, Michigan

Wm. B. Eerdmans Publishing Co.
2140 Oak Industrial Drive NE, Grand Rapids, Michigan 49505
www.eerdmans.com

Published 2017
Printed in the United States of America

26 25 24 23 22 21 20 19 18 17 1 2 3 4 5 6 7 8 9 10

ISBN 978-0-8028-7382-8

Library of Congress Cataloging-in-Publication Data

Names: McKnight, Scot, author.
Title: The Letter to Philemon / Scot McKnight.
Description: Grand Rapids : Eerdmans Publishing Co., 2017. | Series: The New Testament commentary on the New Testament | Includes bibliographical references and index.
Identifiers: LCCN 2017025199 | ISBN 9780802873828 (hardcover : alk. paper)
Subjects: LCSH: Bible. Philemon—Commentaries.
Classification: LCC BS2765.53 .M35 2017 | DDC 227/.86077—dc23
LC record available at https://lccn.loc.gov/2017025199

Contents

TEXT AND COMMENTARY

PHILEMON

"Pastor, what do you think would have happened
if a runaway slave in America
had carried this letter back to his master?"

JAMES A. NOEL
Onesimus Our Brother, 5

General Editor's Preface

As Acts tells the story, the Lord choreographed an encounter between Philip and an Ethiopian eunuch on the road from Jerusalem to Gaza. This Ethiopian, who had a copy of at least some of the Scriptures, was reading from the prophet Isaiah. Hearing him read, Philip inquired, "Are you really grasping the significance of what you are reading?" The Ethiopian responded, "How can I, unless someone guides me?" The result was that Philip shared the good news about Jesus with him and the Ethiopian was baptized as a new Christ-follower (Acts 8:26–40).

It is difficult to imagine a more pressing mandate for the work of a commentary than this: to come alongside readers of Scripture in order to lead them so that they can grasp the significance of what they read—and to do so in ways that are not only informative but transformative. This has been and remains the aim of the New International Commentary on the New Testament. The interpretive work on display in this volume and, indeed, in this commentary series can find no better raison d'être and serve no better ambition.

What distinguishes such a commentary?

First and foremost, we are concerned with the text of Scripture. It does not mean that we are not concerned with the history of scholarship and scholarly debate. It means, rather, that we strive to provide a commentary on the text and not on the scholarly debate. It means that the centerpiece of our work is a readable guide for readers of these texts, with references to critical issues and literature, as well as interaction with them, all found in our plentiful footnotes. Nor does it mean that we eschew certain critical methods or require that each contributor follow a certain approach. Rather, we take up whatever methods and pursue whatever approaches assist our work of making plain the significance of these texts.

Second, we self-consciously locate ourselves as Christ-followers who read Scripture in the service of the church and its mission in the world. Reading in the service of the church does not guarantee a particular kind of interpretation—say, one that is supportive of the church in all times and places or that merely parrots what the church wants to say. The history of interpretation demonstrates that, at times, the Scriptures speak a needed prophetic word of challenge, calling the church back to its vocation as the church. And at other times, the Scriptures speak a word of encouragement, reminding the church of its identity as a people who follow a crucified Messiah and serve a God who will vindicate God's ways and God's people.

We also recognize that, although the Scriptures are best read and understood through prayerful study and in the context of the church's worship, our reading of them cannot be separated from the world that the church engages in mission. C. S. Lewis rightly noted that what we see is determined in part by where we are standing, and the world in which we stand presses us with questions that cannot help but inform our interpretive work.

It is not enough to talk about what God *once said*, for we need to hear again and again what the Spirit, through the Scriptures, *is now saying* to the church. Accordingly, we inquire into the theological significance of what we read, and into how this message might take root in the lives of God's people.

Finally, the New International Commentary on the New Testament is especially for pastors, teachers, and students. That is, our work is located in that place between the more critical commentaries, with their lines of untranslated Greek and Aramaic and Latin, and the homiletical commentaries that seek to work out how a text might speak to congregations. Our hope is that those preparing to teach and preach God's word will find in these pages the guide they need, and that those learning the work of exegesis will find here an exemplar worth emulating.

Joel B. Green

Author's Preface

I am profoundly grateful to Joel B. Green and the editors at Wm. B. Eerdmans Publishing Company, a publisher I have known and with whose editors I have held conversations and dined for more than forty years, for the permission to separate this beautiful Pauline letter from its common companion, Paul's letter to the Colossians. This letter, as my introduction will make clear, deserves today to be given an emancipation because it has a distinctive message for modern-day racism and slaveries of all sorts. In nearly three decades of writing I have never missed a book once finished more than Paul's letter to Philemon.

During the process of researching, reading, and writing this commentary I incurred many debts, not least to the President of Northern Seminary, Bill Shiell, our Dean Karen Walker Freeburg, and the Board of Trustees, one of whom and his wife, Jim and Barb Stellwagen, accompanied me as we toured through Turkey and Greece to visit sites of Paul. My classes have heard me time and again perform Philemon in order for them to catch as much of the social realities of this letter, and my new cohort in New Testament studies will be reading Philemon this year as we work our way into more knowledge of Greek.

One of those students, Justin Gill, asked to work with me and he spent a good block of his time researching modern slavery. His work found its way into the introduction as he helped me think through what Paul would be saying to churches today about slaveries of various sorts. My former graduate assistant, Tara Beth Leach, now the senior pastor at "PazNaz" in Pasadena, in her trustworthy way made copy after copy and found book and article one after the other so I could concentrate on the reading and writing of Philemon. So nervous was she the first time we talked about this book that she somehow pronounced the dear man "Phillymon." He became "Phillymon" in more than one conversation with her.

I have spoken about Philemon more than I have been asked to in the last few years. My wife, Kris, has become an expert on the letter herself. I promise her only that the message of this letter will stick with us even if I will in the future begin to speak about other topics. For now, though, I am a changed person because of this commentary.

Ordinary Time
2016

Abbreviations

AB	Anchor Bible
ABD	Anchor Bible Dictionary
AGJU	Arbeiten zur Geschichte des antiken Judentums und des Urchristentums
AJP	*American Journal of Philology*
ANF	Ante-Nicene Fathers
ANTC	Abingdon New Testament Commentaries
BDAG	Danker, Frederick W., Walter Bauer, William F. Arndt, and F. Wilbur Gingrich. *Greek-English of the New Testament and Other Early Christian Literature.* 3rd ed. Chicago: University of Chicago Press, 2000 (Danker-Bauer-Arndt-Gingrich).
BDF	Blass, Friedrich, Albert Debrunner, and Robert W. Funk. *A Greek Grammar of the New Testament and Other Early Christian Literature.* Chicago: University of Chicago Press, 1961.
Bib	*Biblica*
BJRL	*Bulletin of the John Rylands University Library of Manchester*
BR	*Biblical Research*
BZNW	Beihefte zur Zeitschrift für die neutestamentliche Wissenschaft
CBQ	*Catholic Biblical Quarterly*
CEB	Common English Bible
CGTC	Cambridge Greek Testament Commentary
CurBR	*Currents in Biblical Research*
DNTB	*Dictionary of New Testament Background.* Edited by Craig A. Evans and Stanley E. Porter. Downers Grove, IL: InterVarsity Press, 2000.
DPL	*Dictionary of Paul and His Letters.* Edited by Gerald F. Hawthorne and Ralph P. Martin. Downers Grove, IL: InterVarsity Press, 1993.

EDNT	*Exegetical Dictionary of the New Testament*. Edited by Horst Balz and Gerhard Schneider. ET. 3 vols. Grand Rapids: Eerdmans, 1990–1993.
EFN	Estudios de filología neotestamentaria
EKKNT	Evangelische-katholischer Kommentar zum Neuen Testament
EvQ	*Evangelical Quarterly*
ExpTim	*Expository Times*
FC	Fathers of the Church
FF	Foundation and Facets
HNT	Handbuch zum Neuen Testament
HTR	*Harvard Theological Review*
HUT	Hermeneutische Untersuchungen zur Theologie
ICC	International Critical Commentary
JBL	*Journal of Biblical Literature*
JEH	*Journal of Ecclesiastical History*
JSNT	*Journal for the Study of the New Testament*
JSNTSup	Journal for the Study of the New Testament Supplement Series
JSSR	*Journal for the Scientific Study of Religion*
LCL	Loeb Classical Library
LEC	Library of Early Christianity
L&N	Louw, Johannes P., and Eugene A. Nida, eds. *Greek-English Lexicon of the New Testament: Based on Semantic Domains*. 2nd ed. New York: United Bible Societies, 1989.
LNTS	The Library of New Testament Studies
NCB	New Century Bible
NewDocs	*New Documents Illustrating Early Christianity*. Edited by Greg H. R. Horsley and Stephen Llewelyn. North Ryde, NSW: The Ancient History Documentary Research Centre, Macquarie University, 1981–.
NICNT	New International Commentary on the New Testament
NIDNTTE	*New International Dictionary of New Testament Theology and Exegesis*. Edited by Moisés Silva. 5 vols. Grand Rapids: Zondervan, 2014.
NIGTC	New International Greek Testament Commentary
NIV	New International Version
NovT	*Novum Testamentum*
NPNF[1]	*Nicene and Post-Nicene Fathers*, Series 1
NTOA	Novum Testamentum et Orbis Antiquus
NTS	*New Testament Studies*
NTTS	New Testament Tools and Studies
ÖTK	Ökumenischer Taschenbuch-Kommentar
P.Oxy.	Oxyrhynchus Papyri

PRSt	*Perspectives in Religious Studies*
R&T	*Religion and Theology*
ResQ	*Restoration Quarterly*
SBLDS	Society of Biblical Literature Dissertation Series
SecCent	*Second Century*
SP	Sacra Pagina
TJ	*Trinity Journal*
TLNT	*Theological Lexicon of the New Testament*. C. Spicq. Translated and edited by J. D. Ernest. 3 vols. Peabody, MA: Hendrickson, 1994.
TNTC	Tyndale New Testament Commentaries
TynBul	*Tyndale Bulletin*
USQR	*Union Seminary Quarterly Review*
WMANT	Wissenschaftliche Monographien zum Alten und Neuen Testament
WUNT	Wissenschaftliche Untersuchungen zum Neuen Testament
ZNW	*Zeitschrift für die Neutestamentliche Wissenschaft und die Kunde der älteren Kirche*

Bibliography

I. COMMENTARIES

These commentaries are cited by last name, volume number where appropriate, and page.

Arzt-Grabner, Peter. *Philemon*. Papyrologische Kommentar zum Neuen Testament 1. Göttingen: Vandenhoeck & Ruprecht, 2003.

Barclay, John M. G. *Colossians and Philemon*. New Testament Guides. London: T&T Clark, 2004.

Barth, Markus, and Helmut Blanke. *The Letter to Philemon*. Eerdmans Critical Commentary. Grand Rapids: Eerdmans, 2000.

Bentley, Kristen Plinke. "Philemon." Pages 759–62 in *IVP Women's Bible Commentary*. Edited by Catherine Clark Kroeger and Mary J. Evans. Downers Grove, IL: InterVarsity Press, 2002.

Bird, Michael F. *Colossians and Philemon: A New Covenant Commentary*. Eugene, OR: Cascade, 2009.

Bruce, F. F. *The Epistles to the Colossians, to Philemon, and to the Ephesians*. NICNT. Grand Rapids: Eerdmans, 1984.

Callahan, Allen Dwight. *Embassy of Onesimus: The Letter of Paul to Philemon*. Valley Forge, PA: Bloomsbury T&T Clark, 1997.

Dunn, James D. G. *The Epistles to the Colossians and to Philemon*. NIGTC. Grand Rapids: Eerdmans, 1996.

Felder, Cain Hope. "The Letter to Philemon: Introduction, Commentary, and Reflections." Pages 881–905 in *The New Interpreter's Bible* 11. Edited by Leander E. Keck. Nashville, TN: Abingdon, 2000.

Fitzmyer, Joseph A. *The Letter to Philemon*. AB. New York: Doubleday, 2000.

Gorday, Peter J., ed. *Ancient Christian Commentary on Scripture: Colossians, Thessalonians, Timothy, Titus, Philemon*. Downers Grove, IL: InterVarsityPress, 2000.

Harris, Murray J. *Colossians and Philemon*. Exegetical Guide to the Greek New Testament. Nashville: Broadman & Holman, 2010.

Hübner, Hans. *An Philemon, An Die Kolosser, An Die Epheser*. HNT 12. Tübingen: Mohr Siebeck, 1997.

Iralu, Sanyu. "Philemon." Pages 1705–7 in *South Asia Bible Commentary*. Edited by Brian Wintle. Grand Rapids: Zondervan, 2015.

Lewis, Lloyd A. "Philemon." Pages 437–43 in *True to Our Native Land: An African American New Testament Commentary*. Edited by Brian K. Blount. Minneapolis: Fortress, 2007.

Lightfoot, J. B. *Saint Paul's Epistles to the Colossians and to Philemon*. London: Macmillan, 1879.

Lohse, Eduard. *Colossians and Philemon*. Hermeneia. Philadelphia: Fortress, 1988.

Martin, Ralph P. *Colossians and Philemon*. NCB. Grand Rapids: Eerdmans, 1982.

Moo, Douglas J. *The Letters to the Colossians and to Philemon*. Pillar New Testament Commentary. Grand Rapids: Eerdmans, 2008.

Moule, C. F. D. *The Epistles to the Colossians and to Philemon*. CGTC. Cambridge: Cambridge University Press, 1957.

Osiek, Caroline. *Philippians, Philemon*. ANTC. Nashville: Abingdon Press, 2000.

Pao, David W. *Colossians and Philemon*. Zondervan Exegetical Commentary on the New Testament 12. Grand Rapids: Zondervan, 2012.

Ryan, Judith M., and Bonnie B. Thurston. *Philippians and Philemon*. SP 10. Collegeville, MN: Liturgical Press, 2005.

Soungalo, Soro. "Philemon." Pages 1487–88 in *Africa Bible Commentary*. Edited by Tokunboh Adeyemo. Grand Rapids: Zondervan, 2006.

Stuhlmacher, Peter. *Der Brief an Philemon*. 4th ed. EKKNT 18. Neukirchen-Vluyn: Neukirchener, 2004.

Thompson, James W., and Bruce W. Longenecker. *Philippians and Philemon*. Paideia Commentaries on the New Testament. Grand Rapids: Baker Academic, 2016. (Cited as Longenecker.)

Thompson, Marianne Meye. *Colossians and Philemon*. Two Horizons New Testament Commentary. Grand Rapids: Eerdmans, 2005.

Thurston, Bonnie, and Judith M. Ryan. *Philippians and Philemon*. SP. Collegeville, MN: Liturgical Press, 2005.

Wilson, Robert McL. *Colossians and Philemon*. ICC. Edinburgh: Bloomsbury T&T Clark, 2014.

Winter, Sara C. "Philemon." Pages 301–12 in *Searching the Scriptures 2: A Feminist Commentary*. Edited by Elisabeth Schüssler-Fiorenza. New York: Crossroad, 1997.

Witherington, Ben, III. *The Letters to Philemon, the Colossians, and the Ephesians: A Socio-Rhetorical Commentary on the Captivity Epistles*. Grand Rapids: Eerdmans, 2007.

Wolter, Michael. *Der Brief an Die Kolosser. Der Brief an Philemon*. ÖTK 12. Gütersloh: Gerd Mohn, 1993.

Wright, N. T. *Colossians and Philemon*. TNTC 12. Downers Grove, IL: InterVarsity Press, 2008.

II. ANCIENT SOURCES

Aristotle. *Politics*. Translated by Harris Rackham. LCL. Cambridge: Harvard University Press, 1932.

Columella. *On Agriculture*. Translated by Harrison Boyd Ash, E. S. Forster, and Edward H. Heffner. 3 Vols. LCL. Cambridge: Harvard University Press, 1941–1955.

Cyprian. *To Demetrian*. In vol. 5 of *The Ante-Nicene Fathers*. Translated by Ernest Wallis. Edited by A. Cleveland Coxe. 1886. Repr., Peabody, MA: Hendrickson, 1994.

The Digest of Justinian. Translated by Alan Watson. 4 Vols. Rev. ed. Philadelphia: University of Pennsylvania Press, 2009.

Epictetus. *Discourses*. Translated by W. A. Oldfather. 2 Vols. LCL. Cambridge: Harvard University Press, 1925–1928.

John Chrysostom. *Homilies on Philemon*. In vol. 13 of *The Nicene and Post-Nicene Fathers*, Series 1. Translated and edited by Philip Schaff. 1889. Repr., Peabody, MA: Hendrickson, 1994.

The Orations of Marcus Tullius Cicero. Translated by C. D. Yonge. Vol. 3. London: George Bell & Sons, 1913.

Plato. *Laws*. Translated by R. G. Bury. 2 Vols. LCL. Cambridge: Harvard University Press, 1926.

Saint Basil: Ascetical Works. Translated by M. Monica Wagner. Washington, DC: Catholic University of America Press, 1950.

Seneca. *Moral Epistles*. Translated by Richard M. Gummere. 3 Vols. LCL. Cambridge: Harvard University Press, 1917–1925.

Wiedemann, Thomas, ed. *Greek and Roman Slavery*. Rev. ed. Routledge Sourcebooks for the Ancient World. New York: Routledge, 1989.

III. GENERAL BIBLIOGRAPHY

Aasgaard, Reidar. *"My Beloved Brothers and Sisters!" Christian Siblingship in Paul*. JSNTSup 265. London: T&T Clark, 2004.

Allen, David L. "The Discourse Structure of Philemon: A Study in Textlinguistics." Pages 77–96 in *Scribes and Scripture: New Testament Essays in Honor of J. Harold Greenlee*. Edited by David Alan Black. Winona Lake, IN: Eisenbrauns, 1992.

Anderson, Garwood P. *Paul's New Perspective: Charting a Soteriological Journey*. Downers Grove, IL: InterVarsity Press, 2016.

Arterbury, Andrew. *Entertaining Angels: Early Christian Hospitality in Its Mediterranean Setting*. New Testament Monographs 8. Sheffield: Sheffield Phoenix Press, 2005.

Arzt-Grabner, Peter. "How to Deal with Onesimus? Paul's Solution within the Frame of Ancient Legal and Documentary Sources." Pages 113–42 in *Philemon in Perspective: Interpreting a Pauline Letter*. Edited by D. François Tolmie. BZNW 169. Berlin: de Gruyter, 2010.

———. "Onesimus *erro*: Zur Vorgeschichte des Philemonbriefes." *ZNW* 95 (2004): 131–43.

Atkins, Robert. "Contextual Interpretation of the Letter to Philemon in the United States." Pages 205–21 in *Philemon in Perspective: Interpreting a Pauline Letter*. Edited by D. François Tolmie. BZNW 169. Berlin: de Gruyter, 2010.

Balabanski, Vicky. "Where Is Philemon? The Case for a Logical Fallacy in the Correlation of the Data in Philemon and Colossians 1.1–2; 4.7–18." *JSNT* 38 (2015): 131–50.

Balch, David L. "Household Codes." Pages 25–50 in *Greco-Roman Literature and the New Testament: Selected Forms and Genres*. Edited by David E. Aune. Atlanta: Scholars Press, 1988.

Banks, Robert. *Paul's Idea of Community*. Rev. ed. Peabody, MA: Hendrickson, 1994.

Barclay, John M. G. *Paul and the Gift*. Grand Rapids: Eerdmans, 2015.

———. "Paul, Philemon and the Dilemma of Christian Slave-Ownership." *NTS* 37 (1991): 161–86.

Barnes, Julian. *A History of the World in 10 1/2 Chapters*. New York: Vintage, 1990.

Bartchy, S. Scott. *ΜΑΛΛΟΝ ΧΡΗΣΑΙ. First Century Slavery and the Interpretation of 1 Corinthians 7:21*. SBLDS 11. Atlanta: Scholars Press, 1985.

———. "Philemon, Epistle to." Pages 305–10 in *Anchor Bible Dictionary*. Vol. 5. Edited by David Noel Freedman. New York: Doubleday, 1992.

Bates, Matthew. *Faith as Allegiance Alone: Rethinking Faith, Works, and the Gospel of Jesus the King*. Grand Rapids: Baker Academic, 2017.

Best, Ernest. "Paul's Apostolic Authority–?" *JSNT* 27 (1986): 3–25.

Bieberstein, Sabine. "Disrupting the Normal Reality of Slavery: A Feminist Reading of the Letter to Philemon." *JSNT* 79 (2000): 105–16.

Boers, Hendrikus. "Ἀγάπη and Χάρις in Paul's Thought." *CBQ* 59 (1997): 693–713.

Bohlen, Maren. *Sanctorum Communio: Die Christen als "Heilige" bei Paulus*. BZNW 183. Berlin: de Gruyter, 2011.

Botha, Pieter J. J. "Hierarchy and Obedience: The Legacy of the Letter to Philemon." Pages 251–71 in *Philemon in Perspective: Interpreting a Pauline Letter*. Edited by D. François Tolmie. BZNW 169. Berlin: de Gruyter, 2010.

Bradley, Keith, and Paul Cartledge, eds. *The Cambridge World History of Slavery: 1. The Ancient Mediterranean World*. Cambridge: Cambridge University Press, 2011.

Bradley, Keith R. *Slavery and Rebellion in the Roman World, 140 B.C.–70 B.C.* Bloomington: Indiana University Press, 1989.

———. *Slavery and Society at Rome*. Key Themes in Ancient History. Cambridge: Cambridge University Press, 1994.

———. *Slaves and Masters in the Roman Empire: A Study in Social Control*. Oxford: Oxford University Press, 1987.

Branch, Taylor. *At Canaan's Edge: America in the King Years, 1965–68*. New York: Simon & Schuster, 2006.

———. *Parting the Waters: America in the King Years, 1954–63*. New York: Simon & Schuster, 1988.

———. *Pillar of Fire: America in the King Years, 1963–65*. New York: Simon & Schuster, 1998.

Bruce, F. F. *Paul: Apostle of the Heart Set Free*. Grand Rapids: Eerdmans, 1977.

———. *The Pauline Circle*. Milton Keynes: Paternoster, 1985.

Brueggemann, Walter. *The Psalms and the Life of Faith*. Edited by Patrick D. Miller. Minneapolis: Fortress, 1995.

Burtchaell, James Tunstead. *Philemon's Problem: A Theology of Grace*. Grand Rapids: Eerdmans, 1998.

Byron, John. *Recent Research on Paul and Slavery*. Recent Research in Biblical Studies 3. Sheffield: Phoenix, 2008.

Cadwallader, Alan H. "Name Punning and Social Sterotyping: Re-Inscribing Slavery in the Letter to Philemon." *Australian Biblical Review* 61 (2013): 44–60.

Callahan, Allen Dwight. "'Brother Saul': An Ambivalent Witness to Freedom." Pages 143–56 in *Onesimus Our Brother: Reading Religion, Race, and Culture in Philemon*. Edited by Matthew V. Johnson, James A. Noel, and Demetrius K. Williams. Paul in Critical Contexts. Minneapolis: Fortress, 2012.

———. *Embassy of Onesimus: The Letter of Paul to Philemon*. Valley Forge, PA: Bloomsbury T&T Clark, 1997.

———. "Paul's Epistle to Philemon: Toward an Alternative *Argumentum*." *HTR* 86 (1993): 357–76.

Campbell, Constantine. *Basics of Verbal Aspect in Biblical Greek*. Grand Rapids: Zondervan, 2008.

———. *Colossians and Philemon: A Handbook on the Greek Text*. Waco, TX: Baylor University Press, 2013.

Campbell, Douglas A. *The Deliverance of God: An Apocalyptic Rereading of Justification in Paul*. Grand Rapids: Eerdmans, 2013.

———. *Framing Paul: An Epistolary Biography*. Grand Rapids: Eerdmans, 2014.

———. *The Quest for Paul's Gospel*. London: T&T Clark, 2005.

———. "The Scythian Perspective in Col 3:11: A Response to Troy Martin." *NovT* 39 (1997): 81–84.

———. "Unravelling Colossians 3:11b." *NTS* 42 (1996): 120–32.

Cappon, Lester J., ed. *The Adams-Jefferson Letters: The Complete Correspondence between Thomas Jefferson and Abigail and John Adams*. Chapel Hill, NC: The University of North Carolina Press, 1988.

Chapman, Mark D. "The Shortest Book in the Bible." *ExpTim* 118 (2007): 546–48.

Church, F. Forrester. "Rhetorical Structure and Design in Paul's Letter to Philemon." *HTR* 71 (1978): 17–33.

Clarke, Andrew D. "'Refresh the Hearts of the Saints': A Unique Pauline Context?" *TynBul* 47 (1996): 277–300.

Coffey, John. *Exodus and Liberation: Deliverance Politics from John Calvin to Martin Luther King Jr.* New York: Oxford University Press, 2013.

Cohick, Lynn H. *Women in the World of the Earliest Christians: Illuminating Ancient Ways of Life*. Grand Rapids: Baker Academic, 2009.

Cope, O. Lamar. "On Rethinking the Philemon-Colossians Connection." *BR* 30 (1985): 45–50.

Daube, David. "Onesimos." *HTR* 79 (1986): 40–43.

Davis, David Brion. *Inhuman Bondage: The Rise and Fall of Slavery in the New World*. Oxford: Oxford University Press, 2006.

Decock, Paul B. "The Reception of the Letter to Philemon in the Early Church: Origen, Jerome, Chrysostom and Augustine." Pages 273–87 in *Philemon in Perspective: Interpreting a Pauline Letter*. Edited by D. François Tolmie. BZNW 169. Berlin: de Gruyter, 2010.

DeFelice, John. "Slavery." Pages 191–215 in vol. 4 of in *Dictionary of Daily Life in Biblical and Post-Biblical Antiquity*. Edited by Edwin M. Yamauchi and M. R. Wilson. Peabody, MA: Hendrickson, 2016.

Derrett, J. Duncan M. "The Functions of the Epistle to Philemon." *ZNW* 78 (1987): 63–91.

deSilva, David A. *Transformation: The Heart of Paul's Gospel*. Bellingham, WA: Lexham Press, 2014.

de Villiers, Pieter G. R. "Love in the Letter to Philemon." Pages 181–203 in *Philemon in Perspective: Interpreting a Pauline Letter*. Edited by D. François Tolmie. BZNW 169. Berlin: de Gruyter, 2010.

de Vos, Craig S. "Once a Slave, Always a Slave? Slavery, Manumission and Relational Patterns in Paul's Letter to Philemon." *JSNT* 82 (2001): 89–105.

de Wet, Chris L. *Preaching Bondage: John Chrysostom and the Discourse of Slavery in Early Christianity*. Oakland, CA: University of California Press, 2015.

Doering, Lutz. *Ancient Jewish Letters and the Beginnings of Christian Epistolography*. WUNT 298. Tübingen: Mohr Siebeck, 2012.

Downs, David J. *The Offering of the Gentiles: Paul's Collection for Jerusalem in Its Chronological, Cultural, and Cultic Contexts*. WUNT 2.248. Tübingen: Mohr Siebeck, 2008.

Dunn, James D. G. *Beginning from Jerusalem*. Vol. 2 of *Christianity in the Making*. Grand Rapids: Eerdmans, 2009.

———. *The Theology of Paul the Apostle*. Grand Rapids: Eerdmans, 1998.

du Plessis, Isak J. "How Christians Can Survive in a Hostile Social-Economic Environment: Paul's Mind Concerning Difficult Social Conditions in the Letter to Philemon." Pages 387–413 in *Identity, Ethics, and Ethos in the New Testament*. BZNW 141. Berlin: de Gruyter, 2006.

Edwards, Korie L. *The Elusive Dream: The Power of Race in Interracial Churches*. Oxford: Oxford University Press, 2008.

Ehrensperger, Kathy. *Paul and the Dynamics of Power: Communication and Interaction in the Early Christ-Movement*. LNTS 325. London: T&T Clark, 2007.

Elliott, Scott S. "'Thanks, but No Thanks': Tact, Persuasion, and the Negotiation of Power in Paul's Letter to Philemon." *NTS* 57 (2011): 51–64.

Ellis, E. Earle. "Paul and His Co-Workers." Pages 3–22 in *Prophecy and Hermeneutic in Early Christianity: New Testament Essays*. Grand Rapids: Eerdmans, 1978.

———. *Pauline Theology: Ministry and Society*. Grand Rapids: Eerdmans, 1989.

———. *Prophecy and Hermeneutic in Early Christianity: New Testament Essays*. Grand Rapids: Eerdmans, 1978.

Eltis, David, and Stanley L. Engerman, eds. *The Cambridge World History of Slavery: 3. AD 1420–AD 1804*. Cambridge: Cambridge University Press, 2011.

Evans, Craig A. *From Jesus to the Church: The First Christian Generation*. Louisville: Westminster John Knox, 2014.

Fee, Gordon. *God's Empowering Presence: The Holy Spirit in the Letters of Paul*. Peabody, MA: Hendrickson, 1994.

Feeley-Harnik, Gillian. "Is Historical Anthropology Possible?" Pages 95–126 in *Humanizing America's Iconic Book: Society of Biblical Literature Centennial Addresses 1980*. Edited by Gene M. Tucker and Douglas A. Knight. Biblical Scholarship in North America 6. Chico, CA: Scholars Press, 1982.

Finley, Moses I. *Ancient Slavery and Modern Ideology*. Edited by Brent D. Shaw. Rev. ed. Princeton, NJ: Markus Weiner, 1998.

Fitzgerald, John T. "Theodore of Mopsuestia on Paul's Letter to Philemon." Pages 333–63 in *Philemon in Perspective: Interpreting a Pauline Letter*. Edited by D. François Tolmie. BZNW 169. Berlin: de Gruyter, 2010.

Francis, Fred O. "The Form and Function of the Opening and Closing Paragraphs of James and 1 John." *ZNW* 61 (1970): 110–26.

Friedl, Alfred. "St. Jerome's Dissertation on the Letter to Philemon." Pages 289–316 in *Philemon in Perspective: Interpreting a Pauline Letter*. Edited by D. François Tolmie. BZNW 169. Berlin: de Gruyter, 2010.

Frilingos, Chris. "'For My Child, Onesimus': Paul and Domestic Power in Philemon." *JBL* 119 (2000): 91–104.

Funk, Robert W. "The Apostolic *Parousia*: Form and Significance." Pages 249–68 in *Christian History and Interpretation: Studies Presented to John Knox*. Edited by William R. Farmer, C. F. D. Moule, and Richard R. Niebuhr. Cambridge: Cambridge University Press, 1967.

Galinsky, Karl. "The Cult of the Roman Emperor: Uniter or Divider?" Pages 1–21 in *Rome and Religion: A Cross-Disciplinary Dialogue on the Imperial Cult*. Edited by Jeffrey Brodd and Jonathan L. Reed. Atlanta: Society of Biblical Literature, 2011.

———. "In the Shadow (or Not) of the Imperial Cult: A Cooperative Agenda." Pages 215–25 in *Rome and Religion: A Cross-Disciplinary Dialogue on the Imperial Cult*. Edited by Jeffrey Brodd and Jonathan L. Reed.

Gardner, Jane F., and Thomas Wiedemann, eds. *The Roman Household: A Sourcebook*. New York: Routledge, 1991.

Gaventa, Beverly R. *Our Mother Saint Paul*. Louisville: Westminster John Knox, 2007.

Gehring, Roger W. *House Church and Mission: The Importance of Household Structures in Early Christianity*. Peabody, MA: Hendrickson, 2004.

Getty, Mary Ann. "The Theology of Philemon." Pages 503–8 in *SBL Seminar Papers 1987*. Atlanta: Scholars Press, 1987.

Gielen, Marlis. "Zur Interpretation der Paulinischen Formel Τὴν Κατ' Οἶκον Αὐτῆς Ἐκκλησίαν." *ZNW* 77 (1986): 109–25.

Giles, Kevin. "The Biblical Argument for Slavery: Can the Bible Mislead? A Case Study in Hermeneutics." *EvQ* 66 (1994): 3–17.

Glancy, Jennifer A. "Obstacles to Slaves' Participation in the Corinthian Church." *JBL* 117 (1998): 481–501.

———. "The Sexual Use of Slaves: A Response to Kyle Harper on Jewish and Christian *Porneia*." *JBL* 134 (2015): 215–29.

———. *Slavery as Moral Problem: In the Early Church and Today*. Facet Books. Minneapolis: Fortress Press, 2011.

———. *Slavery in Early Christianity*. Minneapolis: Fortress, 2006.

———. "The Utility of an Apostle: On Philemon 11." *JEH* 5 (2015): 72–86.

Goodman, Martin. *The Roman World: 44 BC–AD 180*. 2nd ed. Routledge History of the Ancient World. London: Routledge, 2012.

Gordon, Lynn Melby, and Sandra Graham. "Attribution Theory." Pages 142–44 in *Encyclopedia of Human Development*. Thousand Oaks, CA: Sage Publications, 2005.

Gorman, Michael J. *Apostle of the Crucified Lord: A Theological Introduction to Paul and His Letters*. 2nd ed. Grand Rapids: Eerdmans, 2016.

———. *Becoming the Gospel: Paul, Participation, and Mission*. Grand Rapids: Eerdmans, 2015.

———. *Cruciformity: Paul's Narrative Spirituality of the Cross*. Grand Rapids: Eerdmans, 2001.

———. *Inhabiting the Cruciform God: Kenosis, Justification, and Theosis in Paul's Narrative Soteriology*. Grand Rapids: Eerdmans, 2009.

Harper, Kyle. "Knowledge, Ideology, and Skepticism in Ancient Slave Studies." *AJP* 132 (2011): 160–68.

———. *Slavery in the Late Roman World, AD 275–425*. Cambridge: Cambridge University Press, 2011.

Harrill, J. Albert. *The Manumission of Slaves in Early Christianity*. HUT 32. Tübingen: Mohr Siebeck, 1995.

———. "Paul and Slavery." Pages 575–607 in *Paul in the Greco-Roman World: A Handbook*. Edited by J. Paul Sampley. Harrisburg, PA: Trinity Press International, 2003.

———. *Slaves in the New Testament: Literary, Social, and Moral Dimensions*. Minneapolis: Fortress, 2005.

———. "Using the Roman Jurists to Interpret Philemon." *ZNW* 90 (1999): 135–38.

Harris, Murray J. *Prepositions and Theology in the Greek New Testament: An Essential Reference Resource for Exegesis*. Grand Rapids: Zondervan, 2012.

———. *Slave of Christ: A New Testament Metaphor for Total Devotion to Christ*. New Studies in Biblical Theology 8. Leicester: Apollos, 1999.

Harris, William V. *Ancient Literacy*. Cambridge: Harvard University Press, 1989.

———. "Towards a Study of the Roman Slave Trade." *Memoirs of the American Academy in Rome* 36 (1980): 117–40.

Haugen, Gary A., and Victor Boutros. *The Locust Effect: Why the End of Poverty Requires the End of Violence*. Oxford: Oxford University Press, 2014.

Haykin, Michael A. G. "Praying Together: A Note on Philemon 22." *EvQ* 66 (1994): 331–35.

Hedrick, Joan D. *Harriet Beecher Stowe: A Life*. Rev. ed. New York: Oxford University Press, 1995.

Heil, John Paul. "The Chiastic Structure and Meaning of Paul's Letter to Philemon." *Bib* 82 (2001): 178–206.

Heilig, Christoph. *Hidden Criticism? The Methodology and Plausibility of the Search for a Counter-Imperial Subtext in Paul*. WUNT 2.392. Tübingen: Mohr Siebeck, 2015.

———. "Methodological Considerations for the Search for Counter-Imperial 'Echoes' in Pauline Literature." Pages 73–92 in *Reactions to Empire: Proceedings of Sacred Texts in Their Socio-Political Contexts*. Edited by John A. Dunne and Dan Batovici. WUNT 2.372. Tübingen: Mohr Siebeck, 2014.

Hellerman, Joseph H. *The Ancient Church as Family*. Minneapolis: Fortress, 2001.

Hengel, Martin. *The Pre-Christian Paul*. Translated by John Bowden. Philadelphia: Trinity Press International, 1991.

———, and Anna Maria Schwemer. *Paul between Damascus and Antioch: The Unknown Years*. Translated by John Bowden. Louisville: Westminster John Knox, 1997.

Hezser, Catherine. "Slavery." Pages 302–19 in *The Oxford Encyclopedia of the Bible and Law*. Vol. 2. Edited by Brent A. Strawn. New York: Oxford University Press, 2015.

Hock, Ronald F. "A Support for His Old Age: Paul's Plea on Behalf of Onesimus." Pages 67–81 in *The Social World of the First Christians: Essays in Honor of Wayne A. Meeks*. Edited by L. Michael White and O. Larry Yarbrough. Minneapolis: Fortress Press, 1995.

Holmes, Michael W., ed. *The Apostolic Fathers: Greek Texts and English Translations*, 3rd ed. Grand Rapids: Baker Academic, 2007.

Horrell, David G. *Solidarity and Difference: A Contemporary Reading of Paul's Ethics*. 2nd ed. London: Bloomsbury T&T Clark, 2015.

Hunter, W. B. "Prayer." Pages 725–34 in *Dictionary of Paul and His Letters*. Edited by Gerald F. Hawthorne, Ralph P. Martin, and Daniel G. Reid. Downers Grove, IL: InterVarsity Press, 1993.

Jacobs, Harriet Ann. *Incidents in the Life of a Slave Girl*. Oxford: Benediction Books, 2011.

Jipp, Joshua W. *Christ Is King: Paul's Royal Ideology*. Minneapolis: Fortress, 2015.

Johnson, Matthew V., James A. Noel, and Demetrius K. Williams, eds. *Onesimus Our Brother: Reading Religion, Race, and Culture in Philemon*. Paul in Critical Contexts. Minneapolis: Fortress, 2012.

Joshel, Sandra R. *Slavery in the Roman World*. Cambridge Introduction to Roman Civilization. Cambridge: Cambridge University Press, 2010.

Joshel, Sandra R., and Lauren Hackworth Petersen. *The Material Life of Roman Slaves*. Cambridge: Cambridge University Press, 2014.

Joubert, Stephan. *Paul as Benefactor: Reciprocity, Strategy and Theological Reflection in Paul's Collection*. WUNT 2.124. Tübingen: Mohr Siebeck, 2000.

Judge, Edwin A. *The Social Pattern of Christian Groups in the First Century*. London: Tyndale, 1960.

Kea, Perry V. "Paul's Letter to Philemon: A Short Analysis of Its Values." *PRSt* 23 (1996): 223–32.

King, Martin Luther, Jr. "Letter from Birmingham City Jail." Pages 289–302 in *A Testament of Hope: The Essential Writings of Martin Luther King, Jr.* Edited by J. M. Washington. San Francisco: Harper & Row, 1986.

———. *A Testament of Hope: The Essential Writings of Martin Luther King Jr.* Edited by J. M. Washington. San Francisco: Harper & Row, 1986.

Klauck, Hans-Josef. *Ancient Letters and the New Testament: A Guide to Content and Exegesis*. Waco, TX: Baylor University Press, 2006.

Knox, John. *Chapters in a Life of Paul*. Nashville: Abingdon Press, 1950.

———. *Philemon among the Letters of Paul*. New York: Abingdon, 1963.

Kuhn, Karl Allen. *Luke: The Elite Evangelist*. Paul's Social Network: Brothers and Sisters in Faith. Collegeville, MN: Glazier, 2010.

Kumitz, Christopher. *Der Brief als Medium der ἀγάπη: Eine Untersuchung zur Rhetorischen und Epistolographischen Gestalt des Philemonbriefes*. Europäische Hochschulschriften 787. Frankfurt am Main: Peter Lang, 2004.

Lampe, Peter. "Affects and Emotions in the Rhetoric of Paul's Letter to Philemon: A Rhetorical-Psychological Interpretation." Pages 61–77 in *Philemon in Perspective: Interpreting a Pauline Letter*. Edited by D. François Tolmie. BZNW 169. Berlin: de Gruyter, 2010.

———. "Keine 'Sklavenflucht' des Onesimus." *ZNW* 76 (1985): 135–37.

Last, Richard. "The Neighborhood (*vicus*) of the Corinthian *ekklēsia*: Beyond Family-Based Descriptions of the First Urban Christ-Believers." *JSNT* 38 (2016): 399–425.

Leech, G. *Principles of Pragmatics*. London: Longman, 1983.

Levison, John R. *Filled with the Spirit*. Grand Rapids: Eerdmans, 2009.

———. *Inspired: The Holy Spirit and the Mind of Faith*. Grand Rapids: Eerdmans, 2013.

Lewis, Lloyd A. "An African American Appraisal of the Philemon-Paul-Onesimus Triangle." Pages 232–46 in *Stony the Road We Trod: African American Biblical Interpretation*. Edited by Cain Hope Felder. Minneapolis: Fortress, 1991.

Lieu, Judith M. "'Grace to You and Peace': The Apostolic Greeting." *BJRL* 68 (1985): 161–78.

Lincoln, Abraham. *Selected Writings and Speeches of Abraham Lincoln*. Edited by T. Harry Williams. n.p.: Hendricks House, 1980.

Lindsay, Dennis R. *Josephus and Faith:* Pistis *and* Pisteuein *as Faith Terminology in the Writings of Flavius Josephus and in the New Testament*. AGJU 19. Leiden: Brill, 1993.

Longenecker, Bruce W. *Remember the Poor: Paul, Poverty, and the Greco-Roman World* (Grand Rapids: Eerdmans, 2010).

Lyons, Kirk D., Sr. "Paul's Confrontation with Class: The Letter to Philemon as Counter-Hegemonic Discourse." *Cross Currents* 56 (2006): 116–32.

MacDonald, Margaret. "New Testament Envoys in the Context of Greco-Roman Diplomatic and Epistolary Conventions: The Example of Timothy and Titus." *JBL* 111 (1992): 641–62.

Malherbe, Abraham J. *Social Aspects of Early Christianity*. 2nd ed. Philadelphia: Fortress, 1983.

Malina, Bruce J. *Timothy: Paul's Closest Associate*. Paul's Social Network: Brothers and Sisters in Faith. Collegeville, MN: Liturgical Press, 2008.

Marchal, Joseph A. "The Usefulness of an Onesimus: The Sexual Use of Slaves and Paul's Letter to Philemon." *JBL* 130 (2011): 749–70.

Marrow, Stanley B. "*Parrhesia* and the New Testament." *CBQ* 44 (1982): 431–46.

Martens, John W. "Ignatius and Onesimus: John Knox Reconsidered." *SecCent* 9 (1992): 73–86.

Martin, Ralph P. "Reconciliation and Forgiveness in the Letter to the Colossians." Pages 104–24 in *Reconciliation and Hope: New Testament Essays on Atonement and Eschatology Presented to L. L. Morris on His 60th Birthday*. Edited by Robert Banks. Grand Rapids: Eerdmans, 1974.

———. *Reconciliation: A Study of Paul's Theology*. New Foundations Theological Library. Atlanta: John Knox Press, 1981.

Martin, Troy. "The Scythian Perspective in Col 3:11." *JBL* 114 (1995): 253.

———. "Scythian Perspective or Elusive Chiasm: A Reply to Douglas A. Campbell." *NovT* 41 (1999): 256–64.

McKnight, Scot. *Jesus and His Death: Historiography, the Historical Jesus, and Atonement Theory*. Waco, TX: Baylor University Press, 2005.

———. *The Letter to Colossians*. NICNT. Grand Rapids: Eerdmans, 2017.

———. *A New Vision for Israel: The Teachings of Jesus in National Context*. Grand Rapids: Eerdmans, 1999.

———. *Turning to Jesus: The Sociology of Conversion in the Gospels*. Louisville: Westminster John Knox, 2002.

———. "The Unexamined Grace." *Books & Culture* (Jan/Feb 2016): 19–21.

Meeks, Wayne A. *The First Urban Christians: The Social World of the Apostle Paul*. 2nd ed. New Haven: Yale University Press, 2003.

Mengestu, Abera M. *God as Father in Paul: Kinship Language and Identity Formation in Early Christianity*. Eugene, OR: Pickwick, 2013.

Meyers, Carol, Toni Craven, and Ross Shepard Kraemer, eds. *Women in Scripture: A Dictionary of Named and Unnamed Women in the Hebrew Bible, the Apocryphal/Deuterocanonical Books, and the New Testament*. Grand Rapids: Eerdmans, 2001.

Miller, Patrick D. *They Cried to the Lord: The Form and Theology of Biblical Prayer*. Minneapolis: Fortress, 1994.

Mitchell, Margaret M. "John Chrysostom on Philemon: A Second Look." *HTR* 88 (1995): 135–48.

Morrice, W. G. *Joy in the New Testament*. Grand Rapids: Eerdmans, 1985.

Morris, Leon L. *Testaments of Love: A Study of Love in the Bible*. Grand Rapids: Eerdmans, 1981.

Mott, Stephen C. "The Power of Giving and Receiving: Reciprocity in Hellenistic Benevolence." Pages 60–72 in *Current Issues in Biblical and Patristic Interpretation: Studies in Honor of Merrill C. Tenney, Presented by His Former Students*. Edited by Gerald F. Hawthorne. Grand Rapids: Eerdmans, 1975.

Moulton, James Hope, and Nigel Turner. *Grammar of New Testament Greek, Vol. 3: Syntax*. Edinburgh: T&T Clark, 1963.

Noll, Mark A. *The Civil War as a Theological Crisis*. Chapel Hill: University of North Carolina Press, 2006.

Nordling, John G. "Onesimus Fugitivus: A Defense of the Runaway Slave Hypothesis in Philemon." *JSNT* 41 (1991): 97–119.

Nida, Eugene A. "Implications of Contemporary Linguistics for Biblical Scholarship." *JBL* 91 (1972): 73–89.

Nida, Eugene A., and Charles R. Taber. *The Theory and Practice of Translation.* Leiden: Brill, 2003.

Novenson, Matthew V. *Christ among the Messiahs: Christ Language in Paul and Messiah Language in Ancient Judaism*. New York: Oxford University Press, 2012.

Oakes, Peter. *Reading Romans in Pompeii: Paul's Letter at Ground Level.* Minneapolis: Fortress, 2009.

Oden, Amy G., ed. *And You Welcomed Me: A Sourcebook on Hospitality in Early Christianity*. Nashville: Abingdon, 2001.

Ollrog, W.-H. *Paulus und Seine Mitarbeiter. Untersuchungen zu Theorie und Praxis der Paulinschen Mission.* WMANT 50. Neukirchen-Vluyn: Neukirchener, 1979.

Omanson, Roger L. *A Textual Guide to the Greek New Testament.* Stuttgart: Deutsche Bibelgesellschaft, 2006.

Orwell, George. *An Age like This 1920–1940: The Collected Essays, Journalism & Letters*. Edited by Sonia Orwell and Ian Angus. Boston: David R. Godine, 2000.

Osiek, Carolyn, and Margaret Y. Macdonald. *A Woman's Place: House Churches in Earliest Christianity*. Minneapolis: Fortress, 2006.

Patterson, Orlando. *Slavery and Social Death: A Comparative Study*. Cambridge, MA: Harvard University Press, 1982.

———, ed. *The Cultural Matrix: Understanding Black Youth.* New Haven: Harvard University Press, 2016.

Pearson, Brook W. R. "Assumptions in the Criticism and Translation of Philemon." Pages 253–80 in *Translating the Bible: Problems and Prospects.* Edited by Stanley Porter and R. S. Hess. JSNTSup 173. Sheffield: Sheffield Academic Press, 1999.

Petersen, Norman R. *Rediscovering Paul: Philemon and the Sociology of Paul's Narrative World.* Philadelphia: Fortress Press, 1985.

Pietri, Charles. "Christians and Slaves in the Early Days of the Church (2nd–3rd Centuries)." Pages 31–39 in *The Dignity of the Despised of the Earth,* edited by Jacques Pohier and Dietmar Mieth. Concilium 130.10. New York: Seabury Press, 1979.

Pohl, Christine D. *Making Room: Recovering Hospitality as a Christian Tradition.* Grand Rapids: Eerdmans, 1999.

Porter, Stanley. *Idioms of the Greek New Testament.* Biblical Languages: Greek 2. Sheffield: JSOT Press, 1992.

———. *Καταλλάσσω in Ancient Greek Literature, with Reference to the Pauline Writings*. EFN 5. Córdoba: Ediciones el Almendro, 1994.

———. "Paul's Concept of Reconciliation, Twice More." Pages 131–52 in *Paul and His Theology*, edited by Stanley Porter. Pauline Studies 3. Leiden: Brill, 2006.

———. "Reconciliation as the Heart of Paul's Missionary Theology." Pages 169–79 in *Paul as Missionary: Identity, Activity, Theology, and Practice*. Edited by Brian S. Rosner and Trevor J. Burke. LNTS 420. London: Bloomsbury T&T Clark, 2011.

Portier-Young, Anathea E. *Apocalypse against Empire: Theologies of Resistance in Early Judaism*. Grand Rapids: Eerdmans, 2011.

Powery, Emerson B., and Rodney S. Sadler, Jr. *The Genesis of Liberation: Biblical Interpretation in the Antebellum Narratives of the Enslaved*. Louisville: Westminster John Knox, 2016.

Punt, Jeremy. "Paul, Power and Philemon. 'Knowing Your Place': A Postcolonial Reading." Pages 223–50 in *Philemon in Perspective: Interpreting a Pauline Letter*. Edited by D. François Tolmie. BZNW 169. Berlin: de Gruyter, 2010.

Quient, Nicholas Rudolph. "Apphia, an Early Christian Leader? An Investigation and Proposal Regarding the Identity of Apphia in Philemon 1:2." *Priscilla Papers*, forthcoming.

Rapske, Brian. *The Book of Acts and Paul in Roman Custody*. Edited by Paul Winter. Vol. 3 of *The Book of Acts in Its First Century Setting*. Grand Rapids: Eerdmans, 1994.

———. "Prison, Prisoner." Pages 827–30 in *Dictionary of New Testament Background*. Edited by Craig A. Evans and Stanley E. Porter. Downers Grove, IL: InterVarsity Press, 1993.

———. "The Prisoner Paul in the Eyes of Onesimus." *NTS* 37 (1991): 187–203.

Reed, Jeffrey T. "Are Paul's Thanksgivings 'Epistolary'?" *JSNT* 61 (1996): 87–99.

Rendtorff, Rolf. *The Covenant Formula: An Exegetical and Theological Investigation*. Translated by M. Kohl. Edinburgh: T&T Clark, 1998.

Rhoads, David M. "Performing the Letter to Philemon." *Journal of Biblical Storytelling* 17 (2008).

Richards, E. Randolph. *Paul and First-Century Letter Writing: Secretaries, Composition and Collection*. Downers Grove, IL: InterVarsity Press, 2004.

———. *The Secretary in the Letters of Paul*. WUNT 2.42. Tübingen: Mohr Siebeck, 1991.

Riesenfeld, Harald. "Faith and Love Promoting Hope: An Interpretation of Philemon v. 6." Pages 251–57 in *Paul and Paulinism: Essays in Honour of C. K. Barrett*. Edited by Morna D. Hooker and S. G. Wilson. London: SPCK, 1982.

Roth, Catharine, trans. *St. John Chrysostom: On Wealth and Poverty*. Crestwood, NY: St. Vladimir's Press, 1984.

Rowe, C. Kavin. *World Upside Down: Reading Acts in the Graeco-Roman Age*. New York: Oxford University Press, 2009.

Russell, David M. "The Strategy of a First-Century Appeals Letter: A Discourse Reading of Paul's Epistle to Philemon." *Journal of Translation and Textlinguistics* 11 (1998): 1–25.

Sanders, E. P. *Jewish Law from Jesus to the Mishnah: Five Studies*. Philadelphia: Trinity Press International, 1990.

———. *Judaism: Practice and Belief. 63BCE—66CE*. Philadelphia: SCM, 1992.

Sanders, J. T. "The Transition from Opening Epistolary Thanksgivings to Body in the Letters of the Pauline Corpus." *JBL* 81 (1962): 348–62.

Sanders, Laura L. "Equality and a Request for the Manumission of Onesimus." *ResQ* 46 (2004): 109–14.

Shaw, Brent D. *Spartacus and the Slave Wars: A Brief History with Documents*. Boston: Bedford/St. Martin's, 2001.

Shiell, William D. *Delivering from Memory: The Effect of Performance on the Early Christian Audience*. Eugene, OR: Pickwick, 2011.

Smith, Mitzi J. "Utility, Fraternity, and Reconciliation: Ancient Slavery as a Context for the Return of Onesimus." Pages 47–58 in *Onesimus Our Brother: Reading Religion, Race, and Culture in Philemon*. Edited by Matthew V. Johnson, James A. Noel, and Demetrius K. Williams. Paul in Critical Contexts. Minneapolis: Fortress Press, 2012.

Snyman, A. H. "A Semantic Discourse Analysis of the Letter to Philemon." Pages 83–99 in *Text and Interpretation: New Approaches in the Criticism of the New Testament*. Edited by P. J. Hartin and J. H. Petzer. Leiden: Brill, 1991.

Soards, Marion L. "Benefitting from Philemon." *Journal of Theology* 91 (1987): 44–51.

———. "Some Neglected Theological Dimensions of Paul's Letter to Philemon." *PRSt* 17 (1990): 209–19.

Spilka, Bernard, Philip R. Shaver, and Lee A. Kirkpatrick. "A General Attribution Theory for the Psychology of Religion." *JSSR* 24 (1985): 1–20.

Stewart, Alistair C. *The Original Bishops: Office and Order in the First Christian Communities*. Grand Rapids: Baker Academic, 2014.

Still, Todd D. "Philemon among the Letters of Paul: Theological and Canonical Considerations." *ResQ* 47 (2005): 133–42.

Stowe, Harriet Beecher. *Uncle Tom's Cabin*. New York: Everyman's Library, 1995.

Stowers, Stanley K. *Letter Writing in Greco-Roman Antiquity*. LEC 5. Philadelphia: Westminster, 1986.

Strauss, Barry. *The Spartacus War*. New York: Simon & Schuster, 2010.

Swartley, Willard M. *Covenant of Peace: The Missing Peace in New Testament Theology and Ethics*. Grand Rapids: Eerdmans, 2006.

Taylor, N. H. "Onesimus: A Case Study of Slave Conversion in Early Christianity." *R&T* 3 (1996): 259–81.

Thiselton, Anthony C. *New Horizons in Hermeneutics*. Grand Rapids: Zondervan, 1992.

Tolmie, D. François, ed. *Philemon in Perspective: Interpreting a Pauline Letter*. BZNW 169. Berlin: de Gruyter, 2010.

———. "Tendencies in the Research on the Letter to Philemon since 1980." Pages 1–28 in *Philemon in Perspective: Interpreting a Pauline Letter*. Edited by D. François Tolmie. BZNW 169. Berlin: de Gruyter, 2010.

Toner, Jerry. *The Roman Guide to Slave Management: A Treatise by Nobleman Marcus Sidonius Falx*. New York: Overlook Press, 2014.

Trebilco, Paul. *The Early Christians in Ephesus from Paul to Ignatius*. Grand Rapids: Eerdmans, 2007.

———. *Self-Designations and Group Identity in the New Testament*. Cambridge: Cambridge University Press, 2012.

Vanhoozer, Kevin J. "Imprisoned or Free? Text, Status, and Theological Interpretation in the Master/Slave Discourse of Philemon." Pages 51–93 in *Reading Scripture with the Church: Toward a Hermeneutic for Theological Interpretation*. Edited by A. K. M. Adam, Stephen E. Fowl, Kevin J. Vanhoozer, and Francis Watson. Grand Rapids: Baker Academic, 2006.

van Unnik, Willem Cornelis. "The Christian's Freedom of Speech in the New Testament." *BJRL* 44 (1962): 466–88.

Wallis, Jim. *America's Original Sin: Racism, White Privilege, and the Bridge to a New America*. Grand Rapids: Brazos Press, 2016.

Webb, William J. *Slaves, Women and Homosexuals: Exploring the Hermeneutics of Cultural Analysis*. Downers Grove, IL: InterVarsity Press, 2001.

Weima, J. A. D. "Paul's Persuasive Prose: An Epistolary Analysis of the Letter to Philemon." Pages 29–60 in *Philemon in Perspective: Interpreting a Pauline Letter*. Edited by D. François Tolmie. BZNW 169. Berlin: de Gruyter, 2010.

Wendland, Ernst. "'You Will Do Even More than I Say': On the Rhetorical Function of Stylistic Form in the Letter to Philemon." Pages 79–111 in *Philemon in Perspective: Interpreting a Pauline Letter*. Edited by D. François Tolmie. BZNW 169. Berlin: de Gruyter, 2010.

Wessels, G. François. "The Letter to Philemon in the Context of Slavery in Early Christianity." Pages 143–68 in *Philemon in Perspective: Interpreting a Pauline Letter*. Edited by D. François Tolmie. BZNW 169. Berlin: de Gruyter, 2010.

White, John L. "The Structural Analysis of Philemon: A Point of Departure in the Formal Analysis of the Pauline Letter." Pages 1–47 in *SBL Seminar Papers 1971*. Missoula, MT: Scholars Press, 1971.

Wickert, U. "Der Philemonbrief—Privatbrief oder Apostolisches Schreiben?" *ZNW* 52 (1961): 230–38.

Wilkerson, Isabel. *The Warmth of Other Suns: The Epic Story of America's Great Migration*. New York: Random House, 2010.

Williams, Demetrius K. "'No Longer as a Slave': Reading the Interpretation History of Paul's Epistle to Philemon." Pages 11–45 in *Onesimus Our Brother: Reading Religion, Race, and Culture in Philemon*. Edited by Matthew V. Johnson, James A. Noel, and Demetrius K. Williams. Paul in Critical Contexts. Minneapolis: Fortress, 2012.

Wilson, Andrew. "The Politics of Politeness and Pauline Epistolography: A Case Study of the Letter to Philemon." *JSNT* 48 (1992): 107–19.

Winter, Sara C. "Methodological Observations on a New Interpretation of Paul's Letter to Philemon." *USQR* 39 (1984): 203–12.

———. "Paul's Letter to Philemon." *NTS* 33 (1987): 1–15.

Witherington, Ben, III. "Christ." Pages 97–98 in *Dictionary of Paul and His Letters*. Edited by Gerald F. Hawthorne, Ralph P. Martin, and Daniel G. Reid. Downers Grove, IL: InterVarsity Press, 1993.

Wolter, Michael. "The Letter to Philemon as Ethical Counterpart of Paul's Doctrine of Justification." Pages 169–79 in *Philemon in Perspective: Interpreting a Pauline Letter*. Edited by D. François Tolmie. BZNW 169. Berlin: de Gruyter, 2010.

Wright, Brian J. "Ancient Literacy in New Testament Research: Incorporating a Few More Lines of Enquiry." *TJ* 36 (2015): 161–89.

———. "Ancient Rome's Daily News Publication with Some Likely Implications for Early Christian Studies." *TynBul* 66 (2016): 161–77.

Wright, N. T. *The Climax of the Covenant: Christ and the Law in Pauline Theology*. Minneapolis: Fortress, 1993.

———. *Paul and the Faithfulness of God*. 2 vols. Vol. 4 of *Christian Origins and the Question of God*. Minneapolis: Fortress, 2013.

Introduction

The letter to Philemon is an important example of how Pauline circles sought to embody a new vision for humanity—the church. Paul and those around him struggled to break down boundaries and establish new creation kingdom realities for conduct and fellowship. The result of this struggle is a deeply disturbing text, the letter to Philemon. Studies of this short letter often exhibit exegetical scrutiny without comparable scrutiny of the moral implications of the letter,[1] beginning by recognizing the phenomenology of slavery. The letter lacks *any* overt appeal from Paul to manumit Onesimus.[2] Perhaps we can lessen our disturbance if we approach the letter from a different angle. Rather than a letter about slavery and manumission, we could approach the letter as one that bears the message of reconciliation. But reconciliation suddenly becomes morally exacerbated when those in need of reconciliation are a slave owner (Philemon) and a slave (Onesimus).

Once reconciliation in Philemon turns its face toward the phenomenology of slavery, this letter stands on knife's edge.[3] A few conclusions

1. For succinct, recent sketches of scholarship on Philemon, each keeping an eye on the moral problem of Philemon, John Byron, *Recent Research on Paul and Slavery*, Recent Research in Biblical Studies 3 (Sheffield: Phoenix, 2008), 116–37; D. François Tolmie, "Tendencies in the Research on the Letter to Philemon since 1980," in *Philemon in Perspective: Interpreting a Pauline Letter*, ed. D. François Tolmie, BZNW 169 (Berlin: de Gruyter, 2010), 1–28; Demetrius K. Williams, "'No Longer as a Slave': Reading the Interpretation History of Paul's Epistle to Philemon," in *Onesimus Our Brother: Reading Religion, Race, and Culture in Philemon*, ed. Matthew V. Johnson, James A. Noel, and Demetrius K. Williams, Paul in Critical Contexts (Minneapolis: Fortress, 2012), 11–45.

2. Perry V. Kea, "Paul's Letter to Philemon: A Short Analysis of Its Values," *PRSt* 23 (1996): 223–32 (225–26). Witherington, 62–64, reads Philemon through the rhetoric of *insinuatio*. He fully believes Paul wanted the manumission of Onesimus. His argument is entirely an inference from the kind of Asiatic rhetoric at work in Philemon.

3. Felder, 885; also Michael J. Gorman, *Apostle of the Crucified Lord: A Theological Introduction to Paul and His Letters*, 2nd ed. (Grand Rapids: Eerdmans, 2016), 454.

from some important scholars of Philemon make our point clear. Thus, Marianne Meye Thompson seems justified to claim that the "most pressing theological issue raised by the epistle to Philemon for modern readers, although likely not for ancient readers, is that of the relationship of the gospel to slavery."[4] Paul, she contends, seeks "to redefine their relationship on the entirely new footing of the gospel."[5] Paul envisions a new kind of relationship on the basis of siblingship, but a brother who is a slave is still a slave, and a master who is a brother remains a master. Whether one likes or does not like what Paul says about reconciling a master and a slave, the substance of this letter leads us into a nightmare when one examines its history of interpretation.[6] Hence Lloyd A. Lewis can say Philemon varies from all the other Pauline letters because "the very subject matter of this letter is controversial." He takes the next step: "What African American readers look for is some vision of how as a church leader Paul understood the gospel's power in the face of this very present social situation [of slavery]." Lewis then gathers the forces of interpretation into a tight knot of reminder: "The letter itself hardly provides a systematic answer."[7] Gillian Feeley-Harnik is more forceful: "Yet it remains agonizingly unclear, even to this day, whether Paul or any other early Christian actually called for the abolition of slavery—or perhaps I should say, agonizingly clear that they did not. They seem able to have developed a theology or theologies that emphasized equality, while being perfectly content to retain what was considered an injustice not only from our perspective but also, the evidence suggests, from their own."[8]

One experiences the same kind of agonizingly clear orientation we find in Paul when one turns to Didache 4:9–11, where we see the author's advice shift from being a Christian father to being a Christian slave owner of some Christian slaves:

4. Thompson, 198.

5. Thompson, 199.

6. Jennifer A. Glancy, *Slavery as Moral Problem: In the Early Church and Today*, Facet Books (Minneapolis: Fortress Press, 2011). A traditionalist view is seen in Murray J. Harris, *Slave of Christ: A New Testament Metaphor for Total Devotion to Christ*, New Studies in Biblical Theology 8 (Leicester: Apollos/InterVarsity, 1999), 47–68.

7. Lewis, 437–38. Along similar lines, see the insightful exploration of John M. G. Barclay, "Paul, Philemon and the Dilemma of Christian Slave Ownership," *NTS* 37 (1991): 161–86; Todd D. Still, "Philemon among the Letters of Paul: Theological and Canonical Considerations," *ResQ* 47 (2005): 138–39.

8. Gillian Feeley-Harnik, "Is Historical Anthropology Possible?," in *Humanizing America's Iconic Book: Society of Biblical Literature Centennial Addresses 1980*, ed. Gene M. Tucker and Douglas A. Knight, Biblical Scholarship in North America 6 (Chico, CA: Scholars Press, 1982), 95–126, quoting 102, where she cites a variety of evidence in support.

> You shall not withhold your hand from your son or your daughter, but from their youth you shall teach them the fear of God. You shall not give orders to your male slave or female servant (who hope in the same God as you) when you are angry, lest they cease to fear the God who is over you both. For he comes to call not with regard to reputation but those whom the Spirit has prepared. And you slaves shall be submissive to your masters in respect and fear, as to a symbol of God.[9]

What then can we make of Philemon when the problem of slavery itself seems to be unnoticed?

Anyone from a privileged location in the USA who interprets this letter without a constant eye on four fields fails.[10] These four are (1) slavery in the Roman Empire, (2) slavery in the New World, (3) modern slavery across the globe and, especially for Americans, and (4) the implications of New World slavery for social conditions in the twentieth and twenty-first century. The interpreter needs to keep an eye on the interpretation of slavery texts in the entire Bible as they impinge upon and have been used by the Bible's interpreters.[11] The slavery inherent to Philemon must be admitted if we wish to read this letter as Scripture.

Philemon was written to persuade a slave owner to create new conditions for a slave who had a pragmatic and depersonalizing name, Onesimus.[12] I can empathize with the interpreters of this letter who think Paul was cowardly to the degree that he did not push harder for manumission. But I cannot empathize with the interpreters who either diminish Roman slavery for whatever reasons or who fail to see the phenomenology of slavery at work in Paul's letter.[13] Paul's vision was expressed in Gal 3:28 ("neither slave nor free") and in Col 3:11 ("no . . . slave or free"). On most readings, Colossians was written simultaneous with or subsequent to Philemon. That means Paul

9. Michael W. Holmes, ed., *The Apostolic Fathers: Greek Texts and English Translations*, 3rd ed. (Grand Rapids: Baker Academic, 2007).

10. On privilege, whiteness, and invisibility, see Korie L. Edwards, *The Elusive Dream: The Power of Race in Interracial Churches* (New York: Oxford University Press, 2008).

11. J. Albert Harrill, *Slaves in the New Testament: Literary, Social, and Moral Dimensions* (Minneapolis: Fortress, 2005), 165–192; Mark A. Noll, *The Civil War as a Theological Crisis* (Chapel Hill: University of North Carolina Press, 2006); Robert Atkins, "Contextual Interpretation of the Letter to Philemon in the United States," in Tolmie, *Philemon in Perspective*, 205–21.

12. Masters often named their slaves; see Varro, *Latin Language* 8.9: "so everyone calls his slave something different after different things, just as he likes" (translation Thomas Wiedemann, ed., *Greek and Roman Slavery*, rev. ed., Routledge Sourcebooks for the Ancient World [New York: Routledge, 1989], 34).

13. E.g., Robert McL. Wilson, *Colossians and Philemon*, ICC (Edinburgh: Bloomsbury T&T Clark, 2014), 327–30.

(or at least a Paulinist) did not expect the manumission of all slaves. This, too, must be admitted.

Philemon should be compared, not with Romans or even with Colossians, but with Nelson Mandela's *Long Walk to Freedom* or Martin Luther King Jr.'s "Letter from Birmingham City Jail."[14] To update Philemon in order to unmask its moral-theological gravity and to expose the voices that deserve to be heard, our letter might be retitled "Paul on Robben Island in Ephesus" or Paul's "Letter from Ephesus City Jail."[15] We would then need to ask how tall Paul stands in comparison with Mandela and King. I believe it is right and fair to imitate the words of others: Paul was no Toussaint Louverture or Frederick Douglass, but there may not have been a Toussaint or Douglass without Paul.[16]

Let us admit the truth about the letter of Philemon. Progressives sometimes accuse the letter of being pro-slavery, morally inferior and in need of rejection and at least updating, or they find it to be a firm first-century step toward manumission or even abolition.[17] Conservatives tend to diminish the significance of slavery in the Roman Empire, routinely claiming it was (sometimes utterly) unlike New World slavery and thereby escaping the moral prob-

14. Nelson Mandela, *Long Walk to Freedom: The Autobiography of Nelson Mandela* (London: Abacus, 1994); Martin Luther King Jr., "Letter from Birmingham City Jail," in *A Testament of Hope: The Essential Writings of Martin Luther King, Jr.*, ed. J. M. Washington (San Francisco: Harper & Row, 1986), 289–302.

15. For some socio-pragmatic and postcolonial interpretations of Philemon that focus on listening to subdued voices, Sabine Bieberstein, "Disrupting the Normal Reality of Slavery: A Feminist Reading of the Letter to Philemon," *JSNT* 79 (2000): 105–16; Jeremy Punt, "Paul, Power and Philemon. 'Knowing Your Place': A Postcolonial Reading," in Tolmie, *Philemon in Perspective*, 223–50; Pieter J. J. Botha, "Hierarchy and Obedience: The Legacy of the Letter to Philemon," in *Philemon in Perspective: Interpreting a Pauline Letter*, ed. D. François Tolmie, BZNW 169 (Berlin: de Gruyter, 2010), 251–71; Matthew V. Johnson, James A. Noel, and Demetrius K. Williams, eds., *Onesimus Our Brother: Reading Religion, Race, and Culture in Philemon*, Paul in Critical Contexts (Minneapolis: Fortress, 2012). For a general introduction to socio-pragmatic hermeneutics, see Anthony C. Thiselton, *New Horizons in Hermeneutics* (Grand Rapids: Zondervan, 1992), 379–470.

16. See below under Paul in the Crucible of New World and Modern Slavery for these two leaders. I imitate words from Bird, 30, who used Wilberforce as his example. The move from ecclesial ethics into public sector ethics in a pluralist society deserves deep discussions, beginning with David G. Horrell, *Solidarity and Difference: A Contemporary Reading of Paul's Ethics*, 2nd ed. (London: Bloomsbury T&T Clark, 2015).

17. Fine expositions of a progressive or redemptive movement hermeneutic are found in Thompson, 261–66; Kevin Giles, "The Biblical Argument for Slavery: Can the Bible Mislead? A Case Study in Hermeneutics," *EvQ* 66 (1994): 3–17; William J. Webb, *Slaves, Women and Homosexuals: Exploring the Hermeneutics of Cultural Analysis* (Downers Grove, IL: InterVarsity Press, 2001). The issue at hand is how deeply intentional such a vision of the future was at work in the Bible and in Paul. Did Paul see this letter or the household regulations as the first step toward abolition? I will argue he did not.

lem itself. They further contend (with progressives) that the text is clearly a first step in the direction of intentional manumission or emancipation. I counter that 1800 years is a long time for the seed of abolitionism to flower. I take such a conservative, Edmund Burkean theory of intentional prescription to be the least likely explanation of what Paul intended. One might well say, and I would agree, that Paul dropped a world-altering stone when he tossed Gal 3:28 and its various parallels into the Mediterranean. One might say it generated ripples that flowed all the way to the *Emancipation Proclamation* and then to the global Civil Rights movement of the last century or toward liberation theology in its many forms, but it is another thing to say Paul intended the ripples. Effects are not always the accurate way to measure intentions. George Orwell's fable *Animal Farm*, adored since its American publication by political conservatives, was created by a man who stood firmly as a Labor Party socialist-leaning critic of totalitarianism and Tories with equal hatred. What one makes of a maker's work does not always match what its maker meant. The same applies to Paul and Philemon.

I want to make it clear what will happen in this commentary. I believe the apostle Paul opens the door into the home of Philemon with a letter that attempts (probably successfully) to persuade Philemon, not to manumit Onesimus, but to welcome him back home after running away and probably swiping some money and goods for his trip. Paul wants Philemon, in other words, not to pursue justice but to create a cycle of grace, forgiveness, restitution, and reconciliation. More tellingly, Paul seeks here to create a new kind of society, a fellowship of equals in which the slave owner and slave were brothers (and sisters) in Christ. I do not know that Paul knew what would happen. Paul wanted an open door for Onesimus to walk through as a forgiven brother.

What this letter then does for us today demands our immediate attention: *the church is to be first space of reconciliation in our communities, first among its own people and second as reconciled people who strive for reconciliation in society.* Reconciled people become agents of reconciliation because they know no other way. Churches form the vanguard of creating a place where those deemed by the world and society and culture as unequals will be welcomed, not in terms of the world but in terms of being in Christ. As a place that embodies reconciliation in space and time, the church generates a new way of life—Christoformity—that is to become paradigmatic of how Christians enter into society and the world. That is, this letter points the way for Christians to become agents that subvert slavery in our world by finding it, by naming it, by fighting against it, and by embodying a way of life that establishes social equality as the ground rules for the new communities in Christ. Hence, we must now enter into two features of slavery: what it meant in the world of Paul and what it means now. Once these are clear, we can see what Paul said and see how we can embody the new society under king Jesus.

I. SLAVERY IN THE ROMAN EMPIRE[18]

John Chrysostom—in the argument to his sermons on Philemon composed more than three centuries after Paul wrote the missive[19]—articulated a par-

18. On slavery in the Roman Empire, see Wiedemann, *Greek and Roman Slavery*; Keith R. Bradley, *Slaves and Masters in the Roman Empire: A Study in Social Control* (New York: Oxford University Press, 1987); Keith R. Bradley, *Slavery and Society at Rome*, Key Themes in Ancient History (Cambridge: Cambridge University Press, 1994); Jo-Ann Shelton, *As the Romans Did: A Sourcebook in Roman Social History*, 2nd ed. (New York: Oxford University Press, 1998), 163–202; Moses I. Finley, *Ancient Slavery and Modern Ideology*, ed. Brent D. Shaw, rev. ed. (Princeton, NJ: Markus Weiner, 1998); Jennifer A. Glancy, *Slavery in Early Christianity* (Minneapolis: Fortress, 2006); Sandra R. Joshel, *Slavery in the Roman World*, Cambridge Introduction to Roman Civilization (Cambridge: Cambridge University Press, 2010); Sandra R. Joshel and Lauren Hackworth Petersen, *The Material Life of Roman Slaves* (Cambridge: Cambridge University Press, 2014); Catherine Hezser, "Slavery," in *The Oxford Encyclopedia of the Bible and Law*, ed. Brent A. Strawn (Oxford: Oxford University Press, 2015), 2:302–19. For a broader look at slavery, see the essay by John DeFelice, "Slavery," in *Dictionary of Daily Life in Biblical and Post-Biblical Antiquity*, ed. Edwin M. Yamauchi and M. R. Wilson, 4 vols. (Peabody, MA: Hendrickson, 2016), 4.191–215; Keith Bradley and Paul Cartledge, eds., *The Cambridge World History of Slavery: 1. The Ancient Mediterranean World* (Cambridge: Cambridge University Press, 2011); David Eltis and Stanley L. Engerman, eds., *The Cambridge World History of Slavery: 3. AD 1420–AD 1804* (Cambridge: Cambridge University Press, 2011).

For methodology of studying slavery, especially as it concerns the cautious use of Roman legal texts for understanding Paul, see J. Albert Harrill, *The Manumission of Slaves in Early Christianity*, HUT 32 (Tübingen: Mohr Siebeck, 1995), 1–67; J. Albert Harrill, "Using the Roman Jurists to Interpret Philemon," *ZNW* 90 (1999): 135–38; J. Albert Harrill, "Paul and Slavery," in *Paul in the Greco-Roman World: A Handbook*, ed. J. Paul Sampley (Harrisburg, PA: Trinity Press International, 2003), 575–607; G. François Wessels, "The Letter to Philemon in the Context of Slavery in Early Christianity," in Tolmie, *Philemon in Perspective*, 143–68; Joshel, *Slavery in the Roman World*, 13–27; Mitzi J. Smith, "Utility, Fraternity, and Reconciliation: Ancient Slavery as a Context for the Return of Onesimus," in *Onesimus Our Brother: Reading Religion, Race, and Culture in Philemon*, ed. Matthew V. Johnson, James A. Noel, and Demetrius K. Williams, Paul in Critical Contexts (Minneapolis: Fortress Press, 2012), 47–58. For a sketch of recent books on slavery, Kyle Harper, "Knowledge, Ideology, and Skepticism in Ancient Slave Studies," *AJP* 132 (2011): 160–68. For a "fictional" but brilliant description of slavery in the Roman world, Jerry Toner, *The Roman Guide to Slave Management: A Treatise by Nobleman Marcus Sidonius Falx* (New York: Overlook Press, 2014).

19. There is some discussion on how integral Chrysostom was to the interpretive tradition about the status of Onesimus. For a challenge to the tradition, followed

ticular form of discourse about slavery and slaves that helped to deepen the theological legitimacy of slavery in Christian rhetoric and society:

> That we ought not to withdraw slaves from the service of their masters. For if Paul, who had such confidence in Philemon, was unwilling to detain Onesimus, so useful and serviceable to minister to himself, without the consent of his master, much less ought we so to act. For if the servant is so excellent, he ought by all means to continue in that service, and to acknowledge the authority of his master, that he may be the occasion of benefit to all in that house. Why dost thou take the candle from the candlestick to place it in the bushel?[20]

Chrysostom's younger contemporary, Basil the Great, was not alone in his support of slavery by encouraging those with the power to do so to return runaways:

> All bound slaves who flee to religious communities for refuge should be admonished and sent back to their masters in better dispositions, after the example of St. Paul who, although he had begotten Onesimus through the gospel, sent him back to Philemon.[21]

This letter on which Chrysostom preaches, Philemon, rode the wave of the Pauline mission and became a significant moral question: How does Christianity's emphasis—not least in the apostle Paul's Magna Carta (Gal 3:28; also 1 Cor 12:13; Col 3:11)—on equality or oneness/unity of all before God *not*

---

by a counter-challenge, see Allen Dwight Callahan, "Paul's Epistle to Philemon: Toward an Alternative *Argumentum*," *HTR* 86 (1993): 357–76; Margaret M. Mitchell, "John Chrysostom on Philemon: A Second Look," *HTR* 88 (1995): 135–48. Mitchell has successfully challenged Callahan's pointing of the finger at Chrysostom's view as "novel and tentative" (140).

On Chrysostom's discourse about slavery, sometimes called "doulology," see Chris L. de Wet, *Preaching Bondage: John Chrysostom and the Discourse of Slavery in Early Christianity* (Oakland, CA: University of California Press, 2015). For the reception history of Philemon in the early church, see Paul B. Decock, "The Reception of the Letter to Philemon in the Early Church: Origen, Jerome, Chrysostom and Augustine," in Tolmie, *Philemon in Perspective*, 273–87; Alfred Friedl, "St. Jerome's Dissertation on the Letter to Philemon," in Tolmie, *Philemon in Perspective*, 289–316; Chris L. de Wet, "Honour Discourse in John Chrysostom's Exegesis of the Letter to Philemon," in Tolmie, *Philemon in Perspective*, 317–31, and John T. Fitzgerald, "Theodore of Mopsuestia on Paul's Letter to Philemon," in Tolmie, *Philemon in Perspective*, 333–63.

20. John Chrysostom, *Homilies on Philemon* (Schaff, *NPNF*[1] 13:546).

21. Wagner, FC 9:261–62. For exposition of others, see Mitchell, "John Chrysostom on Philemon."

interrogate and unravel the Empire's ubiquitous practice of (in)human bondage? Regardless of what one wants to see in Gal 3:28 and in the rather idyllic descriptions by scholars of the first Christian churches, the reality is that three centuries of adherence to and exposition of Paul's letter to Philemon did not provoke belief in manumission as the implication of Paul's teaching. Chrysostom argues that Christianity was being reduced to blasphemy: "Of saying Christianity has been introduced into life for the subversion of everything, masters having their servants taken from them, and it is a matter of violence."[22] Here one hears finally a note of manumission, but manumission is precisely what Chrysostom thinks is blasphemous! No, for him Christianity and the Empire's order of slaves and masters were comfortably compatible, resistance was unacceptable.[23]

A few decades later in the *Code of Theodosius* we discover that the emperor Constantine granted full legal status to anyone who freed a slave "in the bosom of the church" and that "clerics" were given permission to grant manumission to slaves also at their deathbeds. In the interpretation of Constantinian decision, we encounter a clear reminder that slavery not only existed in the Roman Empire but that Christians—including "clerics"—participated in the enslavement of others:

> If anyone wishes to manumit in the holy church, it suffices for him to wish to manumit in the presence of the presbyters, and he will know that when they receive their freedom they become Roman citizens. And if clerics should wish to bestow freedom on their own slaves, they shall attain full and complete freedom as Roman citizens even if the manumission takes place out of the sight of the presbyters, or is simply verbal, without confirmation in writing.[24]

In their massive commentary on Philemon and one that takes this socially conservative ("wise") approach, Markus Barth and Helmut Blanke call many to attention with the following reminder of what actually happens in this letter to Philemon:

22. John Chrysostom, *Homilies on Philemon* (*NPNF*¹ 13:546). Melania, a Christian noblewoman of the fifth century and associate to Augustine, is said to have had some 24,000 slaves. See discussion at Kyle Harper, *Slavery in the Late Roman World, AD 275–425* (Cambridge: Cambridge University Press, 2011), 192–94.

23. Notice, too, the story of Callistus in Hippolytus, *Refutation of All Heresies* 9.7; also Salvian, *Governance of God* 4.3, who turns the behaviors of slaves (stealing, lying, etc.) against Christian slaveowners for doing the same things.

24. *Code of Theodosius* 4.7.1; translation of Wiedemann, *Greek and Roman Slavery*, 50–51.

> Many expositors of [Philemon] . . . have assumed that Paul wrote [Philemon] in order to move the slave owner not only to receive the returning servant kindly but also to manumit him. If this could be proven, Paul would indeed be an early member and protagonist of abolitionism, the Social Gospel movement, and liberation theology. Then it might be claimed that he fought slavery in principle and that any other interpretation reveals the expositor's bourgeois, if not capitalistic, mentality and contributes to future oppression and exploitation. Whether it pleases or displeases, it has to be accepted as a fact that in [Philemon] there is "not one single word" expressing the wish or command that Onesimus be legally emancipated.[25]

The manumission of slaves would have been a major moral accomplishment from Paul. Yet, the evidence is not as favorable as many would like. Notably, Eduard Lohse seemingly sides with the Stoics' approach to slavery (an embodiment that does not touch the soul) and thus frames the moral issue of Philemon in terms of the classic adiaphora:[26]

> There is no doubt that earthly freedom is a great good. Nevertheless, in the last analysis it is of no significance to the Christian whether he is slave or free. The only thing that matters is this: to have accepted God's call and to follow him (1 Cor 7:21–24). The master of a slave also must be obedient to this call, for he, too, is subject to the command of the Kyrios. In this way, the relationship of master and slave has undergone a fundamental change. Although it might seem natural that Philemon grant Onesimus his freedom, the Apostle can leave it to Philemon how he wants to decide. Under all circumstances Philemon is bound to the commandment of love which makes its renovating power effective in any case, since the slave who returns home is now a brother.

Others think Paul opened the door to manumission but did not walk through. Murray Harris is an example:

> Throughout [Philemon] vv. 15–16 Paul is entertaining the possibility that, having forgiven and reinstated Onesimus, Philemon will retain him as a slave. Nowhere in the letter does Paul demand the release of Onesimus or

25. Barth and Blanke, 368. On "wise," see Barth and Blank, 368–69. What one sees as "wise" another will see as lacking courage or failing to be consistent with the vision of Gal 3:28.

26. Lohse, 203. Such a treatment appears morally insensitive. Much better is Bruce, 217, who thinks at least theoretically of Philemon manumitting Onesimus. Also Witherington, 29–30.

even assume that Philemon will set him free. But although the apostle accepts slavery as a social condition and as a legal fact (he returns Onesimus to his rightful owner with a promissory note to cover any indebtedness), he indirectly undermines the institution of slavery by setting the master-slave relation on a new footing when he highlights Onesimus's true status as a dearly loved Christian brother.[27]

Now the questions: What did it mean for Paul to have said there was neither slave nor free in Christ? Did it have any ecclesial-social implications? Was this purely a spiritual equality? Was slavery for Paul a moral issue or not? Did Paul himself work out the theology of Gal 3:28 and Col 3:11 consistently? Did he only begin to work it out? Did he fail to work that theology into the ordinary grind of ordinary life for a Christian household or *oikonomia*? Or did Paul adumbrate, as I think he does in this letter, an early version of what might be called an "Anabaptist" approach, namely, that *in the confines of the Christian* ekklēsia *liberation would rule*?[28] That is, Paul's vision was not for the Roman Empire but for the church, though (of course) what he saw for the *ekklēsia* would obtain as well for the Empire if it were to bow to king Jesus. That is, his vision was not for *manumission of slaves in the Roman Empire*. Rather his view was about something *other than legal manumission*, that is, *a new creation sibling-based fellowship on the basis of adoption as children of God*. For Paul this was a nobler vision and one (for him) more penetrating.[29] For Paul the social revolution was to occur in the

27. Harris, 268.

28. E.g., Reidar Aasgaard, *"My Beloved Brothers and Sisters!" Christian Siblingship in Paul*, JSNTSup 265 (London: T&T Clark, 2004), 254–57. This squares with Paul's understanding of justification transcending all other identity formations; see Michael Wolter, "The Letter to Philemon as Ethical Counterpart of Paul's Doctrine of Justification," in Tolmie, *Philemon in Perspective*, 169–79 (here 176–79).

29. The following works, despite differences, draw some similar conclusions about the ecclesial location of Paul's focus: Lloyd A. Lewis, "An African American Appraisal of the Philemon-Paul-Onesimus Triangle," in *Stony the Road We Trod: African American Biblical Interpretation*, ed. Cain Hope Felder (Minneapolis: Fortress, 1991), 232–46; Craig S. de Vos, "Once a Slave, Always a Slave? Slavery, Manumission and Relational Patterns in Paul's Letter to Philemon," *JSNT* 82 (2001): 89–105; Aasgaard, *My Beloved Brothers and Sisters!*; Isak J. du Plessis, "How Christians Can Survive in a Hostile Social-Economic Environment: Paul's Mind Concerning Difficult Social Conditions in the Letter to Philemon," in *Identity, Ethics, and Ethos in the New Testament*, BZNW 141 (Berlin: de Gruyter, 2006), 387–413; Gorman, *Apostle of the Crucified Lord*, 462–63; Kevin J. Vanhoozer, "Imprisoned or Free? Text, Status, and Theological Interpretation in the Master/Slave Discourse of Philemon," in *Reading Scripture with the Church: Toward a Hermeneutic for Theological Interpretation*, ed. A. K. M. Adam, Stephen E. Fowl, Kevin J. Vanhoozer, and Francis Watson (Grand Rapids: Baker Academic, 2006), 51–93 (esp. 87–88); N. T. Wright, *Paul and the Faithfulness of God*,

church, in the body of Christ, at the local level, and in the Christian house church and household.

The impact of a new creation vision for the *ekklēsia* was as radical for Paul as it was for Philemon, for in this letter Paul eschews his authority and appeals on the basis of love. As such, Paul sets a tone for leadership that counters typical Roman ways.[30] That is, to use the language of Victor Turner, Paul formed some anti-structures to the structures of the world, new anti-structures shaped by personhood and community or fellowship, with the *ekklēsia* being the location.[31] In the anti-structure, Onesimus is no longer a slave but a brother, and Paul (not Philemon) is the father, and Philemon is a brother to Onesimus, and Apphia is a sister to Paul and to Onesimus and Philemon. Paul's concentration was the faith-community and fellowship not the Roman Empire and its structures. I do think Paul offers a "window of hope" for those who ponder the morality of slavery in the context of Philemon.[32] The tension moderns sense in this letter may well be best explained and Paul's own theology and praxis shown to be more consistent, if this distinction between *ekklēsia* and Empire be kept in mind. Revolution occurs in the new relations shaped by love in the *oikonomia* of Philemon in Colossae not with swords and shouts in the Roman forum. Paul did not so much turn a blind eye to the morality of slavery as he did not realize slavery was an issue of morality. He was blind to the immorality of slavery as an institution.

---

vol. 4 of *Christian Origins and the Question of God* (Minneapolis: Fortress, 2013), 1:12. Also, Thompson, 238–46.

Paul's fundamental vision for the fellowship was that they were siblings. He normally uses the term "brother" but implies "brother and sister." He may sustain some fatherly and motherly language, but his bigger vision is not the creation so much of a new "family" but of a new siblinghood. On fathers in Paul: Paul himself (1 Thess 2:11; 1 Cor 4:15; Phil 2:22; with sons—1 Tim 1:2; 2 Tim 1:2; Titus 1:4), Abraham (Rom 4:12, 16), the patriarchs (1 Cor 10:1; Rom 9:5; 11:28; 15:8), Isaac (Rom 9:10), ordinary fathers (Col 3:21; Eph 6:2). On mothers: Gal 4:19, 26; 1 Thess 2:7; 5:3; 1 Cor 3:1–2; Rom 8:22; 1 Tim 5:2.

30. Kirk D. Lyons Sr., "Paul's Confrontation with Class: The Letter to Philemon as Counter-Hegemonic Discourse," *Cross Currents* 56 (2006): 116–32. Lyons contends for a different form of the progressive manumission theory but locates the radical act in Paul's own self-presentation as prisoner and in Paul's appeal to love and partnership rather than power.

31. Employed by Norman R. Petersen, *Rediscovering Paul: Philemon and the Sociology of Paul's Narrative World* (Philadelphia: Fortress Press, 1985), 151–63, and 200–286 (for adoption creating a new symbolic universe for the Pauline churches). See, too, Wright's emphasis on "worldview" in *Paul and the Faithfulness of God*, 1:24–68.

32. Lewis, "Philemon-Paul-Onesimus Triangle," 246. For a more optimistic approach to seeds of abolitionism planted among the early Christians, Charles Pietri, "Christians and Slaves in the Early Days of the Church (2nd–3rd Centuries)," in *The Dignity of the Despised of the Earth*, ed. Jacques Pohier and Dietmar Mieth, Concilium 130.10 (New York: Seabury Press, 1979), 31–39.

Philemon, therefore, both intrigues and disturbs. The first without the second is inaccurate, the second without the first abandons Christian hope. The disturbing nature of Philemon comes to the fore when we examine slavery in the Roman Empire, to which topic we now move, but it is modern slavery that puts the church to the test with this letter in hand, and we will look at modern slavery when our survey of Roman slavery is complete.

A. STATUS AND SLAVES

The Roman Empire with its "compulsion to classify all men as either free or slave" and to dress accordingly expressed status and honor at every turn.[33] *Who one was* and *what one did* were shaped by *where one was located on the social ladder*. The imperial slave was better than the rustic slave on a small farm in central Italy, while the wealthier the master the more slaves and the more specialized the jobs for the slaves. An abundance of slaves was a means to display status and wealth.[34] Status for slaves was determined by the character of the master: good masters were better than the scurrilous and violent (cf. 1 Pet 2:18). Slavery was not connected to race but to social location, and those considered by the Roman elites most naturally born for slavery were Syrians and Jews. Thus, Cicero says, "And as for the miserable farmers of the revenue, (miserable man that I also am, when I see the miseries and sufferings of those men who have deserved so well at my hands,) he handed them over as slaves to the Jews and Syrian nations, *themselves born for slavery*."[35]

The mindset in slave societies is found in quintessential form in Aristotle. Households require tools; "some are lifeless and others living."[36] Aristotle says "the slave is an assistant in the class of instruments of action"[37] so (naturally for him) the relation of a master to a slave is asymmetrical: "whereas the master is merely the slave's master and does not belong to the slave, the slave is not merely the slave of the master but wholly belongs to the master."[38] A slave is "property" and thus "a human being belonging by nature not to himself but to another" (1.2.7) because there are some who are "by nature slaves" (1.2.13). According to Aristotle, "by nature a slave [is] who is capable of belonging to another . . . and who participates in reason so far as

33. Wiedemann, *Greek and Roman Slavery*, 61. At times ancient writers do observe the seeming inconsistency that slaves and free often dressed alike—that a slave could not be known by what was worn (e.g., Appian, *Civil Wars* 2.17).

34. Apuleius, *Apology* 17, illustrates the pervasiveness of this theme in Roman society.

35. Cicero, *On Consular Provinces* 10, my italics (Yonge).

36. Aristotle, *Politics* 1.2.4 (Rackham, LCL).

37. Aristotle, *Politics* 1.2.6.

38. Aristotle, *Politics* 1.2.6.

to apprehend it but not to possess it."[39] His analytics know no boundaries: "the usefulness of slaves diverges little from that of animals."[40] He connects slavery to bodies as some are physically shaped for slavery. For such people "slavery is an institution both expedient and just."[41] Plato had already expressed this deep sense of inferiority on the part of slaves in these words: "that the soul of a slave has no soundness in it, and that a sensible man should never trust that class at all?"[42] Slaves, and this matters intensively for the entire Bible and needs to be admitted by all its readers, had the status of moral and ontological inferiors.

This "classical" view of slaves cannot be relegated to a past period well before the New Testament since it was this classical view that continued to dominate discourse about slavery in the first century CE, of course with adjustments and some more egalitarian (Stoic) rejoinders.[43] This, from Epictetus,[44] is a classic Stoic approach to slavery, one in which the person is distanced from the body, one's status released from power, and the slave can then be "free":

> For the rest, when the tyrant threatens and summons me, I answer "Whom are you threatening?" If he says, "I will put you in chains," I reply, "He is threatening my hands and my feet." If he says, "I will behead you," I answer, "He is threatening my neck." If he says, "I will throw you into prison," I say, "He is threatening my whole paltry body"; and if he threatens me with exile, I give the same answer.—Does he, then, threaten you not at all?—If I feel that all this is nothing to me,—not at all; but if I am afraid of any of these threats, it is I whom he threatens. Who is there left, then, for me to fear? The man who is master of what? The things that

39. Aristotle, *Politics* 1.2.13.

40. Aristotle, *Politics* 1.2.14.

41. Aristotle, *Politics* 1.2.15.

42. Plato, *Laws* 776e (Bury, LCL).

43. Bradley, *Slaves and Masters*, 134, points us to Justinian's *Digest*, where we read "Freedom is one's natural power of doing what one pleases, save insofar as it is ruled out either by coercion or by law. 1. Slavery is an institution of the *jus gentium*, whereby someone is against nature made subject to the ownership of another" (1.5.4. Alan Watson, ed., *The Digest of Justinian*, 4 vols., rev. ed. [Philadelphia: University of Pennsylvania Press, 1998], 1:15. Translation: Notice "against nature" reveals that slavery is not as Aristotle thinks. The Stoics both saw all humans as spiritual, intellectual and moral equals and at the same time saw any physical condition as unworthy of attention since one's happiness was mental, not physical. Hence, there are within Stoicism both the possibility and impossibility of a manumission movement. For discussion, Glancy, *Slavery in Early Christianity*, 30–34. Seneca's expression can be found in *Epistle* 47.

44. Epictetus was a well-known Stoic philosopher of the latter half of the first century and first quarter of the second century CE.

> are under my control? But there is no such man. The man who is master of the things that are not under my control? And what do I care for them?[45]

Neither Epictetus nor his fellow Stoics impacted the embodied normality of Roman slaves. Their airy ideas were inadequate for any movement toward manumission, not to mention manumission itself. Stoicism may well have been attractive to some, but Aristotle's reality ruled the day: those who were slaves were slaves by nature, inferior, and located at the bottom of society.[46]

Rome created a "slave society."[47] Some estimate the percentage of slaves at thirty-five percent.[48] Rome became dependent on slavery. An estimated 250,000 slaves were sold in Rome per year.[49] True to form the Roman world classified this myriad of slaves into orders and ranks, and also true to form there were laws regulating slaves, slave owners, and manumission. As free persons were classified as either born free or manumitted into freedom, so the freed slave could be labeled in three ways: those manumitted into Roman citizenship (usually only after the age of 30), those freed into a status called the Junian Latins (who are less than citizens and cannot make a will or inherit but who, over time, might become citizens), and "subjects" (*dediticii*), those who were no longer slaves but who because of their behaviors in the past could never rise to the level of a citizen.[50] Many, if not most, slaves who were manumitted remained dependent upon their former masters.[51] To illustrate the ongoing relationship of even the freed person to the master, called in Greek the *paramonē*-relationship, the specific example of a manumission inscription from Delphi in the first half of the first century CE provides all we need:[52]

> On the following conditions Sophrona, acting with the consent of her son Sosandros, hands over to the Pythian Apollo to be free the female house-born slave [literally, "body"] named Onasiphoron.

45. Epictetus, *Discourses* 1.29.6–8 (Oldfather, LCL).

46. For more, Wiedemann, *Greek and Roman Slavery*, 224–51. For a typical perception of labor and status, see Cicero, *On Duties* 1.150–51.

47. Bradley, *Slaves and Masters*, 13; Bradley, *Slavery and Society at Rome*, 10–30.

48. Galen said of Pergamum, not far from Colossae, that thirty-three percent of its population were slaves. See Weidemann, *Greek and Roman Slavery*, 79.

49. E.g., William V. Harris, "Towards a Study of the Roman Slave Trade," *Memoirs of the American Academy in Rome* 36 (1980): 117–40 (121–24). Also, Joshel, *Slavery in the Roman World*, 78–110.

50. Discussed in Gaius, *Institutes* 1.1.8–55, a text from the second century CE but at least approximate for the ranks in the first century at Asia Minor.

51. Cf. de Vos, "Once a Slave, Always a Slave?," 89–105 (100).

52. *Fouilles de Delphes* 3.6.36; in Wiedemann, *Greek and Roman Slavery*, 46–47 #23.

> [But notice the nature and life-long length of this *paramonē*-arrangement:] Onasiphoron is to remain with Sophrona for the whole period of the latter's life, doing whatever she is ordered to do without giving cause for complaint. If she does not do so, then Sophrona is to have the power to punish her in whatever way she wishes to. And Onasiphoron is to give Sosandros a child.

One's master determined the slave's location in society and type of labor—slaves of the emperor were much different than the farming slaves. In effect, some if not most imperial slaves lived a much more comfortable life than ordinary freepersons *but* for one unimpeachable reality: slaves were legally non-existent persons, without capacity to marry or to inherit (or pass on inheritance). Powerlessness eventually will produce reaction, rebellion, and revolution.

B. ON DEFINING "SLAVERY"

This definition of slavery in the New World by a fugitive slave, James W. C. Pennington, puts into bold relief the essential features of slavery, New World *and* Roman:

> The being of slavery, its soul and its body, lives and moves in the chattel principle, the property principle, the bill of sale principle; the cart-whip, starvation, and nakedness, are its inevitable consequences.[53]

The "property principle" emerges from the system intended by the powerful. Yet, historians are not satisfied with imposing modern definitions on first-century data. As a result it is necessary to carefully explore the world of Paul and Philemon and Onesimus. The famous *Digest* of Justinian, the code of Roman law, opens with a definition of slavery: "Slavery is an institution of the common law of people (*jus gentium*) whereby someone is against nature made subject to the ownership of another."[54] Focusing on either ownership or on natural law, however, does not go far enough to define slavery. Slavery describes *a perceived inferior human (the other) under the total authority of another perceived superior human, and that perceived (and false) reality is established by power and authority for the sake of profit (for the owner) and publication of the owner's wealth.* Slavery then is about *voluntary exploitation*

53. Found in David Brion Davis, *Inhuman Bondage: The Rise and Fall of Slavery in the New World* (Oxford: Oxford University Press, 2006), 193.

54. From Florentius, *Institutes*, book 9 in Justinian, *Digest* 1.5.4 (Watson).

of an *involuntary* human and in most cases slavery was for life.[55] Slavery is about status, integrity, identity, and utility.

What needs to be repeated over and over is that slavery is a legal status more than it is an occupation. Slaves can be found performing nearly all occupations in the Roman Empire—from farming to philosophizing, from the cruel labor of working in mines to the refined attention on the master's wife,[56] from routine domestic chores to practicing medicine,[57] from being a wet-nurse to being a sexual partner or a prostitute. Slavery was not equated with ignorance and incompetence. Epictetus began life as a slave in the same area of Asia Minor from which the letter to Philemon came to life, and some still believe the Onesimus of our letter became the bishop of Ephesus.

C. FAMILY LIFE FOR THE SLAVE

Slaves lacked legal status. Therefore, when a society is built from the inside out on the basis of families, the family slave enters into the deepest of liminalities. Male slaves remained "boys" and their manhood—connected of course to family and autonomy and inheritance and dignity—was denied. An illustration of this can be found in the terms used in the episode of the healing of the centurion's servant, or was it a boy or a son? Here is how Matthew describes the "servant."

> When he entered Capernaum, a centurion came to him, appealing to him and saying, "Lord, my servant (*pais*) is lying at home paralyzed, in terrible distress." (Matt 8:5–6)
>
> And to the centurion, Jesus said, "Go; let it be done for you according to your faith." And the servant (*pais*) was healed in that hour. (Matt 8:13)

The term *pais* will normally describe a child in relation to a parent, and John's Gospel confirms that interpretation with a powerful Christian twist when the term is not *pais* but *huios* ("son"; cf. John 4:47), someone who could inherit and pass on inheritance. Luke's Gospel, however, calls the male a "slave" (*doulos*; Luke 7:2). The permanent boyhood of a Roman male slave finds its ambiguity in the switching of terms in these gospel texts.[58] All of this is informative for the social realities of Onesimus's world. Why did Paul call him "child" (*teknon*) not "son" (as in NIV) in Phlm 10?

55. Joshel, *Slavery in the Roman World*, 9.

56. Xenophon, *Ways and Means* 1.

57. P.Oxy. 3510 uses the term ἄτεχνοι for two slaves, indicating they were generalists, running errands and fixing this and doing that.

58. Glancy, *Slavery in Early Christianity*, 24–25.

Because slaves had no legal status, and because marriage was a legal act, slaves could not marry so there was a substitute for marriages. Slave "marriages" were not legal marriages but they were permanent arrangements. Such a relationship did not guarantee that either of them could not be sold or that the offspring would not be sold. Slave marriages were contained within the master's economy and, hence even more, the stability of a slave family was contained and exacerbated by the master's economy.

D. THE PRAGMATICS OF MASTERS AND SLAVES

The fundamental relationship of a master to a slave in the Roman Empire maps itself on the spectrum from the absolute authority of the master to the loyalty and obedience of the slave.[59] Valerius Maximus in his famous "Of the Fidelity of Slaves"[60] tells stories of such faithfulness, loyalty, and obedience. Pragmatics, not ideals, ruled the day: masters learned they got more out of their servants the better they treated them, although even that treatment had behind it the dark realities of brutalizing the disloyal and disobedient. Masters provided the necessities of life, including food, clothing, and shelter, the latter often little more than a cell in the household. Notice these pragmatic words from Columella who shows that kind treatment leads to greater profits:

> After all these arrangements have been acquired or contrived, especial care is demanded of the master not only in other matters, but most of all in the matter of the persons in his service. . . . He should be civil in dealing with his tenants, should show himself affable, and should be more exacting in the matter of work than of payments, as this gives less offence yet is, generally speaking, more profitable.[61]

Columella is not alone is urging masters to offer incentives and rewards—like holidays and festivals—along with punishments: "In fact, I now and then avenge those who have just cause for grievance, as well as punish those who incite the slaves to revolt, or who slander their taskmasters; and, on the other hand, I reward those who conduct themselves with energy and diligence."[62] Not a few historians think the aim of such rewards was obedience and loyalty for the sake of peace and profit.[63] Columella writes, "Such justice and consideration on the part of the master contributes easily

59. For discussion and textual support, Bradley, *Slaves and Masters*, 21–45.
60. E.g., Valerius Maximus, *Memorable Doings and Sayings* 6.8.
61. Columella, *On Agriculture* 1.7.1 (Boyd Ash, LCL).
62. Columella, *On Agriculture* 1.8.18–19.
63. Bradley, *Slaves and Masters*, 43–44.

to the increase of his estate."[64] Columella's insight into human nature and giftedness notwithstanding, his blindness to the morality of slavery was typical. Slaves were slaves; masters were masters. The injunctions to loyalty and obedience need to be seen for the social structure they maintained, and hence the early Christian instructions for slaves to be obedient deserve warning.[65]

E. SLAVERY, NO MATTER THE EXPLANATION

Many slaves were captives of war.[66] Others had been rescued from exposure.[67] Some were kidnapped by pirates for the sake of slavery. A rare few chose to sell themselves into slavery for improvement of their social condition.[68] Regardless, the elimination of any sense of status and rights establishes a slave culture of "living death."[69] The evidence of the harsher realities of slaves must not be minimized: slaves were slaves, and the slave's body belonged to the master. The only way to alter the demeaning realities of slavery is to treat the slave as a human being, to create a culture where each person has integrity, respect, and equal standing. No matter how "normal" slavery might be in the Roman Empire, slavery is slavery.

The evidence from the Roman Empire about slaves can be examined through the lens of *embodiment*, revealing that the slave's body was the master's body and that slave's body became in some ways a surrogate for the master's.[70] Revelation 18:11–13 lists what Rome's merchants sold:

> And the merchants of the earth weep and mourn for her, since no one buys their cargo anymore . . . wine, olive oil, choice flour and wheat, cattle and sheep, horses and chariots, *slaves*—and human lives.

But behind the word "slaves" is the Greek term *sōmatōn*, not *douloi* or even *diakonoi*. The merchants were trading what could be translated "bodies."[71]

64. Columella, *On Agriculture* 1.8.19.

65. See also Glancy, *Slavery in Early Christianity*, 34–38.

66. E.g., Josephus, *Jewish War* 6.420, where we read that during the war some 97,000 were taken as prisoners, which means most became slaves.

67. Suetonius, *Grammarians* 21.

68. On self-sale, which is not as common as is sometimes said in the literature, see now Glancy, *Slavery in Early Christianity*, 80–85.

69. The expression is thematized at times in Bradley, *Slavery and Society at Rome*, 25. On kidnapping, see Pausanias, *Description of Greece* 5.21.10; Suetonius, *Augustus*. 32; Wiedemann, *Greek and Roman Slavery*, 113–14.

70. Glancy, *Slavery in Early Christianity*.

71. See discussion in Glancy, *Slavery in Early Christianity*, 10–11.

So the beginning point for embodied slavery is slave trading.[72] Near the Roman forum, at the Temple of Castor, slaves were traded. Here we could have observed the indignity of embodied humiliation of inspecting slaves as an item of purchase and observed that slaves often had a note hanging around the neck that clarified any details legally about the slave's suitability.[73] Slaves were not only traded; they were commonly exploited and physically abused with violence.[74] Slave bodies were branded, shackled, their hands were cut off, and their legs broken; sometimes they were castrated[75] and iron collars imposed on them. The slave was always punished more severely than the citizen and free person, so the *Digest* will tell us.[76] Slaves were cremated alive, crucified, and handed over to wild animals in the amphitheater. The bodies of slaves, if we could but gaze upon them, could tell the story of slavery better than the literary and archaeological record.

Seneca reminds of the awful and embodied sexual reality of the *male* slave:

> Another, who serves the wine, must dress like a woman and wrestle with his advancing years; he cannot get away from his boyhood; he is dragged back to it; and though he has already acquired a soldier's figure, he is kept beardless by having his hair smoothed away or plucked out by the roots, and he must remain awake throughout the night, dividing his time

72. Slaves in Asia Minor were often imported from the Caucasus, which invites speculation about the meaning of "Scythian" in Col 3:11 and its possible parallel to "slaves" in the following "slave, free." See Douglas A. Campbell, "Unravelling Colossians 3:11b," *NTS* 42 (1996): 120–32; Douglas A. Campbell, "The Scythian Perspective in Col 3:11: A Response to Troy Martin," *NovT* 39 (1997): 81–84. In contrast, see Troy Martin, "The Scythian Perspective in Col 3:11," *JBL* 114 (1995): 253; Troy Martin, "Scythian Perspective or Elusive Chiasm: A Reply to Douglas A. Campbell," *NovT* 41 (1999): 256–64.

73. Bradley, *Slaves and Masters*, 115–16. Citing *Papyrus Turner* 22, Bradley provides an illustration of the sale of a ten-year-old slave girl named Abaskantis, and the text says she was "prone neither to wandering nor running away, and is free of epilepsy." Bradley, *Slaves and Masters*, 2. See also Justinian, *Digest* 21.1.12.1–4, where Ulpian (a later recorder of early Roman laws) discusses what disqualifies a slave and what does not. It is worth noting in passing that Roman *law* and what law was practiced in the provinces are not identical, however much the Romans set the precedents and the provinces the pattern of imitation. Nonetheless, one cannot assume Roman law was uniformly applied in every province or city or village or court. This conclusion mutes the sound of Roman law in the specific case of Colossae, Ephesus, Philemon, and Onesimus.

74. For a sampling of texts, see Wiedemann, *Greek and Roman Slavery*, 167–87. Note especially Juvenal, *Satires* 6.474–94.

75. For discussion of the Roman legal shifts on castrations, see Bradley, *Slaves and Masters*, 128–29.

76. Justinian, *Digest* 48.19.28.16.

> between his master's drunkenness and his lust; in the chamber he must be a man, at the feast a boy.[77]

If with males, how much more with *female* slaves?[78] They were torn from families at times to become sexual property, they became available to the master of the house—as well as the sons and other males in the household, including other slaves, or they became items to sell at a profit.[79] Part of their existence depended on their ability to satisfy the desires of the master. Some have suggested that at times slaves—male and female—used their sexuality to gain not only favor but to win manumission.

With regard to Onesimus, were there marks of abuse on his body? Had he been sexually used and abused? What kind of master was Philemon? More broadly, and a bit of a source of debate today, did Paul or the apostles expect converted masters to refrain from sex with their female slaves?[80]

F. THE OPTIONS FOR THE SLAVE

In thinking of Onesimus as a possible case of injustice, what were the options for a slave?[81] Appeal to the courts was possible but uncommon; court decisions rarely went in favor of the slave.[82] Open revolt by a mass of slaves had been tried and defeated by way of mass crucifixion of some 6,000 slaves. The memory of Spartacus cast a long, chilling, and dark shadow.[83] However, rarely was even a minor revolt an option during the Empire. So what could a slave do? Here are the options:

77. Seneca, *Epistle* 47 (Gummere, LCL).

78. Lynn H. Cohick, *Women in the World of the Earliest Christians: Illuminating Ancient Ways of Life* (Grand Rapids: Baker Academic, 2009), 257–84.

79. Apuleius, *The Golden Ass* 7.9.

80. Not all think so, and the topic now has its own booth for discussion. See Jennifer A. Glancy, "Obstacles to Slaves' Participation in the Corinthian Church," *JBL* 117 (1998): 481–501; Glancy, *Slavery in Early Christianity*, 49–70; Joseph A. Marchal, "The Usefulness of an Onesimus: The Sexual Use of Slaves and Paul's Letter to Philemon," *JBL* 130 (2011): 749–70; Kyle Harper, "*Porneia*: The Making of a Christian Sexual Norm," *JBL* 131 (2012): 363–83; Jennifer A. Glancy, "The Sexual Use of Slaves: A Response to Kyle Harper on Jewish and Christian *Porneia*," *JBL* 134 (2015): 215–29.

81. Bradley, *Slavery and Society at Rome*, 107–31. For a sampling of the texts on resistance and rebellion, Wiedemann, *Greek and Roman Slavery*, 188–223.

82. For discussion, Bradley, *Slaves and Masters*, 123–29.

83. Brent D. Shaw, *Spartacus and the Slave Wars: A Brief History with Documents* (Boston: Bedford/St. Martin's, 2001); Barry Strauss, *The Spartacus War* (New York: Simon & Schuster, 2010). Alongside Shaw's own translations, important texts are gathered in Wiedemann, *Greek and Roman Slavery*, 198–223.

> Those forms ranged from violent acts, such as suicide or murderous assaults on slave owners (often provoked by excessively brutal treatment), to the far less extreme actions of lying, cheating and stealing, of pretending to be sick or working at a calculatedly slow pace, of resorting in fact to any form of petty sabotage thinkable in order to indicate that slaves would not cooperate with their masters on a day to day basis, that they would cause their owners constant annoyance and frustration, and that they would take for themselves whatever relief from oppression was possible. In between was the ubiquitous practice of running away, either to gain temporary respite from slavery or in the hope of escaping servitude forever.[84]

Two extreme options for the slave were suicide or murder of the master.[85] At the time of Paul's letter to Philemon a city prefect Lucius Pedanius Secundus was murdered by his slave (Tacitus, *Ann.* 14.42–45). Masters kept slaves in their own social order by fear, punishments, disciplines, execution, and the constant threat of dissolving any kind of familial relationships. For these, and other reasons, some chose to run.

G. THE RUNAWAY[86]

Assuming the conclusion that Paul wrote the letter from a prison in Ephesus (rather than Rome) and that Onesimus was a runaway, the slave had traveled some one hundred miles when he "found" Paul, not an unusual distance for travel in that day. However, an escaping slave needed to acquire food, drink, and shelter. The fear of being caught—made doubly more difficult because slave catchers were on the prowl—was constant. In general, runaways escaped either to locations where they could be protected or to a large city where they could go undercover and find work. Hence, Epictetus summarizes the runaway's journey in these terms:

> Aren't you ashamed to be more cowardly and ignoble than a runaway slave? How do they, when they run off, leave their masters? in what estates or slaves do they put their confidence? Do they not steal just a little bit to last them for the first few days, and then afterwards drift along over land

84. Bradley, *Slavery and Society at Rome*, 110.

85. There is a well-known epitaph telling the story of a slave murdering his master, the slave then burning down the house to cover the evidence, the discovery of the perpetrator, the entire city mourning, and the crucifixion of the slave. See the text and a discussion in *NewDocs* 8:1–3.

86. For an excellent discussion, see *NewDocs* 8:9–46.

> or sea, contriving one scheme after another to keep themselves fed? And what runaway slave ever died of hunger?[87]

To flee required enormous courage, ingenuity, and emotional stamina on the part of the slave.

Slave owners were protected, of course, by laws and principles to return runaways to their owners.[88] Paul would have been expected to act in accordance with the laws. In the Roman Empire masters frequently posted information in public places to help find their runaways, the post offering a physical description of the runaway. One papyrus describes a runaway in these terms:

> Ignorant of Greek, tall, thin, smooth-shaven, on the left side of his head having a [small] wound, honey-complexion, pale, with scanty beard—altogether not having hair on his chin, smooth-skinned, narrow in the jaws, with a long nose, [being] a weaver by trade, always awkwardly speaking with a shrill voice of a pretentious person. He is about 32 years of age. He wears a ragged coat.[89]

Not uncommonly the notices described the materials the slave had pilfered, which, when attempted to be sold, could be used to identify the runaway. Following the description of the slave an injunction to find the person is given, a reward is mentioned, and information for contacting the slave owner provided, either through officials or more directly. Sometimes the government officials were involved in the search while at other times the task fell on the shoulders of the owner. Roman law made attempts to hide, employ (unless his master did not claim the slave in time), or sell runaways injurious to the one not returning the runaway. The runaway who was apprehended was sometimes bound hand and foot to secure the slave until he or she was returned to the master.[90] We can assume Onesimus—perhaps alone and perhaps with another runaway—knew Philemon was searching for him and from that we can infer that he needed an advocate and Paul was that person.

A final observation about runaways: owners assumed that what one slave did the others knew. Hence, *all slaves became responsible for the actions of the runaway*. Every slave in a household had a direct interest in the choice of the others and could be punished. A runaway then not only required cour-

87. Epictetus, *Discourses* 3.26.1–2 (Oldfather, LCL).

88. Thus, Justinian, *Digest* 11.4.1–5.

89. *NewDocs* 8:9. See also *NewDocs* 6:55–60.

90. *NewDocs* 8:24.

age but put all other slaves in jeopardy. When Paul sends a letter not only to Philemon, Apphia, and Archippus but also to "the church that meets in your home," one is entitled to speculate that other slaves and servants in the home were attentive to what Paul had to say.

H. MANUMISSION

There was a far more promising option for slaves than rebellion or runaway: manumission to become a freeperson. What then of the legal process and act of manumission as an option? While there are not a few comments in the ancient world indicating widespread manumission or at least a reasonably relaxed opportunity to acquire one's freedom, the path to manumission was far from easy and life after manumission often far more difficult. Most slaves were never manumitted:

> The elements of time involved—having to survive until the requisite age, having to await the death of the master for testamentary emancipation, having to wait for the accumulation of cash within the *peculium* to buy freedom; the location of the individual slave in the spectrum of servile statuses; and above all, the caprice of the slave-owner; all of these factors conditioned the eventual acquisition of liberty and made it a far more difficult proposition than the strict letter of the law suggests.[91]

And the promise to be manumitted for participation in a war or in some dangerous expedition could be added to the above conclusions.[92] Manumission did not lead immediately or even commonly to citizenship nor did it lead to a change of character.[93] It led to being a "freeperson," which is not the same as a citizen. As stated already, there was a legal category called *Junian* status in which a slave was both set free but rebound to the master in a kind of mandatory employment. That is, the slave's status or condition may have changed but the life did not change.

Defining descriptions of the manumission ceremony are found in Epictetus. A fundamental expression for manumission is "turning around" the slave in the presence of the praetor or legal authority:

91. Bradley, *Slaves and Masters*, 111 (see the discussion 81–112).

92. E.g., Dio Cassius 49.12; *Code of Theodosius* 7.13.8, 16.

93. Though his study assumes the correspondence between the stereotype of a slave's character and the actual character of slaves, de Vos's study illuminates an important dimension of manumission: it did not change character. See de Vos, "Once a Slave, Always a Slave?," 94–95.

> When, therefore, in the presence of a praetor a man turns his own slave about, has he done nothing?
>
> He has done something.
>
> What?
>
> He has turned his slave about in the presence of the praetor.
>
> Nothing more?
>
> Yes, he is bound to pay a tax of five percent of the slave's value.
>
> What then?
>
> Has not the man to whom this has been done become free?[94]

At this point Epictetus, who shows his Stoicism in full regalia, considers even such manumission to be unimportant when compared to freedom from all things—and he points at the slave owners who are owned by money and desires. In addition to turning around the slave, one finds inscriptions that use "hand over" to the gods as the official language of manumission.[95] In the ceremony, a tax would be imposed on the slave owner and payment made to the Roman court system. All this followed by promises about freedom and obligations or non-obligations of the freed person to the slave owner.

Epictetus both knows the experience and imagines his way into the thought processes of a slave being manumitted:

> "If I am set free," [the slave] says, "immediately it is all happiness, I shall pay no attention to anybody, I talk to everybody as an equal and as one in the same station in life, I go where I please, I come whence I please, and where I please."

But what happens?

> Then he (the slave) is emancipated, and forthwith, having no place to which to go and eat, he looks for someone to flatter, for someone at whose house to dine. Next he either earns a living by prostitution, and so endures the most dreadful things, and if he gets a manger at which to eat he has fallen into a slavery much more severe than the first; or even if he grows rich, being a vulgarian he has fallen in love with a chit of a girl, and is miserable. And laments, and yearns for his slavery again. "Why, what was wrong with me? Someone else kept me in clothes, and shoes, and supplied me with food, and nursed me when I was sick; I served him in only a few matters. But now, miser-

94. Epictetus, *Discourses* 2.1.25–27 (Oldfather, LCL).
95. *Fouilles de Delphes* 3.6.36; see Wiedemann, *Greek and Roman Slavery*, 46–47.

able man that I am, what suffering is mine, who am a slave to several instead of one!"[96]

We perhaps need to know then that manumission was not immediate success in life—it could lead as much to hardship then as it did when New World slaves found themselves on the Underground Railroad with rear-view mirrors suddenly haunting their every moment. Even more, our sense of social and civic freedom was not what the manumitted slave expected; furthermore, pressing the letter to Philemon to speak into that kind of freedom is to press it to do what it could not and did not do.

Even more, the critical language in manumission ceremonies of turning around is simply not found in Paul's letter to Philemon. Epictetus's Stoicism aside, there is no evidence in this letter that Paul envisions Philemon manumitting Onesimus. We do not find language about handing over or of turning around. We do not find him even hinting at public spaces or a courtroom or a praetor. We also hear nothing of taxation or payment to a court official. We see no description of the legal condition after the act of manumission. Rather, we find encapsulated space, the household of Philemon, and we find language like "welcome," "more than a brother," and "son/child" and we find terms like Paul paying Philemon as an act of restitution. These are the terms used by Paul to describe social realities, but they are not the terms or the social realities of manumission. Most notable of all, the word "freedom" is loudly absent in Philemon.

Three laws come into play in the discussion about manumission: The *lex Fufia Caninia*, the *lex Aelia Sientia*, and the *lex Junia*. The first created a "sliding scale" that determined the percentage of slaves that could be manumitted when the master died; the second stipulated that a master had to be twenty to manumit while the slave needed to be thirty (achieving thirty was hardly an assumption for first-century slaves). The final law, the *lex Junia*, created the category of a slave that was both manumitted but without full citizenship.[97] These laws were less concerned with expanding manumission than they were with protecting Roman citizenship.

One of the more illustrative careers of a slave is the story of Quintus Remmius Palaemon as told by Suetonius in his collection of stories about the lives of the illustrious.[98] The capacity of a few slaves to be liberated and to become famous was extensive and expansive. Were these stories not told

96. Epictetus, *Discourses* 4.1.34–37 (Oldfather, LCL).

97. Bradley, *Slavery and Society at Rome*, 156–57.

98. Suetonius, *Grammarians* 23. Another story, from a time after Philemon, of a slave rising to the heights of the Empire under Vespasian is a man known only as the "father of Claudius Etruscus." See Statius, *Silvae* 3.3.

among slaves to excite their hope? Epictetus, eventually an illustrious Stoic philosopher, was born a slave in the middle of the first century in Hierapolis. Was he buoyed up by stories of slaves becoming somebody in the Roman Empire?

We must come down from these utopian mountains to the reality. Freedom, at least as we have come to understand it—especially since the French Revolution at the hands of folks like the Baron Montesquieu or Thomas Paine with the connotations of self-determination and individual autonomy—was the condition of very few in the Roman Empire.[99] Only those at the top of power—emperors, senators, and equestrians—experienced what we would recognize as freedom and the rest were shaped by their location in the household. Hence, the sense of freedom that often drives the moral agenda in modern studies about Paul and the institution of slavery in the letter to Philemon was neither on the minds nor in the hearts of either the slaves or the Christian visionaries. Paul does not need to be seen as offering deliberate ambiguity in a rhetorical exploration or some kind of dualistic anthropology. The facts are these: (1) Paul clearly does not seem bothered by Christians masters or slaves (1 Cor 7:21–24, see below), despite Gal 3:28; (2) if Colossians and Ephesians are after Philemon (and scholars differ) then Paul did not manumit slaves for slaves are addressed in the household regulations and one might add that 1 Peter does the same; and (3) there is no evidence that earliest Christianity saw any demand to manumit slaves (as any number of early fathers demonstrates). Freedom in Christ, then, seemed to be lined up like bricks and cement with slavery and owning slaves. A place to stand, a status with some recognition, a family to call one's own, a siblingship in a household, a task that was ennobling—these are far more the hopes of slaves and the Christian visionaries like Paul. *We* are driven by culture to evaluate Paul's moral message on the basis of the later *abolition from slavery and freedom of slaves*, but we are not to equate *our* drives with *Paul's first-century Christian realities*.

A variety of explanations have been brought to the table to explain slavery in the New Testament, not least in Paul's own writings.[100] Thus, Christian interpreters have said slavery was part of the order of the Roman world, that protest against slavery was impossible for someone like Paul (or most anyone else). Christians were asked to treat slaves in a Christian manner. Such treatment would, in time, effect some change in the culture of Roman slavery. Following these typical explanations has been a routine claim that Paul planted seeds for the growth of an anti-slavery and eventual abolition

99. For a good discussion of freedom's senses, Thompson, 255–61.

100. Williams, "'No Longer as a Slave,'" 30–34. Many think Paul has here planted a seed for abolitionism (e.g., Bruce, 197–98; Harris, 268; Soungalo, 1487–88).

movement.[101] My response is terse: *if he did, Christians did not listen well and neither did Paul for he simply does not see slavery in itself as a moral problem.* To extend the metaphor, if Paul was planting seeds no one watered them. Such a viewpoint of planting seeds as the beginning of a new movement admittedly accords both with modern Christian beliefs as well as with social agendas. Yet, I am entirely unconvinced this was Paul's agenda. Paul was not unafraid to speak his mind; on this issue he did not speak his mind in favor of manumission.

The drive then to see if Paul was urging manumission is more the concern and privilege of post-French Revolution moderns than it was Roman or Jewish. While concentrating on a desire for freedom after manumission we miss the precise aim Paul had in mind: ennoblement, integrity, respect, status, honor and vocation. We need then to keep in mind not just the possibility of manumission but even more the vision Paul had for Onesimus, Philemon, and the church that met in his house. If we find in Paul an "ambivalent witness" about slavery and manumission,[102] we find in him at the same time an important ecclesial center for a new reality *that is not yet complete after nearly two millennia.* This we do know: liberation is created by Christ and in Christ. It is the church's responsibility to create spaces of liberation, both in the church itself and in culture.

101. Here is a brief breakdown of positions about manumission in Philemon, though it is not always clear if some authors fit into the first or second view so the nuances have to be blunted to get the discussion started:

1. Paul pleads for manumission: Witherington, 80, 86; Petersen, *Rediscovering Paul*, 280–86; Sara B. C. Winter, "Paul's Letter to Philemon," *NTS* 33 (1987): 1–15 (11–12); S. Scott Bartchy, "Philemon, Epistle to," *ABD* 5:308; Laura L. Sanders, "Equality and a Request for the Manumission of Onesimus," *ResQ* 46 (2004): 109–14; du Plessis, "How Christians Can Survive," 408–11. Also, Winter, 306–8. Paul implies, suggests, hints, and plants seeds for manumission: Bruce, 197–98; Harris, 268; Wright, 169–70; Fitzmyer, 122; Soungalo, 1488; Moo, 424–25, 436; Wessels, "Letter to Philemon," 164–68; Wright, *Paul and the Faithfulness of God*, 1:15.
2. Paul does not bother with slavery because either one is to live above it as in Stoicism or the eschaton is so imminent that slavery is diminished: Marion L. Soards, "Benefitting from Philemon," *Journal of Theology* 91 (1987): 44–51.
3. Paul is himself unsure or deliberately ambiguous: Dunn, 306; Osiek, 142; Barclay, "Dilemma of Christian Slave-Ownership," 175.
4. Paul thinks in terms of ecclesial revolution. Wolter, 271; Arzt-Grabner, 26; de Vos, "Once a Slave, Always a Slave?," 102–4.

102. Allen Dwight Callahan, "'Brother Saul': An Ambivalent Witness to Freedom," in *Onesimus Our Brother: Reading Religion, Race, and Culture in Philemon*, ed. Matthew V. Johnson, James A. Noel, and Demetrius K. Williams, Paul in Critical Contexts (Minneapolis: Fortress, 2012), 143–56.

I. CHRISTIANS AND SLAVES[103]

Cyprian, bishop in the third century CE, said the following in his address *To Demetrian*:

> You complain that the fountains are now less plentiful to you, and the breezes less salubrious, and the frequent showers and the fertile earth afford you less ready assistance; that the elements no longer subserve your uses and your pleasures as of old. But do you serve God, by whom all things are ordained to your service; do you wait upon Him by whose good pleasure all things wait upon you? From your slave you yourself require service; and though a man, you compel your fellow-man to submit, and to be obedient to you; and although you share the same lot in respect of being born, the same condition in respect of dying; although you have like bodily substance and a common order of souls, and although you come into this world of ours and depart from it after a time with equal rights, and by the same law; yet, unless you are served by him according to your pleasure, unless you are obeyed by him in conformity to your will, you, as an imperious and excessive exactor of his service, flog and scourge him: you afflict and torture him with hunger, with thirst and nakedness, and even frequently with the sword and with imprisonment. And, wretch that you are, do you not acknowledge the Lord your God while you yourself are thus exercising lordship?[104]

I call our attention, then, to the stunning contradiction between belief in a "fellow-man," the "same lot in respect of being born," and most especially a "common order of souls" in combination with a lack of hesitation to flog, scourge, and deprive the slave of food, water, and clothing. Such "lordship" is not afraid either of the "sword" or "imprisonment." Cyprian seems to take the Stoic approach to slavery, insensitive though it was (and is) to far too many realities and the effects his view would generate. Many have wondered if the widespread use of "slave" as an image for the Christian life has not been tragically detrimental to the slave.[105] If sin is a kind of slavery, one is entitled to declare that slavery is a kind of sin.

I mention now but one other text, namely 1 Cor 7:21–24:

103. On slavery and the NT, see Harrill, *Slaves in the New Testament*; Byron, *Paul and Slavery*. For a marvelous sketch of slavery and Christianity, see Glancy, *Slavery as Moral Problem*.

104. Cyprian, *To Demetrian* 8 (Wallis, *ANF* 5:459–60).

105. Bradley, *Slavery and Society at Rome*, 151.

> Were you a slave when you were called? Do not let it trouble you—although if you can gain your freedom, *do so*.[106] For the one who was a slave when called to faith in the Lord is the Lord's freed person; similarly, the one who was free when called is Christ's slave. You were bought at a price; do not become slaves of human beings. Brothers and sisters, each person, as responsible to God, should remain in the situation they were in when God called them.

Does Paul mean pursue manumission or does he mean to say the slaves are not to be bothered by their status as a slave? Notice, first, that Paul is not urging a revolt or a revolution as he says "Do not let it trouble you." And then he says "*if* you can gain your freedom." Thus, the "do so" suggests to slaves that if they can get the opportunity they are to "use their freedom."[107] Despite some debate, this reading has the support of most modern exegetes. What is clear is that in a letter (1 Corinthians) dated to the approximate time of Philemon Paul is not *pressing for manumission* as the *inevitable conclusion of liberation in Christ* but urging slave-Christians to pursue manumission if possible. This, I would contend, is as close as Paul gets to the modern notion of abolitionism. But abolitionism it is not.

The above sketch of Roman slavery brings to the surface the profound moral issue that simmers throughout the entire letter to Philemon as well as the New Testament. Readers of this commentary are not merely interested in a text "back then" but also in this text as it can speak to the "here and now." Times may have changed and slave societies like Rome have all but disappeared, but there are profound human captivities in our world that deserve a brief hearing in a commentary that has one eye on the first century and the other on the twenty-first century. This commentary is not a moral treatise nor can it fully engage modern slavery. Yet, a brief discussion of modern slavery is necessary. Unfortunately, it is customary for modern Christians to diminish the slavery of the Roman world while admitting the horrors of New World slavery. As demonstrated above, the life of a slave in the Greco-Roman world was extraordinarily difficult, at times horrific.

106. The issue revolves around this expression: μᾶλλον χρῆσαι.

107. See Harrill, *Manumission of Slaves*, 68–128 (esp. 122 and 194). For a survey of scholarship, see Byron, *Paul and Slavery*, 92–115.

II. PHILEMON IN THE CRUCIBLE OF NEW WORLD SLAVERY AND SLAVERY TODAY[108]

The richest country in the world, the USA, hoisted itself above all others by standing on the backs of black slaves—Africans were bought or captured and then transported under unimaginable conditions. The *leitmotif* of America's founders was liberty, but that proud theme was hypocritically blind to the enslavement of its working class. As one of America's great historians of slavery, David Brion Davis, states it,

> The strongest card in the hands of American abolitionists was their ability to indict the entire American nation for what appeared to be the most hypocritical contradiction in all human history: A nation conceived in liberty and dedicated to the proposition "that all men are created equal" happened also to be the nation, by the mid-nineteenth century, with the largest number of slaves in the Western Hemisphere—a nation whose most valuable exports, particularly cotton, were produced by slaves.[109]

How did a nation that prided itself on liberty, freedom, and equality become a nation that enslaved millions of Africans? A heavy handful of fingers can be pointed at many: from seventh- and eighth-century Muslim transportation of sub-Saharan Africans into slavery north and east of the Mediterranean, to the Portuguese and Spanish, who in developing trade with the New World exploited slaves, to west African black traders who sold captured Africans to European merchants, to the seventeenth century's fixation of slavery with black skin, to the European obsession with consumerist capitalistic economic developments in exploiting slave labor to produce sugar, coffee, tobacco, and cotton, and *perhaps most painfully* to the widespread justification of slavery on the back of both the Bible (e.g., Exod 21:21; Lev 19:20–22; 25:44–46; Col 3:22–4:1) and the highly influential discussions of slavery in Aristotle's *Politics*. In most cases, European and American (North and South) Christians—clerics and laity—were at the heart of this moral collapse. Blame is diffuse. The conditions from Maine through the Caribbean and down to Brazil varied, but the conditions of slaves overwhelmingly entailed personal, physical, sexual, and familial violence as well as exploitation. Davis sums up these conditions with this: "Much of the New World, then, came to resemble the Death Furnace of the ancient god Moloch—consuming African slaves so increasing numbers

108. The literature on slavery is extensive. An introduction by a specialist historian that interacts with the scholarship is Davis, *Inhuman Bondage*. Also, Eltis and Engerman, *The Cambridge World History of Slavery*.

109. Davis, *Inhuman Bondage*, 175.

of Europeans (and later, white Americans) could consume sugar, coffee, rice, and tobacco."[110]

Much attention has been given to abolitionists like William Garrison, William Wilberforce, and John Woolman, who deserve much credit for courage and according to some a profound and costly altruism, but it was not until the Haitian Revolution of 1791–1794 that the tide began to turn. Abolitionists had arguments and theories and power, but the slaves themselves created the groundswell of resentment, resistance, and at times rebellion. The freed slave Frederick Douglass in a famous speech called everyone's attention to Haiti's history-shifting moment in these words:

> Until Haiti spoke, Douglass pointed out, "no Christian nation had abolished Negro slavery. . . . Until she spoke, the slave trade was sanctioned by all the Christian nations of the world, and our land of liberty and light included. . . . Until Haiti spoke, the church was silent, and the pulpit dumb."[111]

Douglass, along with others of the formerly enslaved who wrote out their painful freedom narratives, reinterpreted the Bible of the slave owners to announce liberation for the enslaved.[112] These conflicting interpretations simultaneously illustrate the ambivalence of the Bible about slavery and therefore its capacity for exploitation by the slave owners. Philemon, of course, played its part. It also revealed that the Puritans who wrested themselves from their own slavery in England, once established in the colonies, propagated the same slave conditions in the United States. The unconscionable irony is that African American slaves learned to read the Bible just as the Puritans had read it—as an instrument of liberation. Here is the summary of Emerson Powery and Rodney Sadler, Jr. as they describe subversive African American slave hermeneutics:

> Early African Americans found that they could benefit from employing the Bible as it:
>
> 1. Gave them hope that God would act without human (political) intervention to provide justice for enslaved Africans;
> 2. Grounded subversive arguments against the type of Christianity practiced by Southern slaveholders;

110. Davis, *Inhuman Bondage*, 99.

111. Davis, *Inhuman Bondage*, 158. On the famous line about altruism by W. E. H. Lecky because of the economic cost to Britain in abolishing slavery, see Davis, *Inhuman Bondage*, 234.

112. Emerson B. Powery and Rodney S. Sadler, Jr., *The Genesis of Liberation: Biblical Interpretation in the Antebellum Narratives of the Enslaved* (Louisville: Westminster John Knox, 2016). See also John Coffey, *Exodus and Liberation: Deliverance Politics from John Calvin to Martin Luther King Jr.* (Oxford: Oxford University Press, 2013).

3. Provided a mythic system that could explain their plight and a symbolic world that resonated with their own while demonstrating God's fidelity to those similarly situated (slaves, exiles, sufferers);
4. Allowed them the latitude to emphasize or exclude portions of Scripture based upon their needs without compromising the core of the Christian message;
5. Envisioned human origins in a manner that allowed them to discern a glorious past for African peoples and discern positive dimensions of African identity;
6. Continued to be flexible enough to address their evolving plight in America (slavery, segregation, persistent inequality, etc.).[113]

One can only ask if Onesimus and his slave comrades heard the same messages when they heard Scriptures read in the household of Philemon.

Protests by abolitionists like Harriet Beecher Stowe's *Uncle Tom's Cabin* pressured slave owners, gave hope to slaves, and cornered politicians, including presidents.[114] Abraham Lincoln's famous "House Divided Speech" as well as *The Emancipation Proclamation* on January 1, 1863, expressed a moderate and politically savvy President's beliefs as his convictions were also to preserve the union of the Northern and Southern states.[115] Lincoln pushed open the legal door for abolition but Reconstruction retrenched into Jim Crow laws, racism continued to simmer in a cauldron of inequality, suppression, and systemic injustice. The Civil Rights Movement in the United States exposes what David Brion Davis calls "America's greatest historical contradiction"[116]—the ongoing impact of slavery by way of Jim Crow laws rather than the true exhibition of liberty and justice for all. Martin Luther King Jr.—whether one points to his "Letter from Birmingham City Jail" or to his "I Have a Dream" (both from 1963)—prophetically denounced systemic systems of racism, the ugly shadow of race-based slavery in North Amer-

113. Powery and Sadler, *The Genesis of Liberation*, 3–4. On the evocative "talking back to the Talking Book" and the regular choice to avoid or repudiate some texts in the Bible, see Powery and Sadler, *The Genesis of Liberation*, 113–43. These freedom narratives brought into expression "a communal hermeneutics of suspicion" that the slaveowning "preacher imposed his own ideological slant onto the biblical text" and thus led the slave community to notes of liberation. See Powery and Sadler, *The Genesis of Liberation*, 169. For an appeal for us to continue to listen to this talking book, Mark D. Chapman, "The Shortest Book in the Bible," *ExpTim* 118 (2007): 546–48.

114. Harriet Beecher Stowe, *Uncle Tom's Cabin* (New York: Everyman's Library, 1995); Joan D. Hedrick, *Harriet Beecher Stowe: A Life*, rev. ed. (Oxford University Press, 1995).

115. Abraham Lincoln, *Selected Writings and Speeches of Abraham Lincoln*, ed. T. Harry Williams (n.p.: Hendricks House, 1980), 53–61, 199–201.

116. Davis, *Inhuman Bondage*, 11.

ica.[117] Isabel Wilkerson's tale of the migration of some six million African Americans from southern conditions to slightly better northern conditions continues the story.[118]

Slavery in the antebellum period fostered cultures of primary socialization that—in spite of *The Emancipation Proclamation*, the Civil Rights Movement, and the legal ending of Jim Crow—have their impact today. One needs merely to point to white flight, urban sprawl, inner city poverty, food ghettoes, the rise of the Black Lives Matter movement, and the attempt to understand black youth in what Orlando Patterson calls the "cultural matrix."[119] America's greatest contradiction remains what social activist Jim Wallis is calling "America's original sin."[120] One of the finest studies on Philemon available today derives its energy from the evil of racism and gives Philemon the opportunity to speak again.[121]

I repeat: there is no reason for us to vest all of our theological needs in this letter to Philemon. Yet, the Pauline theology that is worked out in this letter leads to three major working premises for Christianity in our world:

(1) liberation begins in the act of God in Christ through the Spirit,
(2) liberation is embodied in cross-cultural, ethnic, racial and gendered fellowship, and
(3) the embodied experience of liberation in the church is to expand its way into our world as Christians live out what it means to be brothers and sisters in Christ and under Christ in a world marked by global slavery and systemic injustices of all kinds.

This letter challenges each church with this question: Are we, in our churches, welcoming marginalized others into a world of reconciliation for all? Are we expressing that reconciliation in our community and world? Is it then not the case that the letter to Philemon opens the door for an ecclesial liberation theology? (I believe so.)

117. Martin Luther King Jr., *A Testament of Hope: The Essential Writings of Martin Luther King Jr.*, ed. J. M. Washington (San Francisco: Harper & Row, 1986), 217–20 and 289–302. For biography, see Taylor Branch, *Parting the Waters: America in the King Years, 1954–63* (New York: Simon & Schuster, 1988); Taylor Branch, *Pillar of Fire: America in the King Years, 1963–65* (New York: Simon & Schuster, 1998); Taylor Branch, *At Canaan's Edge: America in the King Years, 1965–68* (New York: Simon & Schuster, 2006).

118. Isabel Wilkerson, *The Warmth of Other Suns: The Epic Story of America's Great Migration* (New York: Random House, 2010).

119. Orlando Patterson, ed., *The Cultural Matrix: Understanding Black Youth* (New Haven: Harvard University Press, 2016).

120. Jim Wallis, *America's Original Sin: Racism, White Privilege, and the Bridge to a New America* (Grand Rapids: Brazos Press, 2016).

121. See the book of Callahan.

Slavery cannot be reduced to the USA because slavery's modern reality remains a global condemnation of humans exploiting humans.[122] The United Nations estimates—and the number staggers—that twenty-one million people are in slavery today,[123] while one of the leading non-government organizations raises it to thirty-five million.[124] The percentage of two particular slave subgroups remains consistent: twenty-five percent of all slaves are forced into commercial sex services[125] and about thirty percent of all slaves are under the age of eighteen.[126] Males make up about forty-six percent and females fifty-four percent of modern slaves.[127]

The global distribution deserves consideration as well:[128]

- Western Europe: 566,000 (2%)
- Russia & Eurasia: 2,600,000 (7%)
- Asia Pacific: 23,543,000 (67%)
- Sub-Saharan Africa: 5,620,000 (16%)
- Middle East and North Africa: 2,178,000 (6%)
- The Americas: 1,285,000 (3%)

While modern slavery is primarily present in the developing world, those in more developed nations need to be aware of the hundreds of thousands of slaves within their own societies. This includes more than 150,000 slaves throughout Europe[129] and more than 60,000 slaves within the borders of the USA.[130] In the USA, sex trafficking has begun to surpass drug trafficking as the preferred revenue stream by gangs.[131] Because of the rise in slave revenue incentives, the National Center for Missing and Exploited Children reported in 2014 that one in six runaways in the USA were in danger of being sex trafficked. Nearly seventy percent of runaways are in the care of social services at the time of running away.[132]

122. My student assistant, Justin Gill, wrote up his own research on modern slavery. The following section depends on his work.

123. Havocscope, *Human Trafficking: Prices and Statistics of the Modern Day Slave Trade* (n.p.: Havocscope, 2015), under "74," Amazon Kindle edition.

124. "The Global Slavery Index." See http://www.globalslaveryindex.org/.

125. Havocscope, under "81."

126. Havocscope, under "332."

127. Havocscope, under "72."

128. "The Global Slavery Index."

129. *The Globalization of Crime: A Transnational Organized Crime Threat Assessment* (Vienna: United Nations Office on Drugs and Crime, 2010). See http://www.unodc.org/unodc/en/data-and-analysis/tocta-2010.html.

130. "The Global Slavery Index."

131. Havocscope, under "197."

132. "Polaris." See https://polarisproject.org/facts.

The economic "contribution" of slaves to the global economy is small but much of the reality is unknown. Still, the deep economic reverberations of low costs in foods, textiles, computers, and other components gain the attention of companies that buy such goods in mass.[133] It was originally estimated at the turn of the millennium that slave labor only contributed about $20 billion directly into economies. But fifteen years later that number has ballooned to more than $150 billion, with $100 billion coming from the forced commercial sex trade alone.[134] Sex trafficking has become the most profitable market for slavery because a slaveholder can make five times more profit than any other form of forced work.[135] Even while sex slaves only make up twenty-five percent of the overall slave population, they create more than two-thirds of the profit generated by slaveholders globally. The numbers for current profit margins are seemingly low, but when the context of the poor developing world and the low overhead costs of slaves is taken into account, the allure of modern slavery becomes clearer:[136]

- Annual Profit from Sexual Exploitation Victim: $21,800;
- Annual Profit from Labor Exploitation Victim: $4,800;
- Annual Profit from Exploiting Agriculture Worker: $2,500;
- Annual Profit from Exploiting Domestic Helper: $2,300.

Traffickers and slave owners exploit government corruption. Every level of government is susceptible to bribery, but those involved in the slave trade depend upon the collusion of police.[137] In Thailand, the potential income from bribery is a motivating reason for males to enter into the police work.[138] Because of these tendencies of corruption by local police, the poor of the world often view police as another gang that preys on them for their own financial gains and career self-advancement.[139] Why are these law enforcement systems so bad in protecting their communities from exploitation? They were never intended to protect the poor in the first place but were created to protect colonial rulers, and then shifted to protecting the elite and powerful of the people group when the Empires left.[140]

133. Kevin Bales, *Disposable People: New Slavery in the Global Economy* (Berkeley: University of California Press, 1999), 23–24.

134. Havocscope, under "81."

135. Havocscope, under "184–91."

136. Havocscope, under "184."

137. Bales, *Disposable People*, 29–31.

138. Bales, *Disposable People*, 54.

139. Gary A. Haugen and Victor Boutros, *The Locust Effect: Why the End of Poverty Requires the End of Violence* (Oxford: Oxford University Press, 2014), 87, 94, 135.

140. Haugen and Boutros, *The Locust Effect*, 174–76.

Three specific examples show the diversity and particularity of modern slavery:

Thai Fishing Ships. Thailand's fishing economy is the third largest in the world, which has created a massive need for cheap labor on the fishing ships. Because of accounts of brutal forced labor, such as sixty percent of the 2 million workers claim to have seen a captain kill a worker,[141] the government created an oversight task force. This task force only raids registered ships, which is less than twenty percent of all Thai fishing ships. Yet, the task force lacks resources, such as interpreters.

Child Sex Slaves. Yearly, at least 2 million children are exploited as sex slaves[142] with 400,000 being boys.[143] All forms offer impersonal sexual pleasure at cheap prices to working class males.[144]

Forced Marriages. Yearly, more than 10 million children, ages five to eighteen, are forced into marriages.[145] Most modern slavery is greed-based exploitation, but forced marriage exploits children based on gains in religious, cultural, and social statuses.

Modern slavery is different from the past in its deception, its technological sophistication, and its disregard for ethnicity and race. Modern slavery takes advantage of those unable to protect themselves through resources such as education, finances, and social systems. It is the combination of poverty, weakness, and lawlessness that creates modern slavery and exploitation. At the same time, there must be profitable enough markets available that slaveholders believe the risks of trafficking and using slaves are justified.[146] These contexts must be addressed by governments and communities in order to liberate slaves, and humanity, from modern slavery. The church ought both to embody liberation and fight for liberation on all fronts.

The question lingering at the far edge of this section now comes into view: *What can Philemon say to the modern versions of slavery? What would Paul say in our world to our churches?* I repeat what I already stated: the apostle Paul held a vision where the powers of redemption were shattering the status and power symbols of the Roman Empire. Paul's kingdom reality was to take root in a local *ekklēsia beginning in the household.* From there a new form of primary socialization could take root that would, could or should work its way into the whole of society. What Philemon begins to say already then is that the assault on modern slavery needs to begin with justice in the church that spreads into justice for all.

141. Havocscope, under "629–31."

142. Havocscope, under "462."

143. "The Story," Blackbox International. See http://www.blackboxinternational.org/#/about/the-story.

144. Bales, *Disposable People*, 44–48.

145. Havocscope, under "599–607."

146. Bales, *Disposable People*, 31–32.

III. AUTHORSHIP AND DATE

Few scholars dispute Paul's authorship of Philemon (Phlm 1, 19).[147] However, the date of composition is disputed. In the commentary on Colossians, I presented a case for that letter deriving from Paul's imprisonment in Ephesus (cf. Phlm 22) and, since Philemon accompanied Colossians—just before Colossians, at the same time, or Colossians just after Philemon—Philemon, too, also was written while Paul was under loose guard in Ephesus.[148] This puts the date as well at the same time, roughly 53–55 CE. It is highly probable that Onesimus is from Colossae (Col 4:9), and, as a slave of Philemon, we infer Philemon's *oikos* was in Colossae.

IV. THE SOCIAL REALITIES OF PHILEMON: RUNAWAY OR SLAVE IN SEARCH OF A MEDIATOR?

What George Orwell once said of his experience in India can be said of Philemon: "a story always sounds clear enough at a distance, but the nearer you get to the scene of events the vaguer it becomes."[149] Onesimus and his relation to Philemon and Paul can be reduced to five options, leaving us with that vagueness of proximity:[150]

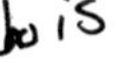

1. As messenger of the church, Onesimus (or the letter only) is sent officially to Paul.[151]
2. As a runaway (*fugitivus*) Onesimus finds himself in prison with Paul, whom he knows or does not know.

147. Dunn, 299–300.

148. Scot McKnight, *The Letter to the Colossians*, NICNT (Grand Rapids: Eerdmans, 2017), 34–39. For two recent introductions to Philemon, see Stanley Porter, *The Apostle Paul: His Life, Thought, and Letters* (Grand Rapids: Eerdmans, 2016), 375–84; Gorman, *Apostle of the Crucified Lord*, 454–70.

149. From the famous essay called "Shooting an Elephant," in George Orwell, *An Age like This 1920–1940: The Collected Essays, Journalism & Letters*, ed. Sonia Orwell and Ian Angus (Boston: David R. Godine, 2000), 237.

150. A variation upon Brian Rapske, "The Prisoner Paul in the Eyes of Onesimus," *NTS* 37 (1991): 187–203 (here 187). I was only able to skim Bruce Longenecker's judicious new commentary as it came too late to be used in this commentary, but I was pleased by our many convergences.

151. Sara B. C. Winter, "Methodological Observations on a New Interpretation of Paul's Letter to Philemon," *USQR* 39 (1984): 203–12; Winter, "Paul's Letter to Philemon"; Winter, 301–12; Sanders, "Equality and a Request"; Scott S. Elliott, "'Thanks, but No Thanks': Tact, Persuasion, and the Negotiation of Power in Paul's Letter to Philemon," *NTS* 57 (2011): 51–64.

3. An associate of Paul happens upon the runaway Onesimus and brings him to the imprisoned Paul.
4. As a runaway Onesimus becomes needy and casts himself upon Paul to importune Philemon for mercy.
5. As an asylum seeker (*erro*), not a runaway (*fugitivus*), Onesimus flees to Paul as Onesimus's advocate, and Paul, as a friend of the master (*amicus domini*), might plea for mercy to Philemon or perhaps Paul might help Onesimus find a new and kinder master.

The traditional view, that Onesimus was a runaway slave (2, 3, or 4 above), has as much and more to commend it as any other view though a recent theory has gained some momentum (5 above).[152] The fourth and fifth options merge into one another. This newer view (in the form of 5 above) rests upon two solid inferences: the *seeming absence* of indicators that Onesimus was a runaway[153] and, even more significantly, the *incongruence* of a runaway happening upon Paul—Philemon's brother and fellow gospel minister—in prison, however loosely he was imprisoned. How and why would a runaway get so close to the institutions that could capture him and send him back to his slave owner? Hence, some have argued in effect that Onesimus was not a *fugitivus* but an

erro, not a runaway but a slave whose intention was never to run away but to find a mediator whom he knew could get Onesimus off the hook for some failure on his part or his fear of his master's wrath or retribution.[154] In addition, an *erro* had every intention to return to his master but under new and usually forgiven conditions.[155] Proculus, as cited in Justinian's *Digest* 21.1.17.4, has the famous line that required those involved to discern the motive of the slave who had run away: "one has to assess the man's [slave's] purpose in so acting." If the motive was to find justice and return to the house, the slave was not a *fugitivus*.

152. For a solid defense of the *fugitivus* theory, John G. Nordling, "Onesimus Fugitivus: A Defense of the Runaway Slave Hypothesis in Philemon," *JSNT* 41 (1991): 97–119.

153. If one presses Phlm 18–19 into stereotypical theft by a runaway, there is no absence of evidence for the runaway hypothesis.

154. For technical discussion, see Harrill, *Slaves in the New Testament*, 8–11.

155. Peter Lampe, "Keine 'Sklavenflucht' des Onesimus," *ZNW* 76 (1985): 135–37; Rapske, "Prisoner Paul," 197–98; Bartchy, "Philemon," *ABD* 5:309. Some of Rapske's counterarguments to the *fugitivus* theory lack the flexibility (and imagination) of reality. Paul the Roman citizen, for example, could harbor a *fugitivus* if the slave were remorseful and seeking mediation with Paul and if Paul's intent were to return Onesimus to Philemon in due course. In this case, the fourth option above can slide quite naturally into the fifth option. In addition, too much is made of Philemon's presumed wrath in the *amicus domini* theory when not a word of that is found in Philemon. Philemon's character comes off as kind and compassionate in the letter. In addition, Paul was even more attuned to the common Jewish tendency to treat slaves better, which suggests that had Philemon mistreated Onesimus Paul would have said something. On this, Hezser, "Slavery," 313–16.

However, in favor of the runaway hypothesis are both the external evidence (including Pliny's letter to Sabinianus)[156] as well as the long history of interpretation (including Jerome, Ambrose, and John Chrysostom). Furthermore, the stereotype that runaways absconded with goods for their journey has strong support in Philemon itself (v. 18). This view then, once assumed, is shored up by indicators in the letter that Onesimus's departure was not willed by Philemon, that it can now be seen as having a divine purpose (v. 15), and that Paul is returning (v. 12) the man to his master. Against the runaway theory, so far as I can see, is only the lower probability that Onesimus would accidentally run into one of Philemon's associates (Paul) and jeopardize his own security. Furthermore, against the *erro* hypothesis are these observations: it relies too heavily upon Roman legislation,[157] Greek or local Ephesian law might obtain more to this situation, and, most significantly, in this letter Paul is not as much Philemon's friend as Onesimus's advocate. Finally, that Onesimus committed an injustice and that Paul would repay the costs suggest less of a flight for mediation than a runaway. The evidence and inferences are not completely balanced and both theories are capable of explaining all the evidence, but until more support can be found for the *erro* theory and against the *fugitivus* theory, I am inclined to think Onesimus was a runaway.

V. THE EVENTS AT WORK IN THE LETTER TO PHILEMON[158]

One of the most fascinating dimensions of this short letter is the attempt to reconstruct what happened, to whom it happened, and in what order. Here is one such attempt to reconstruct in chronological order:

1. Philemon incurs a debt to Paul, probably by being converted (v. 19)
2. Paul is imprisoned in Ephesus for his gospel ministry (vv. 1, 9, 10, 13, 23)
3. Onesimus the slave runs away, committing an injustice (vv. 11–13, 15, 18–19)

156. Pliny, *Epistle* 9.21.

157. Harrill, "Using the Roman Jurists."

158. I have revised slightly the discussion of Petersen, *Rediscovering Paul*, 43–88 (here 70). I have added 9 and 12. Peterson compares the sequences of his events (without my 9 and 12) events, events at times not mentioned but implied (3 and 5 above), as referred to in the texts with the poetic order, that is, the order of these events as they appear in the text. The poetic order is 5, 2, 4, 6, 3, 7, 1, 8, 9, and 10. For other sketches, see Pao, 343–47; Barclay, 98–102; Gorman, *Apostle of the Crucified Lord*, 458–59.

4. Onesimus "finds" Paul and is converted under Paul (vv. 10, 13)[159]
5. Paul hears of Philemon's love and faith from Onesimus and Epaphras (vv. 4–7)
6. Paul sends Onesimus back to Philemon (v. 12)
7. Paul sends Onesimus to Philemon with the letter (vv. 17–19)
8. Onesimus and letter arrive
9. The letter is read publicly to the *oikonomia-ekklēsia* of Philemon
10. Philemon responds to Paul's letter (vv. 20–21)
11. Paul anticipates visit to Philemon (v. 22)
12. Philemon welcomes Onesimus, restores him, and then Onesimus perhaps (?) returns to Paul. (Depending on the order of Colossians and Philemon, it is possible Onesimus then later visits Philemon as a minister to Paul [Col 4:9].)

Not all agree about this reconstruction. There are a few distinct theories about how to reconstruct the events in play in this letter and they deserve to be mentioned. I begin with John Knox's theory and variations of it.[160] Paul sent this letter not to Philemon but to Archippus, who was both the *paterfamilias* and the master of Onesimus. Philemon was himself the church leader of the Lycus Valley and could exert some pressure on Archippus to heed Paul's requests. Hence, Paul is sending the case of Onesimus up to Philemon in a quasi-legal sense. What then was Paul's request? To return Onesimus to Paul for the work of the ministry—that is, he was asking *for* Onesimus not *about* him. In addition, Knox believed Onesimus became the bishop of Ephesus mentioned in Ignatius's letter to the Ephesians.[161] Sara C. Winter understands the thanksgiving section to express what is most important to the substance to follow (i.e., Paul praises Philemon's generosity).[162] She contends that the church at Colossae had sent Onesimus as an emissary to Paul and Paul was requesting that he be retained on a permanent basis to serve the gospel.[163] There are a number of problems with the theories of Knox and Winter. They

159. Some have made much of Paul's legal dilemma in harboring Onesimus; see David M. Russell, "The Strategy of a First-Century Appeals Letter: A Discourse Reading of Paul's Epistle to Philemon," *Journal of Translation and Textlinguistics* 11 (1998): 1–25.

160. John Knox, *Philemon among the Letters of Paul* (New York: Abingdon, 1963). For those who follow him with variations: O. Lamar Cope, "On Rethinking the Philemon-Colossians Connection," *BR* 30 (1985): 45–50; Harrill, *Manumission of Slaves*; Harrill, *Slaves in the New Testament*.

161. Against Knox, see John W. Martens, "Ignatius and Onesimus: John Knox Reconsidered," *SecCent* 9 (1992): 73–86.

162. Hence, for her this means his sending of Onesimus to serve Paul.

163. Winter, "Methodological Observations"; Winter, "Paul's Letter to Philemon." Also, Winter, 303.

will be discussed in more detail below.[164] John Barclay's question gets to the heart of the emissary theory: "Would Philemon's church employ a 'useless' non-Christian slave, in bad odour with his master, for an important service to Paul?"[165]

While these theories have not been compelling to most Philemon scholars, the *status* of Onesimus is another matter altogether: it is, as we indicate above, reasonable to think he was a runaway. Yet, it is also possible he fled to Paul for mediation. Allen Callahan, however, has offered another theory: Onesimus was never status-wise a slave but only metaphorically a slave; he was not a runaway; Philemon was not a slave owner, nor was Archippus or Apphia.[166] Rather, Onesimus and Philemon are blood brothers in need of reconciliation. Paul sends Onesimus back to Philemon to represent Paul in the ministry of Colossae—assured as well that Paul will pay whatever tab arises. His approach, with which I disagree, will be mentioned in the commentary below as well.

VI. STRUCTURE, RHETORIC AND CLARITY OF PHILEMON[167]

Most think the letter's basic organization has three sections: vv. 1–7 (vv. 1–3, 4–7), vv. 8–22, and vv. 23–25. There is some dispute whether the second unit ends at v. 19 or at v. 21 or at v. 22 but the general consensus is clear (vv. 1–7, vv. 8–19/21/22, and vv. 23–25). A typical structure, then, looks like this:[168]

1. Letter opening (vv. 1–3)
2. Thanksgiving (vv. 4–7)
3. Letter Body (vv. 8–18)
4. Letter closing (vv. 19–25)

164. Barclay, 100.

165. Barclay, 100. This gets complicated for others. Pao, 347, for example, is not convinced the "son" of v. 10 refers to conversion but to rededication (see Commentary at v. 10).

166. Callahan, "Paul's Epistle to Philemon"; Callahan, 16–19; Callahan, "'Brother Saul.'"

167. Overall and as long as one does not force Philemon to fit a typological ideal, Philemon falls naturally into a genre mailbox called "Letters of Mediation." See Stanley K. Stowers, *Letter Writing in Greco-Roman Antiquity*, Library of Early Christianity 5 (Philadelphia: Westminster, 1986), 153–65; Ernst Wendland, "'You Will Do Even More than I Say': On the Rhetorical Function of Stylistic Form in the Letter to Philemon," in Tolmie, *Philemon in Perspective*, 81–85.

168. J. A. D. Weima, "Paul's Persuasive Prose: An Epistolary Analysis of the Letter to Philemon," in Tolmie, *Philemon in Perspective*, 29–60.

Disagreements quickly enter when one factors in how this letter actually works: chiasms,[169] the epistolary units,[170] various performance[171] and rhetorical movements,[172] text linguistics,[173] and for Philemon the parallel in Pliny's letter to Sabinianus, a letter that is both like and quite unlike Philemon (*Epistle* 9.21),[174] as well as Ignatius's *Ephesians* (2:1–2), in which he appeals to retain Burrhus. One might claim that we cannot interpret Philemon until we have sorted out its structure. Yet, that claim is countered by all these con-

169. John Paul Heil, "The Chiastic Structure and Meaning of Paul's Letter to Philemon," *Bib* 82 (2001): 178–206.

170. Weima, "Paul's Persuasive Prose." An older study is John L. White, "The Structural Analysis of Philemon: A Point of Departure in the Formal Analysis of the Pauline Letter," in *SBL Seminar Papers 1971* (Missoula, MT: Scholars Press, 1971), 1–47.

171. On performance criticism, William D. Shiell, *Delivering from Memory: The Effect of Performance on the Early Christian Audience* (Eugene, OR: Pickwick, 2011). On Philemon and performance, David M. Rhoads, "Performing the Letter to Philemon," *Journal of Biblical Storytelling* 17 (2008).

172. Of the more expansive studies and in addition to those mentioned above on performance criticism, see F. Forrester Church, "Rhetorical Structure and Design in Paul's Letter to Philemon," *HTR* 71 (1978): 17–33; Andrew Wilson, "The Politics of Politeness and Pauline Epistolography: A Case Study of the Letter to Philemon," *JSNT* 48 (1992): 107–19; Peter Lampe, "Affects and Emotions in the Rhetoric of Paul's Letter to Philemon: A Rhetorical-Psychological Interpretation," in Tolmie, *Philemon in Perspective*, 61–77; Wendland, "You Will Do Even More than I Say."

In addition to how rhetorical theory impacts Philemon one must consider as well literacy rates among Christians and Romans for one must assume the reader of this letter was not employed as a professional reader/performer but that Onesimus (or someone else) performed the letter as someone competent to read. Harris estimated that about ten percent of Jews could read. Despite his influence, Harris's argument has rightly been challenged. See William V. Harris, *Ancient Literacy* (Cambridge: Harvard University Press, 1989); Brian J. Wright, "Ancient Literacy in New Testament Research: Incorporating a Few More Lines of Enquiry," *TJ* 36 (2015): 161–89; Brian J. Wright, "Ancient Rome's Daily News Publication with Some Likely Implications for Early Christian Studies," *TynBul* 66 (2016): 161–77.

173. David L. Allen, "The Discourse Structure of Philemon: A Study in Textlinguistics," in *Scribes and Scripture: New Testament Essays in Honor of J. Harold Greenlee*, ed. David Alan Black (Winona Lake, IN: Eisenbrauns, 1992), 77–96 (here 83). He proposes twenty-two sentences with these divisions: vv. 1–3, 4–7, 8–16, 17–20, 21–22, and 23–25. Also, A. H. Snyman, "A Semantic Discourse Analysis of the Letter to Philemon," in *Text and Interpretation: New Approaches in the Criticism of the New Testament*, ed. P. J. Hartin and J. H. Petzer, NTTS 15 (Leiden: Brill, 1991), 83–99. Snyman varies markedly from Allen, dividing Philemon into the following cola: vv. 1–2, 3–5, 6–9, 10–14, 15–19, 20–25. See also Russell, "The Strategy of a First-Century Appeals Letter."

174. Discussed in most every study of Philemon; e.g., Barclay, 104–11; Wright, *Paul and the Faithfulness of God*, 1:3–7.

tentious disagreements.[175] To add another layer, behind and under this letter are at least three vital stories: the story of Philemon, the story of Onesimus, and the story of Paul—and there are a host of questions surrounding each in their relation to one another.[176] Elements of each of these stories surface in this letter only to the degree that they are deemed necessary for the letter, but one must assume that each of these persons had a story to tell and that their stories may well have not meshed neatly.

Rhetorical criticism finds other ways to sort out this letter but there is little consensus beyond the basic agreement on the big elements of the outline and the genuine sense that in the letter Paul "piles on his charm."[177] Once again there is very little agreement among those who study the rhetoric of Philemon. Assumptions play more role in rhetorical criticism than perhaps they deserve. For instance, one may intuit the entire gamut of emotions at work behind and in this letter: anger for Philemon, fear for Onesimus, trust of Onesimus in Paul and Paul's responding love for Onesimus, pity by Philemon for Paul in prison at his old age, respect and admiration for Paul by Philemon along with some sense of indebtedness to and thankfulness for Paul, and the very Roman sense of honor and shame—all topped off by the congregation's (slaves and non-slaves) curiosity about what Philemon will do![178]

There is a fine line of non-difference between conscious rhetoric and the common acquisition of persuasion by those untrained but gifted in the art. The untrained may be doing what the rhetoric manuals teach without any idea that such maneuvers are being performed. The Latin and Greek manuals of rhetoric, after all, like laws, render into consciousness what has either been formed intuitively or what has become the standard mode of operation. While some terms for rhetoric will come into play in this commentary, I state up front that I am not entirely convinced Paul "knew what he was doing" in the sense of knowing rhetorical moves.[179] Perhaps, but Paul does not have to know either Roman or Greek or Asiastic rhetoric in order to make such rhetorical moves.[180] Rather, the great orators and teachers of orators, Cicero and

175. A sorting out of these disagreements can begin with Wendland, "You Will Do Even More than I Say," 85–88, where he examines compositional breaks and how the various translations disagree.

176. A good sketch of the questions can be found in Bartchy, "Philemon," *ABD* 5:305–10 (esp. 306).

177. Barclay, 100.

178. Lampe, "Affects and Emotions," 65–66.

179. For the state of scholarship on Philemon and rhetoric—though he has ignored the important rhetorical (Asiatic) explanations by Witherington (4–11, 75)—see Tolmie, "Tendencies," 11–16.

180. Church, who examines the rhetoric of Paul, admits as much and seeks to show how theoretical rhetoric illuminates Philemon. See Church, "Rhetorical Structure," 21.

Quintilian, famously put into words what good rhetoricians or speakers or preachers or prophets were doing, and Paul—who was probably not trained in Greek or Latin rhetoric in Tarsus or Jerusalem though he was trained in the arts of argument in a Jewish mode of thinking —accomplished what famous rhetoricians would approve of![181]

I have for a long time believed in the theory of indirection that some rhetorical critics (like Witherington) propose for Philemon. However, as a result of my last few years of working closely with Philemon, I am convinced the theory of indirection is too subtle because it must assume everything it concludes. Instead of thinking that manumission is the aim but never expressed—and one must emphasize that Paul does not mention manumission—and that indirection is the mode of rhetoric and thus not obvious, I propose that Paul is habitually clear and routinely to the point.[182] I believe Paul says exactly what he wants to say in this letter, that his rhetoric is not nearly as indirect as some would like to think, and that his aim is not the *manumission* of Onesimus. Instead, what we find in this letter is a revolutionary plea for *the reconciliation of Philemon and Onesimus, which means a kind of liberation of Onesimus in the household of Philemon*.[183] To manumit a slave, as already discussed above, was not a radical action—many slaves were manumitted, especially when they had become cost-ineffective. Hence, an appeal for manumission does not need to be a closeted topic for Paul fit only for indirection.[184] The gravity of the letter then falls on these important but revolutionary expressions: "no longer as a slave, but . . . a dear brother" and "brother in the Lord" (v. 16) and "welcome" (v. 17). Paul's revolution, then, is not at the level of the Roman Empire but at the level of the household, not at the level of the *polis* but at the level of the *ekklēsia*. Instead of thinking that this bold apostle's argument was enveloped in *insinuatio* (indirection) I contend Paul was up front, personal, and clear. In the letter he never pleads for Onesimus's manumission.[185]

It has been claimed that Philemon contains a "strange phenomenon." What might that be? That the "letter is skillfully designed to constrain Philemon to accept Paul's request, and yet, at the same time, it is extremely

181. On Paul's education, Martin Hengel, *The Pre-Christian Paul*, trans. John Bowden (Philadelphia: Trinity Press International, 1991); Martin Hengel and Anna Maria Schwemer, *Paul between Damascus and Antioch: The Unknown Years*, trans. John Bowden (Louisville: Westminster John Knox, 1997). For an alternative view, E. P. Sanders, *Paul. The Apostle's Life, Letters, and Thought* (Minneapolis: Fortress, 2015), 13–82.

182. A point also made by Wright, *Paul and the Faithfulness of God*, 1:10.

183. For a strong statement that Philemon is about reconciliation, see Wright, *Paul and the Faithfulness of God*, 1:3–74.

184. A point made by others, including Kea, "Paul's Letter to Philemon," 230–32.

185. So others, including Iralu, 1705; Pao, 347–48.

unclear what precisely Paul is requesting!"[186] Further, that Paul is ambiguous because "*he did not know exactly what to recommend.*"[187] I agree with some of these claims as well as elements in the "politeness" theory for explaining Paul's rhetoric.[188] Yet, I contend Paul is not unclear: he says what he wants and what he wants is for Philemon to "welcome" Onesimus back as "a brother" *and all that such a welcome entails for the fellowship in Philemon's household.* One can multiply the problems in interpretation through the grid of indirect discourse and so contend the request is not clear except to the one trained in rhetoric. Or, as I believe, one can read the problems in this letter through the clear imperative to welcome Onesimus into the household and many of the problems crumble into clarity. What is more: Nearly all the discoveries of ambiguity in this letter are created by the hope that Paul somehow advocates for the manumission of Onesimus. If that hope is relinquished as we think it should be, a new clarity is discovered in the simple command "welcome."[189]

One might think we are settling for too little in thinking Paul's letter is not about manumission, but if so we ought then to point a long finger at Paul for failing to live up to his Magna Carta lines in Gal 3:28, 1 Cor 12:13 and Col 3:11. Rather, I want to contend that we are not settling for anything less than Paul's socio-ecclesial revolutionary kingdom reality in the house churches themselves. It is a grass-roots level revolution; it is concerned with the *ekklēsia*. We must conclude then that Paul was not disturbed by slavery as an institution.

Because both epistolary and rhetorical features are next to impossible to incorporate into a recognizable outline, I will use a basic outline and note both epistolary and rhetorical features in the commentary.

I. Introduction (vv. 1–7)
  A. Authors (v. 1a)
  B. Addressees (vv. 1b–2)
  C. Salutation (v. 3)
  D. Thanksgiving (vv. 4–7)
    1. Thanksgiving (v. 4)
    2. Cause (v. 5)
    3. Purpose of the prayer (v. 6)
    4. Emotional claim on Philemon (v. 7)

186. Barclay, "Dilemma of Christian Slave-Ownership," 170–71.

187. Barclay, "Dilemma of Christian Slave-Ownership," 175 (italics his).

188. Wilson, "The Politics of Politeness," 115–17 (illustrating the maxims of modesty and generosity).

189. I do not dispute Barclay's sketch of the problems of what it would mean for a slaveowner to treat a slave as a brother; see "Dilemma of Christian Slave-Ownership," 175–82.

II. Paul's Appeal for Onesimus (vv. 8–22)
   A. First Appeal in the Sketch of the Scene (vv. 8–11; appeal in v. 10)
   B. Second Appeal in the Presentation of Onesimus (vv. 12–16; appeal in vv. 15–16)
   C. Third Appeal in Their Partnership (vv. 17–21; appeal in vv. 17, 20–21)
   D. Final Appeal in a Presence (v. 22)

III. Conclusion (vv. 23–25)

The Letter to PHILEMON

Text and Commentary

I. INTRODUCTION: AUTHORS, ADDRESSEES, AND SALUTATION (1–3)[1]

1*Paul, a prisoner of Christ Jesus,*[a] *and Timothy our brother, To Philemon our dear friend and fellow worker*[b]*—* 2*also to Apphia our sister and Archippus our fellow soldier—and to the church that meets in your home:* 3*Grace and peace to you*[c] *from God our Father and the Lord Jesus Christ.*

a. As with *Colossians,* I will compare the NIV (the printed text in the Commentary and abbreviated as NIV) to the Common English Bible (CEB) and highlight significant differences. The simpler "a prisoner of Christ Jesus" (NIV) is made more explicit in the "who is a prisoner *for the cause* of Christ Jesus" (CEB).

b. CEB: "our dearly loved coworker."

c. CEB postpones "to you" (NIV) until the end to form "be with you."

The length of Philemon, a mere 335 words in Greek, approximates the average length of a letter in the Roman, Greek, and Jewish worlds of the first century CE. Unlike the other canonical letters of Paul, Philemon is less overtly theological. Yet, the letter is highly suggestive of what theology looks like on the ground level as the apostle becomes pastor and friend. In spite of the brevity and practicality of Philemon, it too contains the standard elements of a Pauline letter:[2] salutation or greeting,[3] a thanksgiving,[4] and the main body.[5] The

1. Some sections and terms in Phlm, esp. in vv. 1–7, overlap with Colossians so much that I will use explanations and footnotes from my commentary on *Colossians* when appropriate.

2. Weima, "Paul's Persuasive Prose," 30–39.

3. Rom 1:1–7; 2 Cor 1:1–2; Gal 1:1–5; Eph 1:1–2; Phil 1:1–2; 1 Thess 1:1; 2 Thess 1:1–2.

4. Col 1:3–8; Rom 1:8–15; 1 Cor 1:4–9; Phil 1:3–11; 1 Thess 1:2–10; 2 Thess 1:3–12.

5. E.g., the rough contemporary of Paul, the Roman orator Cicero, wrote numerous letters that begin with his name followed immediately by the person to whom the letter was

terms Paul uses are theologically evocative. They tempt the reader into seeing more than needs to be seen: "grace and peace" after all are the apostle's terms for "greetings."[6]

Philemon 1–3 are designed not only to communicate the necessary information about the authors and addressees but also to set the tone for the rhetoric and content that will follow, especially in vv. 8–22. In no other letter written by Paul is his personal presence (*parousia*) to be felt more than in the public reading of this letter to the church at Colossae.[7] If Onesimus or Tychicus is the reader and if he looked at Philemon in the name of Paul when he got to vv. 8–22, then his eyes were the eyes of the apostle himself. In addition, the letter itself is a medium through which the apostle Paul expresses his personal presence and love for Philemon and for Onesimus. He expresses his love by becoming an advocate for Onesimus in his appeal to Philemon to act honorably.[8]

A. AUTHORS (1A)

1a The letter opens with "Paul, a prisoner of Christ Jesus, and Timothy our brother." This typical opening indicates dual authorship.[9] As with Colossians

---

sent. On letter writing and Paul, see John L. White, *Light from Ancient Letters*, FF (Philadelphia: Fortress, 1986); Stowers, *Letter Writing*; Hans-Josef Klauck, *Ancient Letters and the New Testament: A Guide to Content and Exegesis* (Waco, TX: Baylor University Press, 2006); E. Randolph Richards, *The Secretary in the Letters of Paul*, WUNT 2.42 (Tübingen: Mohr Siebeck, 1991); E. Randolph Richards, *Paul and First-Century Letter Writing: Secretaries, Composition and Collection* (Downers Grove, IL: InterVarsity Press, 2004). Also *NewDocs* 5:48–57; 7:1–57. A recent case has been made that Pauline letters reflect traditions of Jewish letters. See Lutz Doering, *Ancient Jewish Letters and the Beginnings of Christian Epistolography*, WUNT 298 (Tübingen: Mohr Siebeck, 2012). On the greeting, see more at Judith M. Lieu, "'Grace to You and Peace': The Apostolic Greeting," *BJRL* 68 (1985): 161–78.

6. The anarthrous states of nouns in salutations like Phlm 3 are not necessarily indefinite, but compressed due to the formality of a greeting.

7. Robert W. Funk, "The Apostolic *Parousia*: Form and Significance," in *Christian History and Interpretation: Studies Presented to John Knox*, ed. William R. Farmer, C. F. D. Moule, and Richard R. Niebuhr (Cambridge: Cambridge University Press, 1967), 249–68. Paul's presence in this letter is experienced both in the letter and in the envoys whom he sends, including Onesimus himself. Cf. Margaret MacDonald, "New Testament Envoys in the Context of Greco-Roman Diplomatic and Epistolary Conventions: The Example of Timothy and Titus," *JBL* 111 (1992): 641–62.

8. Christopher Kumitz, *Der Brief als Medium der* ἀγάπη: *Eine Untersuchung zur Rhetorischen und Epistolographischen Gestalt des Philemonbriefes*, Europäische Hochschulschriften 787 (Frankfurt am Main: Lang, 2004).

9. Cf. Acts 15:23; 23:26.

(1:1; 4:18) so with Philemon (1, 19), someone else physically *wrote* this letter on papyrus.[10] We are to imagine Paul at work sketching ideas, talking to his companions, someone composing drafts of letters, Paul hiring at considerable cost a secretary or scribe for the more official writing with a copy or two for himself, and then hiring or finding a letter carrier to deliver the letter—in this case probably Tychichus and Onesimus (Col 4:7–9). Paul probably did not write out by hand any of his letters, each of his letters reflects the grammar, style, and contribution of his secretary and companions in the process. Paul's letters were drafted in conversation and debate with his companions. He did not simply dictate his letters to a secretary and probably did not write out letters in one sitting.

In contrast to Colossians where Paul calls himself "apostle," Paul here calls himself "prisoner."[11] If there is a pattern already established—and this depends in part on the dating of Paul's letters—the use of "prisoner" would be atypical (but cf. Rom 1:1; Phil 1:1; Titus 1:1).[12] Paul does not anchor himself in "saber-rattling" apostolic authority (e.g., Galatians).[13] Rather, he relies upon a rhetorical strategy that both solicits sympathy for his condition of imprisonment and demonstrates the authenticity of his message. The result is a summons for Philemon to exercise an obedience similar to Paul.[14] Of note, in the Greco-Roman world, prison was normally a temporary holding station prior to a trial, not a final punishment. Noticeably, Philemon and the others are not in prison. His stated appeal emerges from

10. Compare 1 Cor 1:1 (Paul and Sosthenes) and 16:21 (in his own hand). 1 Corinthians 1:1–16:20 was written out by someone else, perhaps a professional scribe or amanuensis or even perhaps a coworker with such a skill.

11. δέσμιος, BDAG 219; for similar terms, L&N 1:485, 486, 551–52. The term is found only in the later Pauline letters (Phlm 1, 9, 13; Eph 3:1; 4:1; 2 Tim 1:8). It is unlikely that this term designates metaphorical slavery to Christ; against Stuhlmacher, 29; Moule, 140; Wilson, 332. For more analysis, see Harris, *Slave of Christ*. For discussion of scholarship on the metaphors for slavery in Paul, note Byron, *Paul and Slavery*, 77–91. On Paul in prison, see McKnight, *Colossians*, 101–5, at Col 1:7–8; 4:12. Compare also Phil 1:7, 13, 14, 17; 4:22; 2 Cor 6:5; 11:23. In the summary statements about prisons, I am dependent upon Brian Rapske, *The Book of Acts and Paul in Roman Custody*, vol. 3 of *The Book of Acts in Its First Century Setting* (Grand Rapids: Eerdmans, 1994), 9–70, 177–82, 195–422. See also Brian Rapske, "Prison, Prisoner," *DNTB*, 827–30.

12. Both Romans and Titus add apostolic credentials to "servant" status.

13. On "saber-rattling," see Callahan, 23–24. Note the critique in Weima, "Paul's Persuasive Prose," 33. In a stronger form, a case has been made that Paul asserts himself in this letter as the *paterfamilias*: see Chris Frilingos, "'For My Child, Onesimus': Paul and Domestic Power in Philemon," *JBL* 119 (2000): 91–104. It is, therefore, unwise to restrict the claim to authority to the term "apostle" as has been argued by Ernest Best, "Paul's Apostolic Authority–?," *JSNT* 27 (1986): 3–25.

14. On the rhetoric, Witherington, 53–54; Pao, 363.

his confined location, their freedom, and the bond of friendship.[15] One thinks of John the Baptist in prison similarly appealing to Jesus (Matt 11:2–3), just as one thinks of Jesus urging his followers to care for those in prison (25:31–46). *The term "prisoner" also intentionally identifies Paul with the analogous marginal condition of Onesimus*, who could well have experienced the humiliation of being shackled: one "in bonds" in prison is far closer to the slave Onesimus than Philemon.[16] In the letter to Philemon, Paul presents himself in other terms: "old man" (v. 9), "prisoner" (vv. 1, 9, 10), the spiritual parent of Onesimus (v. 10), brother of Onesimus (v. 16), and the brother, fellow gospel minister, partner, and future guest of Philemon (vv. 1, 6, 17, 22). As a prisoner, Paul is dependent upon others for support, including his need for food and water. Under the best circumstances, he would only have received a minimum of both from the prison guards. If chained or underground—both common in Roman prisons—Paul was in pain and deprived of natural light and almost certainly living in horrendous conditions.

Paul is a prisoner of "Christ Jesus."[17] Some think "Christ" is not so much Jesus's role as Messiah as a second name with barely a whiff of the historic role as Messiah. However, recent studies have concluded that whenever Paul uses *christos* he never loses touch with the historic claim that Jesus is the Messiah of Israel.[18] To call Jesus "Messiah" moves in two directions at once. Jesus, as Messiah, changes Israel's story; Jesus, as Messiah, pushes against Roman honor. Romans despised having a king (*rex*). From the days of the republic through Julius Caesar until the period of Octavian (Caesar Augustus)—who established not a "kingdom" but the *Principate* (symbolizing the one true Roman senator/citizen leading and representing all true Roman citizens), the Romans would not call their leader *rex*. To call Jesus "Messiah" was evocative of sinister intentions against Romans. The early Christians proclaimed Jesus

15. Harris, 244; Fitzmyer, 84; Moo, 380.

16. Barth and Blanke, 132; Thompson, 206; Lewis, 439.

17. The genitive expresses an ambiguous relationship: it can be possessive, causal, purposive or more generally relational (see Harris, 244; Moo, 380).

18. See Ben Witherington III, "Christ," *DPL*, 97–98; Matthew V. Novenson, *Christ among the Messiahs: Christ Language in Paul and Messiah Language in Ancient Judaism* (New York: Oxford University Press, 2012); Wright, *Paul and the Faithfulness of God*, 2:817–36; Joshua W. Jipp, *Christ Is King: Paul's Royal Ideology* (Minneapolis: Fortress, 2015). For an earlier statement by Wright, "ΧΡΙΣΤΟΣ as 'Messiah' in Paul: Philemon 6," in *The Climax of the Covenant: Christ and the Law in Pauline Theology* (Minneapolis: Fortress, 1993), 41–55. That proper names are often anarthrous is sometimes used as the argument that anarthrous *christos* is a personal name. See BDF §260.1. I have examined "Christ" and its connection to atonement in Scot McKnight, *Jesus and His Death: Historiography, the Historical Jesus, and Atonement Theory* (Waco, TX: Baylor University Press, 2005), 60–68, 161–71, 207–24.

was "king" and that he was bringing a "kingdom," terms that burned with deep suspicion.[19] It is best not to affirm that Paul was "anti-empire." Rather, Paul's claims were not so much an *anti*-imperial critique as they were a *supra*-imperial critique.[20]

Timothy contributed to this letter in content,[21] thus the inclusion of his name in the epistolary prescript.[22] Timothy is Paul's best friend, closest co-worker and associate, and a man about whom we know plenty even if he is always in the background.[23] To take a maximalist view of the evidence about him: Timothy's father was a Gentile but his mother a Jew; he probably came to believe in Christ during Paul's first missionary journey to Lystra where Timo-

19. For one important discussion, C. Kavin Rowe, *World Upside Down: Reading Acts in the Graeco-Roman Age* (New York: Oxford University Press, 2009), 91–137.

20. Karl Galinsky, "The Cult of the Roman Emperor: Uniter or Divider?" in *Rome and Religion: A Cross-Disciplinary Dialogue on the Imperial Cult,* ed. Jeffrey Brodd and Jonathan L. Reed (Atlanta: Society of Biblical Literature, 2011), 1–21, and Karl Galinsky, "In the Shadow (or Not) of the Imperial Cult: A Cooperative Agenda," in *Rome and Religion: A Cross-Disciplinary Dialogue on the Imperial Cult,* in Jeffrey Brodd and Jonathan L. Reed (Atlanta: Society of Biblical Literature, 2011), 215–25. The same expressions could be used for manumission in Philemon and Paul: he was not so much *anti*-slavery as *supra*-slavery.

21. That Timothy contributed or co-wrote or participated in the letter to Philemon see Dunn, 311; Fitzmyer, 85–86; Thompson, 207; for those who think he is an add-on for strategic reasons, Lohse, 189; Bruce, 205; Wright, 172; Harris, 244–45; Barth and Blanke, 249–50 (but they speak then of "brotherly agreement" [250]), Stuhlmacher, 30; Ryan, 210; Moo, 380–81. Most who exclude Timothy from writing the letter appeal to the first person in the rest of the letter (e.g., Lohse, 189). Grammatically it is impossible to excerpt Timothy from co-authorship at some level, so one must consider Timothy to be behind the Pauline "I" in Philemon. On this topic, and the inclusion of others in authorship, see the very important study of Richards, *Paul and First-Century Letter Writing.* On Timothy as contributor, see 1 Thess 1:1; 2 Thess 1:1; 2 Cor 1:1; Col 1:1; notice Eph 1:1; but see again Phil 1:1. Timothy, then, had his hand in six of the ten letters prior to the Pastorals. Two others are purportedly sent to Timothy (1 and 2 Tim). Galatians and Romans have no others in the salutation; 1 Thess and 2 Thess each include Silas; 1 Cor 1:1 has Sosthenes. I would infer that when Timothy was present with Paul, he was involved in the production of any letter. As co-author, Timothy is a "contributing" but not the main author, indicated by Paul's first person references. Thus, Col 1:1–9, 28; 4:3; as well the central section of 2 Corinthians (e.g., 2 Cor 2:12–13; 7:8–12).

22. One suspects at times that we are in need of retooling the clear evidence that Paul believed in power-with, or that he shared power; on this important topic, see Kathy Ehrensperger, *Paul and the Dynamics of Power: Communication and Interaction in the Early Christ-Movement,* LNTS 325 (London: T&T Clark, 2007). An important observation: "Thus the power-over operative between Paul and the communities is aimed at rendering itself obsolete, in that their asymmetrical relationship will be transformed and Paul should eventually become one among many siblings" (62).

23. On Timothy, F. F. Bruce, *The Pauline Circle* (Milton Keynes: Paternoster, 1985), 29–34; Bruce J. Malina, *Timothy: Paul's Closest Associate,* Paul's Social Network: Brothers and Sisters in Faith (Collegeville, MN: Liturgical Press, 2008).

thy surely saw Paul being stoned; Timothy's mother was a believer; Paul chose Timothy to be with him on his second missionary journey and he received a special endowment of the Spirit through the laying on of hands; to regulate his status, Paul had Timothy circumcised; when Paul traveled in Athens, Timothy stayed with Silas in Berea and then joined Paul in Athens. In addition, Timothy encouraged the Christians in Thessalonica and reported good news about the Thessalonians to Paul later, part of that good news expressed by a gift of money for the poor saints in Jerusalem. Timothy helped Paul write both 1 and 2 Thessalonians, assisted in the evangelization of Corinth, and helped write 2 Corinthians (probably also Romans). He traveled with Paul to Jerusalem as Lystra's delegate to the Jerusalem church, and then helped Paul in writing Colossians, Philemon, and Philippians. Later Paul may have sent Timothy to Philippi. Timothy was encouraged to stay in Ephesus and to eventually meet Paul in Rome (?) during winter. In addition, Timothy was imprisoned for the gospel and eventually released.[24] What Lewis and Tolkien were to one another and Bethge was to Bonhoeffer is what Timothy was to Paul.

Timothy is "our brother,"[25] a term that indicates spiritual and real kinship in the church as well as a coworker in the gospel.[26] Furthermore, the term evokes Paul's special love for Timothy (1 Cor 4:17; Phil 2:19–23). We see in this designation not a hierarchy of relations but coordination in a mutual calling to the gospel. This term resonates throughout the letter (cf. vv. 2, 7, 9, 10, 12, 16, 17, 20).[27]

B. ADDRESSEES (1B–2)

1b–2 As the authors are plural, so too the addressees: "To Philemon our dear friend and fellow worker—also to Apphia our sister and Archippus our fellow soldier—and to the church that meets in your home." The addressees

24. See Acts 14:19–20; 16:1–3; 17:14–16; 18:5; 19:22; 20:4; 1 Thess 1:1; 3:1–6; 2 Thess 1:1; 1 Cor 4:17; 16:10–11; 2 Cor 1:1, 19; 11:9; Rom 16:21; Col 1:1; Phlm 1; Phil 1:1; 2:19, 23; 1 Tim 1:3, 18; 4:12, 14; 2 Tim 1:5–6; 3:11, 15; 4:13, 21; Heb 13:23.

25. The Greek does not indicate a plural as in "our." The Greek text contains a simple definite article ("the brother"). The article is rendered in the NIV as indicating the brother of us all. I am inclined to see it more as "my" than "our." That ἀδελφοί may indicate a ministry of coworkers has been argued in E. Earle Ellis, "Paul and His Co-Workers," in *Prophecy and Hermeneutic in Early Christianity: New Testament Essays* (Grand Rapids: Eerdmans, 1978), 3–22 (esp. 13–22).

26. Joseph H. Hellerman, *The Ancient Church as Family* (Minneapolis: Fortress, 2001); Aasgaard, *My Beloved Brothers and Sisters!* It is commonly said it is "fictive" kinship, which term is fine as long as it does not mean pretend. This new kinship is real (Fitzmyer, 85).

27. Lewis, "Philemon-Paul-Onesimus Triangle," 239–46.

in Greek are neatly coordinated: To (1) Philemon, (2) Apphia, (3) Archippus, and (4) to the church. Philemon is mentioned first because of his primary importance in the letter. It is likely that "the church that meets in your [masculine] home" is Philemon's. Hence, as can be seen in the translation above, the NIV brackets Apphia and Archippus so it can connect the house church to Philemon.

Philemon,[28] otherwise unknown in the NT, is both a "dear friend" and a "fellow worker."[29] Philemon was a convert of Paul (v. 19). This new relationship reconfigures Philemon's household and Paul becomes the *paterfamilias.*[30] Being "dear friend" (or, "loved") creates the need in honor-shame as well as benefaction cultures to reciprocate in loving friendship (i.e., sending Onesimus back to Paul):[31] thus, v. 9: "I prefer to appeal to you on the basis of

28. A common name; cf. BDAG 1057; Lightfoot, 303–7. A recent theory is that Philemon's home was actually in Rome. See Vicky Balabanski, "Where Is Philemon? The Case for a Logical Fallacy in the Correlation of the Data in Philemon and Colossians 1.1–2; 4.7–18," *JSNT* 38 (2015): 131–50.

29. τῷ ἀγαπητῷ καὶ συνεργῷ ἡμῶν. The single article unites both terms and the final possessive applies to both of the substantives as well (Harris, 245). On "dear friend" (τῷ ἀγαπητῷ), see Commentary at Phlm 5 on "love." For other uses of "beloved" for both churches and individuals, 1 Thess 2:8; 1 Cor 4:17; 10:14; 15:58; Eph 5:1; 6:21; Phil 2:12; 4:1; 1 Tim 6:2; 2 Tim 1:2; esp. also Col 1:7; 4:7, 9, 14, and Phlm 16. On "coworkers," and fellow ministers, see James D. G. Dunn, *Beginning from Jerusalem*, vol. 2 of *Christianity in the Making* (Grand Rapids: Eerdmans, 2009), 566–72; Ellis, *Prophecy and Hermeneutic*, 3–22; Bruce, *The Pauline Circle*, 81–90; Ehrensperger, *Paul and the Dynamics of Power*, 35–62. For an exposition, Barth and Blanke, 251–53. The shared assumptions and communal evocations in the term "our," which grammatically refers to Paul and Timothy, along with the new conditions created by this new kind of community, has been sketched by Mary Ann Getty, "The Theology of Philemon," in *SBL Seminar Papers 1987* (Atlanta: Scholars Press, 1987), 503–8.

30. For now, see Frilingos, "For My Child, Onesimus." Also, Petersen, *Rediscovering Paul*, 92–93. On first-century households in the Roman Empire, see Jane F. Gardner and Thomas Wiedemann, eds., *The Roman Household: A Sourcebook* (New York: Routledge, 1991); David L. Balch, "Household Codes," in *Greco-Roman Literature and the New Testament: Selected Forms and Genres*, ed. David E. Aune (Atlanta: Scholars Press, 1988), 25–50. For a refreshing expansion of the early Christian households to the neighborhood, see now Richard Last, "The Neighborhood (*vicus*) of the Corinthian *ekklēsia*: Beyond Family-Based Descriptions of the First Urban Christ-Believers," *JSNT* 38 (2016): 399–425. Last's work needs to be nuanced with Peter Oakes, *Reading Romans in Pompeii: Paul's Letter at Ground Level* (Minneapolis: Fortress, 2009).

31. Examined with care in John M. G. Barclay, *Paul and the Gift* (Grand Rapids: Eerdmans, 2015); Bruce W. Longenecker, *Remember the Poor: Paul, Poverty, and the Greco-Roman World* (Grand Rapids: Eerdmans, 2010); Stephan Joubert, *Paul as Benefactor: Reciprocity, Strategy and Theological Reflection in Paul's Collection*, WUNT 2.124 (Tübingen: Mohr Siebeck, 2000); David J. Downs, *The Offering of the Gentiles: Paul's Collection for Jerusalem in Its Chronological, Cultural, and Cultic Contexts*, WUNT 2.248 (Tübingen: Mohr Siebeck, 2008). An older, but still valuable, study is Stephen C. Mott, "The Power of Giving and Receiving:

love." Paul calls Philemon a "fellow worker" and so Philemon is now in a long list: Urbanus and Timothy (Rom 16:9, 21), Apollos (1 Cor 3:9), Titus (2 Cor 8:23), Epaphroditus (Phil 2:25), Euodia, Syntyche, and Clement (Phil 4:2–3), Timothy (1 Thess 3:2), as well as Mark, Aristarchus, Demas, and Luke (Phlm 24). A coworker of Paul serves various ministries alongside Paul in God's mission, which means evangelizing, teaching, planting churches, administrating, pastoring and discipling—as well as working with one's hands and showing hospitality.[32] To call Philemon a "fellow worker" then implicates Philemon in the ministry of Paul and pulls him deeper into the rhetorical circle Paul creates here: "If you are a coworker," Paul is arguing, "then you will support my need for Onesimus."

Most important for this letter, however, is that Philemon *is a slave owner*. He owns Onesimus and has him in his power. It is because he is slave owner that Paul addresses Philemon as a mediator for Onesimus.[33] We repeat the operative definition of slavery to clarify social realities about Philemon:

> Slavery by definition is a means of securing and maintaining an involuntary labour force by a group in society which monopolizes political and economic power.[34]

As a slave owner, Philemon is implicated in the widespread, socially-accepted, and culture-shaping institution of slavery; he is implicated in the power, authority, and force used to maintain that system; he had political and economic power over Onesimus, his slave. Since slave owners used fear to intimidate and to control their slaves, one can assume that at some level Philemon exercised fear-producing actions and Onesimus knew Philemon's powers. One can speculate that Philemon had used violence against Onesimus; one can guess Philemon may have made use of Onesimus sexually. We do not know how Philemon obtained Onesimus but we are safe to infer he either purchased Onesimus in a slave market or that Philemon's female slave gave birth to Onesimus. (We do not, for instance, know that Apphia was not a

---

Reciprocity in Hellenistic Benevolence," in *Current Issues in Biblical and Patristic Interpretation: Studies in Honor of Merrill C. Tenney, Presented by His Former Students*, ed. Gerald F. Hawthorne (Grand Rapids: Eerdmans, 1975), 60–72.

32. Phlm 22; see Callahan, 25.

33. Much can be and has been said about Paul as a reconciler here. Recently in a sermon, my pastor Jay Greener, beautifully connected Paul's reconciling work with Benjamin Rush, a man who sought to reconcile John Adams and Thomas Jefferson. See Lester J. Cappon, ed., *The Adams-Jefferson Letters: The Complete Correspondence between Thomas Jefferson and Abigail and John Adams* (Chapel Hill, NC: The University of North Carolina Press, 1988), 284–86.

34. Bradley, *Slaves and Masters*, 18.

female slave or that, even if she were, she had married Philemon or had given birth to Onesimus as Philemon's sexual partner.) We can assume Philemon's power extended far enough for Onesimus to fear being sold. Inasmuch as Onesimus could be a runaway, we can infer he ran out of fear or, to put a different and Christian liberation face on the problem, perhaps he escaped because he believed in manumission as a result of Pauline statements (like Col 3:11 or Gal 3:28; cf. 1 Cor 12:13). We can assume Philemon hung up notices in various places describing Onesimus his runaway and requested those who found him to contact officials with the promise of a reward. Furthermore, Onesimus would have known he might be branded and bear a scar the rest of his life or be forced to wear a collar for running away.[35] These generalizations or inferences from reasonable descriptions of masters and slaves are only that, but they need to be present in all explanations of this letter of Paul's. To avoid including the brutality, barbarity, or even lesser forms of violence is to ignore the obvious. We should not assume Philemon was a one-of-a-kind master or that Onesimus had lived the good life. That Philemon was a Christian can be assumed; that it transformed his attitude toward slavery and toward Onesimus can neither be assumed nor inferred from this letter. That Philemon was a good and kind man is clear from the letter. What can be inferred is that *even though Philemon was a Christian* Onesimus still sought shelter elsewhere. We can also infer that *Philemon was enough of a Christian and had enough respect for Paul that he would listen to Paul's fresh instructions to consider Onesimus a brother*. In that we begin to see the light of gospel transformation, but whether it led to liberation in the household or manumission in society are matters of speculation.

This personal letter to Philemon is not merely a private letter but instead a public-personal letter: it was sent to Philemon but also to Apphia, Archippus, and the church that meets in Philemon's house.[36] The public reading of the letter undoubtedly heightened the rhetoric. Apphia is a "sister" in Christ (cf. 1 Cor 7:15; 9:5; 1 Tim 5:2) and joins Phoebe (Rom 16:1) in the family of Christ.[37] She also becomes a witness in the public reading of the letter.[38] Des-

35. E.g., Petronius, *Satyricon* 103; one such Latin inscription shows a slave collar with the initials. See Wiedemann, *Greek and Roman Slavery*, 194 no. 221.

36. U. Wickert, "Der Philemonbrief—Privatbrief oder apostolisches Schreiben?," *ZNW* 52 (1961): 230–38. Also, Fitzmyer, 89–90; Lewis, 440; Pao, 365; Bieberstein, "Disrupting the Normal Reality of Slavery," 111–12; Weima, "Paul's Persuasive Prose," 37–38. Hence, I cannot agree with David Allen's claim that "Secondary participants are mentioned in the text but play no significant role." Allen, "Discourse Structure," 77–96 (here 82).

37. See Nicholas Rudolph Quient, "Apphia, an Early Christian Leader? An Investigation and Proposal Regarding the Identity of Apphia in Philemon 1:2," *Priscilla Papers*, forthcoming.

38. Bieberstein, "Disrupting the Normal Reality of Slavery," 115–16.

ignating females as being “in Christ” reflects Paul’s ecclesial principle that there is “not male and female” (Gal 3:28). Many think Apphia is the wife of Philemon,[39] although the term “wife” would have made that clearer. If she was his wife, her role as *materfamilias* would include special responsibilities in managing slaves, like Onesimus.[40] There is nothing in this text to establish the precise relationships of these persons. Apphia may have been mentioned because of her status as a leader in the church.[41] Philemon and Apphia may have been a couple in ministry.[42]

Archippus is a “fellow soldier” along with Epaphroditus (Phil 2:25). The term “fellow soldier” indicates loyalty, discipline, and courage in the face of opponents.[43] In Colossians, Archippus—probably the same person—was instructed by Paul to “complete the ministry you have received in the Lord” (Col 4:17), which perhaps concerns the collection.[44] Some have guessed that Archippus is the son of Philemon and Apphia;[45] others consider him to be the direct recipient of the letter.[46] Some even posit him as bishop of the church, following Epaphras.[47] No one knows. In fact, it is speculative to assume Paul addresses a single household—that of Philemon, his wife Apphia and his son Archippus. These individuals could be three different leaders in the church at Colossae from different households. Archippus’s connection with ministry in Col 4:17 might tip the evidence toward three leaders instead of three family members.

The fourth addressee is the “church that meets in your home.”[48] The

39. More or less so: Lightfoot, 306; Lohse, 190; Bruce, 206; Harris, 245; Bentley, 759–62 (here 759). Winter thinks seeing Apphia as a wife rather than as a “sister” in her own right is an example of “androcentric gender bias”; see Winter, “Methodological Observations,” 207. She backtracks later to say “perhaps (but not necessarily) married to Philemon” in Winter, “Paul’s Letter to Philemon,” 2.

40. Emphasized by Bentley, 760–61.

41. In general, see Cohick, *Women in the World of the Earliest Christians*. For Apphia as a leader, see Bird, 134; extensively argued by Quient, “Apphia.”

42. Andronicus and Junia (Rom 16:7) and Aquila and Priscilla (16:3–4).

43. Barth and Blanke, 258–59.

44. See McKnight, *Colossians*, 398–99.

45. Lightfoot, 308–9; Bruce, 206. Hübner, 28, rejects the idea that he was Philemon’s son as “reine Spekulation”; so too Fitzmyer, 88.

46. John Knox, *Chapters in a Life of Paul* (Nashville: Abingdon Press, 1950); Knox, *Philemon among the Letters of Paul*, 58; Winter, “Paul’s Letter to Philemon,” 2.

47. Martin, 158–59; Soungalo, 1487 (“senior pastor”).

48. On early house churches, Edwin A. Judge, *The Social Pattern of Christian Groups in the First Century* (London: Tyndale, 1960); Bruce, *The Pauline Circle*, 91–100; Marlis Gielen, “Zur Interpretation der Paulinischen Formel Τὴν Κατ’ Οἶκον Αὐτῆς ’Εκκλησίαν,” *ZNW* 77 (1986): 109–25; E. Earle Ellis, *Pauline Theology: Ministry and Society* (Grand Rapids: Eerdmans, 1989), 139–45; Robert Banks, *Paul’s Idea of Community*, rev. ed. (Peabody, MA: Hendrickson, 1994), 26–36; Abraham J. Malherbe, *Social Aspects of Early Christianity*, 2nd ed.

term "your" is masculine and means we are to look either to the closest reference (Archippus) or the more remote referent, Philemon. There is nothing in the grammar that yields clarity except the priority of first mention.[49] Nothing in Col 4:17, where Archippus is mentioned, suggests his home is the house church. Although one might argue that the group might have met at Archippus's home, since no other house church in Colossae is mentioned (Nympha's at Laodicea is mentioned in Col 4:15),

The term *ekklēsia* ("church") refers to the gathered body from the community, gathered together here for instruction, prayer, worship, edification, and fellowship.[50] Paul's mission was not simply to increase the church's numbers through evangelism but to bring Gentiles to the table with Jews to form a new family called the church (*ekklēsia*). For Paul, the church was an expansion of Israel into Gentile territory. Perhaps most notable here is that "church" in the Prison Letters signifies the church universal (so also Eph 1:22–23). Such a meaning for "church," however, is not innovative to these letters—the same sense is found at 1 Cor 12:27.[51] Nor should one think Paul has dropped the local expression as the body: it is a particularization of the universal church gathered.[52] In this context one must also think the term *ekklēsia* will have evoked a political assembly of citizens; as such, the use of the term by Paul for a Christian kind of politics under Jesus had some overtones of a political alternative if not subversive activity.

(Philadelphia: Fortress, 1983), 60–91; Wayne A. Meeks, *The First Urban Christians: The Social World of the Apostle Paul*, 2nd ed. (New Haven: Yale University Press, 2003); Roger W. Gehring, *House Church and Mission: The Importance of Household Structures in Early Christianity* (Peabody, MA: Hendrickson, 2004); Carolyn Osiek and Margaret Y. Macdonald, *A Woman's Place: House Churches in Earliest Christianity* (Minneapolis: Fortress, 2006); Oakes, *Reading Romans in Pompeii*. A recent attempt to expand the house church to the neighborhood, with bibliographical discussion, can be found in Last, "The Neighborhood." For a sketch of the rise of the church, see Craig A. Evans, *From Jesus to the Church: The First Christian Generation* (Louisville: Westminster John Knox, 2014).

49. Joining many: Lohse, 191; Harris, 245–46; Barth and Blanke, 260; Fitzmyer, 89; Osiek, 133; Thompson, 209; Ryan, 213. The thesis of Knox and others is rooted in the natural antecedent being Archippus. See Knox, *Philemon among the Letters of Paul*, 62; Cope, "Rethinking," 47.

50. James D. G. Dunn, *The Theology of Paul the Apostle* (Grand Rapids: Eerdmans, 1998), 533–623; Paul Trebilco, *Self-Designations and Group Identity in the New Testament* (Cambridge: Cambridge University Press, 2012), 164–207. Also *NIDNTTE* 2:134–44.

51. Trebilco, *Self-Designations and Group Identity in the New Testament*, 178–80.

52. Banks, *Paul's Idea of Community*, 37–46. Banks, however, presses too hard against organizational relationships between churches. For an alternative understanding of how the church institutions developed, see Alistair C. Stewart, *The Original Bishops: Office and Order in the First Christian Communities* (Grand Rapids: Baker Academic, 2014).

C. SALUTATION (3)

3 Here, Paul and Timothy establish their strategy by way of a greeting:[53] "Grace and peace to you from God our Father and the Lord Jesus Christ."[54] Translation theorists argue that the meaning of a text in a given context is limited to what is required,[55] suggesting that we may need to minimize the theological weight apportioned to "grace and peace." However, since the apostle Paul at nearly the same time of writing uses a more mundane word for typical greetings—*aspazomai* (Col 4:10, 12, 14, 15) —we are inclined to think that "grace" and "peace" are more than typical greetings, an inclination made more sure by the source: "from God our Father and our Lord Jesus Christ."[56] In this greeting, Paul turns Timothy and himself into priestly mediators of divine blessings. Such blessings are "fatherly," an Old Testament term for God (e.g., Hos 11:1; 2 Sam 7:14; Ps 2:7) and an especially sensitive New Testament term for God (Matt 6:9; Gal 4:7; Rom 8:15–17).[57]

53. Many commentaries say "See the commentary at Col 1:2." Words require contexts and inasmuch as the contexts of Colossians and Philemon are substantively different, the words will take on different evocations. Overlaps exist but, for example, "grace" in Col 1:2 has a different evocation than in Phlm 3. For the importance of this blessing for the letter, Barth and Blanke, 264; Thompson, 211.

54. See similar greetings at Gal 1:3; 2 Thess 1:2; 1 Cor 1:3; 2 Cor 1:2; Eph 1:2; Phil 1:2; Titus 1:4; also 1 Pet 1:2; 2 Pet 1:2; Rev 1:4.

55. Eugene A. Nida, "Implications of Contemporary Linguistics for Biblical Scholarship," *JBL* 91 (1972): 73–89. Nida writes, "the correct meaning of any term is that which contributes least to the total context, or in other terms, that which fits the context most perfectly" (86). Cf. Eugene A. Nida and Charles R. Taber, *The Theory and Practice of Translation* (Leiden: Brill, 2003).

56. For theologically robust perception of the terms in the greeting, Moo, 384. That Paul's letters stand out from other Jewish letters because of "grace" (vs. "mercy") is noted by Dunn, 51. The *theology* of Philemon has been neglected in much literature, and one who draws out the theology, combining exegesis with rhetorical analysis and historical reconstruction, is Marion L. Soards, "Some Neglected Theological Dimensions of Paul's Letter to Philemon," *PRSt* 17 (1990): 209–19. He draws these four conclusions about God in Philemon: God takes initiative, intervenes in human affairs, transforms persons in relationships, and God redirects lives. See also Still, "Philemon among the Letters of Paul," 133–42 (here 136–38).

57. *Contra* convention among many Christians who think Jesus was the first to address God as father, father is part of a deep biblical (and Jewish) tradition: Deut 32:6; Isa 63:16; Jer 3:4, 19; 31:9; Hos 11:1; Mal 1:6. But this does not deny a distinctiveness to Jesus and the early church; see Scot McKnight, *A New Vision for Israel: The Teachings of Jesus in National Context* (Grand Rapids: Eerdmans, 1999), 49–65. On God as father, see further in the important works of Marianne Meye Thompson, *The Promise of the Father: Jesus and God in the New Testament* (Louisville: Westminster John Knox, 2000); Abera M. Mengestu, *God as Father in Paul: Kinship Language and Identity Formation in Early Christianity* (Eugene, OR: Pickwick, 2013).

"Grace" refers to God the Father's goodness and redemptive work showered upon unworthy, non-status humans who are transformed by that grace into saints. Consequent to that grace they become grateful, contributing members of the body of Christ.[58] Hence, in terms of benefaction, for the Father to show grace or give a gift is to form a social bond with the receiver and to implicate the receiver in an obligatory reciprocal gift. "Peace" refers to general well-being, including material flourishing as well as inner and relational wholeness of God's people now that they have found themselves in Christ.[59] The theological weight of these terms packs more than a hint of rhetorical implication. Grace is a gift given to those without regard to worth, status, and honor. Yet, the lexical evidence suggests that grace given entailed *reciprocation*.[60] That is, the receiver of a gift was expected to respond with a reciprocal gift in kind or in gratitude. Paul lays the foundation for Philemon to act out the gift he has already experienced through Paul by reciprocating with the gifts of forgiveness, reconciliation, and probably release of Onesimus to Paul for further ministry. In such a context "peace" too evokes both reconciliation between master and slave as well as the eschatological kingdom taking root in the *ekklēsia* of Colossae.[61]

The Christology of Paul comes through in two ways: in coordinating Jesus with the Father as the source of grace, Paul demonstrates an implicit Christology that evokes the deity of Christ: "Lord Jesus Christ." To call Jesus "Lord" evokes the lordship of Jesus over Philemon and perhaps turns a gaze on Caesar.[62] It is, however, more accurate to speak of Paul's *supra*-imperial stance toward Rome than of his *anti*-imperial stance.[63] Paul was typically

58. See Rom 3:23–24; Eph 2:8–9. The full possibilities of grace include its superabundance, singularity, priority, incongruity, efficacy, non-circularity, and I have called attention above to grace's superabundance, priority, incongruity, efficacy, and reciprocity, see Barclay, *Paul and the Gift*, 183–88, with 575–82. See McKnight, *Colossians*, 46–48, for a brief introduction. For a more extensive review, see Scot McKnight, "The Unexamined Grace," *Books & Culture* (Jan/Feb 2016): 19–21. For an expansive understanding of grace in Phlm 3, note Barth and Blanke, 266–67. For the view that Paul's theology of grace is unsystematic, see Hendrikus Boers, "Ἀγάπη and Χάρις in Paul's Thought," *CBQ* 59 (1997): 693–713.

59. E.g., Luke 2:14; Eph 2:14. On peace, see Willard M. Swartley, *Covenant of Peace: The Missing Peace in New Testament Theology and Ethics* (Grand Rapids: Eerdmans, 2006). Also, Ryan, 213–14.

60. Barclay, *Paul and the Gift*, 24–50 (esp. 45–51).

61. Hübner, 29; Barth and Blanke, 267.

62. Harris, 246: "Of no mere human being could it be said that, together with God, he was a fount of spiritual blessing: the deity of Christ is thus implicitly affirmed." Dunn, 314, sees an extraordinary Christology at work, too; also Barth and Blanke, 265–66.

63. See Galinsky, "The Cult of the Roman Emperor: Uniter or Divider?" and "In the Shadow (or Not) of the Imperial Cult: A Cooperative Agenda." See also now the careful methodological exploration of detecting anti-imperialism in Paul in Christoph Heilig,

Jewish, which means he believed in the one creator God of all and that meant the idols of the nations were not Israel's God (Josephus, *Ant.* 14.228). Further, these idols were false gods and their rulers were, at worst, rebellious overlords or, at best, destined someday to surrender to Israel's God.[64] Hints of such themes reverberate from the words "Lord" and "Christ," which means "Messiah" or "King."

II. THANKSGIVING (4–7)

4*I always thank my God as I remember you*[a] *in my prayers,* 5*because I hear*
about your love for all his holy people and your faith in the Lord Jesus.[b] 6*I pray*
that your partnership with us in the faith may be effective in deepening[c] *your*
understanding of every good thing we share for the sake of Christ. 7*Your love has*
given me great joy and encouragement, because you, brother, have refreshed the
hearts of the Lord's people.

a. CEB creates a vocative by opening v. 4 with "Philemon," specifying the identity of "you." The Greek points us to one male (σου).

b. The NIV apportions love to "all his holy people" and faith to "the Lord Jesus," while the CEB follows the Greek word order more closely: "because I've heard of your love and faithfulness, which you have both for the Lord Jesus and for all God's people."

c. NIV adds "in deepening" as something implied.

There is a long and rich history of thanksgiving in the Bible on which these eucharistic words of Paul rest.[65] Paul's thanksgiving—theocentric and enchanted to the core—brings to expression the theology of all that follows in this letter:[66] his thanksgiving expresses gratitude to God, constant prayers

"Methodological Considerations for the Search for Counter-Imperial 'Echoes' in Pauline Literature," in *Reactions to Empire: Proceedings of Sacred Texts in Their Socio-Political Contexts*, ed. John A. Dunne and Dan Batovici, WUNT 2.372 (Tübingen: Mohr Siebeck, 2014), 73–92; Christoph Heilig, *Hidden Criticism? The Methodology and Plausibility of the Search for a Counter-Imperial Subtext in Paul*, WUNT 2.392 (Tübingen: Mohr Siebeck, 2015).

64. Anathea E. Portier-Young, *Apocalypse against Empire: Theologies of Resistance in Early Judaism* (Grand Rapids: Eerdmans, 2011); Wright, *Paul and the Faithfulness of God*, 1:279–347.

65. E.g., Lev 7:12–13, 15; 22:29; 1 Chr 25:3; 2 Chr 5:13; 33:16; Neh 12:8, 46; Pss 42:4; 50:14, 23; 69:30; 95:2; 100:4; 107:22; 116:17; 147:7; Isa 51:3; Jer 30:19; Jonah 2:9. See also 1QM XV, 5; 4Q260 X, 5.

66. For a fuller study of epistolary, introductory and thanksgivings, see Fred O. Francis, "The Form and Function of the Opening and Closing Paragraphs of James and 1 John," *ZNW* 61 (1970): 110–26; Jeffrey T. Reed, "Are Paul's Thanksgivings 'Epistolary'?," *JSNT* 61 (1996): 87–99. Note David W. Pao, "Gospel within the Constraints of an Epistolary Form:

for the person or church, the attributes of the person or church that earns his commendation, and a prayer request. In the logic of Philemon, Paul builds on Philemon's "faith" to appeal for him to activate his "love" toward Onesimus.

Paul's manner of presentation in this letter—and surely brought to the surface in the public performance and reading of this letter in Philemon's presence—can be described as "politeness."[67] Politeness is marked by six features: tact (minimize cost to Philemon, maximize benefit to Philemon), generosity (maximize cost to Paul, minimize benefit to Paul), approbation (minimize dispraise of Philemon, maximize praise of Philemon), modesty (minimize praise of Paul, maximize dispraise of Paul), agreement (minimize disagreement with Philemon, maximize agreement with Philemon), and sympathy (minimize antipathy for Philemon, maximize sympathy for Philemon). Various items on this list surface in vv. 4–7. Most significantly, these verses exhibit approbation, which means Paul and Timothy want to minimize criticism of Philemon and maximize praise.

The thanksgiving can be understood in two ways: first, a *consecutive* (if not always overt) logic moves from thanksgiving (v. 4) to cause (v. 5), to the purpose of the prayer (v. 6), and then to an emotional claim on Philemon (v. 7). Second, a *chiastic* arrangement begins with a thanksgiving (v. 4), the cause of thanksgiving in love (A) and faith (B; v. 5), a commentary on the implications of that faith (B´; v. 6), and a commentary on that love (A´; v. 7).[68] Through this chiastic exposition of love and faith Paul sets up the request found in vv. 8–22.

4 The first person plural "we" shifts noticeably in Phlm 4 to singular: "*I* always thank *my* God as *I* remember you in *my* prayers."[69] The "I" of this

Pauline Introductory Thanksgivings and Paul's Theology of Thanksgiving," in *Paul and the Ancient Letter Form*, ed. Stanley Porter and Sean A. Adams, Pauline Studies 6 (Leiden: Brill, 2010), 101–28. Also, Weima, "Paul's Persuasive Prose," 39–46.

67. Wilson, "The Politics of Politeness," 111. Wilson uses the categories of G. Leech, *Principles of Pragmatics* (London: Longman, 1983).

68. Dunn, 316; Fitzmyer, 95–96, is careful to note that some manuscripts in the textual tradition vary in word order, a variance that counts against too neat of a chiastic explanation.

69. Similar at 1 Cor 1:4; Rom 1:8; Phil 1:3. Many suggest an echo of Psalms in "my" God (Pss 3:7; 7:1, 3, 6, etc.). Εὐχαριστῶ τῷ θεῷ μου πάντοτε μνείαν σου ποιούμενος ἐπὶ τῶν προσευχῶν μου. The present aspects make more vivid to the listeners the act of thanksgiving; the participle is temporal ("when" or "whenever"); both verb and participle are intensified temporally by the use of πάντοτε. On aspectual theory for understanding Greek tenses, see two introductions, one elementary and the other more advanced: Constantine Campbell, *Basics of Verbal Aspect in Biblical Greek* (Grand Rapids: Zondervan, 2008); Stanley Porter, *Idioms of the Greek New Testament*, Biblical Languages: Greek 2 (Sheffield: JSOT Press, 1992). Aspectual theory examines *the action depicted by the author* (or the author's viewpoint) and not the relation of the action to temporal reality. The ἐπί in ἐπὶ τῶν προσευχῶν μου is equivalent to ἐν, but could mean "on the occasion of my prayers" (see Harris, 249).

letter is Paul.[70] The letter becomes the voice of Paul himself and is directed at Philemon personally, but this does not mean Timothy's voice is erased or Apphia and Archippus are ignored. That is, the letter becomes a conversation between Paul and Philemon with Timothy standing next to Paul as Apphia and Archippus stand alongside Philemon—with the whole church functioning (perhaps) as the Greek choir. Paul forms this thanksgiving for rhetorical reasons: by depicting Philemon as a gift from God[71] Paul relocates Philemon from being *paterfamilias* and slave owner into being a brother in Christ's family where Paul is the agent of God's grace to Philemon and Philemon comes under the social customs of reciprocal exchange. This rhetorical move creates space for the gift of reception of Onesimus as a brother and not as a slave.

One is led in this thanksgiving into the quiet of Paul's chambers to overhear him mentioning all those for whom he regularly prayed. Paul could have said "I thank God for you in my prayers" but instead adds "as I remember you," an expression that evokes the rich heritage of "remembrance" in the Hebrew Bible and Jewish tradition. Remembrance involves the mentioning of a person's name in God's presence, the history of that person or event, and the importance of intercession in solidarity with God's mission.[72] In fact, the term used here (*mneia*) often means "mention."[73] A good reminder of the term (or its cognate) is found in the name of one of our prophets, Zechariah. That name means "YHWH remembers." Also, God "remembered" Hannah because she pleaded with God to "remember" her, and so God gave her one of Israel's brilliant leaders, Samuel (1 Sam 1:11, 19). Nehemiah wants God to remember Israel's good deeds—to bless them, and he wants God to remember the enemy's wicked deeds—to conquer them (Neh 5:19; 6:14; 13:14, 22). But the prophets famously ask God to remember the covenant's promises to save and sanctify Israel. And Israel is to live faithfully by remembering God's covenant love and faithfulness. This context for Paul suggests that remembering ushers others into the presence of God. Paul "mentions" and "remembers" Philemon in order for God to open him to the sacred space of forgiving and reconciling grace.

The temporal participle behind "as I remember you," translated in the CEB as "every time I mention you,"[74] could be rendered either "when I remember you" or more likely "whenever I remember you." Beside the rather

70. Thus, cf. Phlm 7, 8–11, 14, 19–21.

71. On εὐχαριστῶ, see BDAG 415–16; *NIDNTTE* 2:334–36.

72. On μνεία, BDAG 654. Cf. 1 Thess 1:2; Rom 1:9; Eph 1:16; Phil 1:3; 2 Tim 1:3. For discussion, Barth and Blanke, 270–71; Moo, 386; Pao, 367.

73. 1 Thess 1:2; Eph 1:16; Rom 1:9. Wilson, 336: "remembrance through mention in intercessory prayer."

74. ποιούμενος. See BDF §310.1.

obvious problem sometimes generated by well-meaning preachers who want Christians to pray more often and who speak here of Paul's "always" remembering, we need to remember that Paul's prayer life was determined by the Shema-based hours of prayer along with the afternoon prayer of thanksgiving (at the temple). Hence, "always"[75] mentioning you does not signal Paul's mentioning Philemon's name before God all day long but more probably doing so "at the set hours of prayer."[76]

5 Paul's thanksgiving in Phlm 4 now specifies the cause of the thanksgiving. Here is a schematic that presents the logic of our passage:[77]

I always thank...

Remember you in my prayers (v. 4)
Because I hear about your love and faith (v. 5)
[So that] your partnership in the faith (v. 6)
[By the way, to comment back on love in v. 5,] your love (v. 7)

As can be seen, the verb ("I always thank") in Phlm 4 unfolds into when that occurs (v. 4b); the participle opening Phlm 5, translated with "because," ties into either the thanks of v. 4 or into remembering in prayer in v. 4b or, which is more likely, into the more general connection of both thanksgiving *and* remembering in prayer.

Paul gives thanks to God because he has heard (from Epaphras? Onesimus? Tychicus?) of Philemon's love and faith.[78] The grammar of Phlm 5 is

75. Does the adverb πάντοτε modify "thank" (always thank; NIV; Lightfoot, 334; Moule, 140; Harris, 249; Hübner, 29) or "remember" (always remember)? Word order creates the puzzle; I prefer to connect it to "remember" (CEB). Barth and Blanke, 269–70, think a false dichotomy is at work in forcing a distinction; perhaps the two verbal ideas are so connected it can function with both (Moo, 386).

76. On Paul in prayer, see W. B. Hunter, "Prayer," *DPL*, 725–34. On prayer in Judaism, see E. P. Sanders, *Jewish Law from Jesus to the Mishnah: Five Studies* (Philadelphia: Trinity Press International, 1990), 72–77; E. P. Sanders, *Judaism: Practice and Belief 63BCE–66CE*, new ed. (Minneapolis: Fortress, 2016), 321–23; Patrick D. Miller, *They Cried to the Lord: The Form and Theology of Biblical Prayer* (Minneapolis: Fortress, 1994); Walter Brueggemann, *The Psalms and the Life of Faith*, ed. Patrick D. Miller (Minneapolis: Fortress, 1995).

77. The order is unusual for Paul: 1 Thess 1:3; Col 1:4, 8; Eph 1:15; 1 Cor 13:13. See Barth and Blanke, 273–74.

78. ἀκούων σου τὴν ἀγάπην καὶ τὴν πίστιν. The participle (cf. Col 1:4; Eph 1:15) is taken by most to be causal (Harris, 249), and its present tense puts Paul's act of praying more vividly into the mind of Philemon and all those who heard the letter read. It is noticeable to aspectual theorists that the parallel in Col 1:3–4 uses an aorist participle while Phlm uses a present—the same temporal relation is no doubt in view but aspect drives attention to how

open to interpretation. Literally, it reads "Having heard of your love and faith, which [faith or love or both?] for the Lord Jesus [surely Jesus is the object of "faith" and perhaps "love"] and for all the holy people [surely the object of love but not faith]." The final clause in Greek in the NIV reads "for all his holy people" (or "saints"). It needs to be the completion of one of the terms: love or faith (or both). Some think Philemon has *both* love and faith for *both* Christ and the saints, but what does it mean to have "faith" for all the saints?[79] Or, one could think of love and faith as inseparable virtues and therefore both virtues extend toward Christ and the saints: a loving-faith in Christ and a loving-faith toward the saints.[80] Others mix the options: love and faith are directed to Christ while only love applies to the saints.[81] These explanations trip ultimately over the oddity of expressing faith in the saints. The consensus sees here a chiasm: Paul thanks God for Philemon's love and faith, his faith is in Christ and his love is for the people.[82] Thus, love (A), faith (B), faith (B′) and love (A′). More schematically and using my own translation:

Because I have heard of your:

(A) love and
(B) faithfulness,
Which (B′) faith/faithfulness you have in the Lord Jesus and
Which (A′) love you have for all the saints.

Love lacks definition in most discussions and hence assumptions often creep into our perceptions.[83] First, it is not true, regardless of the number of

---

the author depicts the action rather than the temporal relations. The verb can have its object in either accusative or genitive in NT Greek (cf. BDAG). On Epaphras, cf. Col 1:7, 8; 4:12. On Tychicus, cf. Acts 20:4; Col 4:7; Eph 6:21; 2 Tim 4:12; Titus 3:12.

79. Dunn, 317–18. On the tension of "faith" with "saints," Moo, 388.

80. Barth and Blanke, 272.

81. Hübner, 29–30.

82. Lightfoot, 334–35; Moule, 141; Lohse, 193; Wolter, 253; Moo, 387–89; Harris, 249–50, for full discussion. See further at James Hope Moulton and Nigel Turner, *Grammar of New Testament Greek, Vol. 3: Syntax* (Edinburgh: T&T Clark, 1963), 345–47.

83. On love, see Leon L. Morris, *Testaments of Love: A Study of Love in the Bible* (Grand Rapids: Eerdmans, 1981); Dunn, *Theology of Paul the Apostle*, 649–61; Boers, "Ἀγάπη and Χάρις in Paul's Thought." Also *TLNT* 1:8–22. For Philemon's emphasis on love, see Pieter G. R. de Villiers, "Love in the Letter to Philemon," in Tolmie *Philemon in Perspective*, 181–203. de Villiers, "Love in the Letter to Philemon," defines love as follows: "love is about a person-to-person relationship. It is a sharing and giving of oneself, unconditionally, in relationship to the other as a human being" (196). This relationship is formed in union with Christ (197), is relationally transformative (199–200), sacrificial (200–201), and ecclesial (201–2).

times repeated, that *agapē* is to be radically distinguished from *philia*. The two words overlap in meaning and any distinction is dependent upon a specific author's use. Second, love is central to the Christian ethic—from Jesus's great commandments (Mark 12:28–33) and the upper room discussion (John 13:34–35) to Paul (Gal 5:6, 13, 22; Rom 13:10; 1 Cor 13; 16:14; Eph 5:2; 1 Tim 1:5; here in Col 2:2; 3:14). Third, love is defined in the Bible by how God loves. Love then is a *covenantal relationship*, or a commitment to someone. Thus, we are to think of Gen 12, 15, 17, 22; Exod 19–24; 2 Sam 7 and then eventually to the new covenant of Mark 14:24, not to ignore Gal 4:24; 1 Cor 11:25; 2 Cor 3:6, 14 and Eph 2:12.[84] God's covenant then needs to be spelled out to comprehend what love means: as a covenant, God's love is a commitment of presence, advocacy and protection, and God's commitment entails both summoning his people into, and providing for, their transformation into holiness and love, which in the New Testament can be summed up as Christlikeness. All of this is at work in Israel's covenant formula.[85] Fourth, Paul knows Philemon's love is "for *all* his holy people."[86] The Gentile mission created ecclesial space for Jewish Christians to love Gentiles, males to love females, slaves to love the free, and Scythians to love barbarians (Col 3:11). In our context, the expansion of the family and siblinghood puts special pressure on Philemon to love the slave Onesimus as a brother (Phlm 16) and vice versa. Finally, the paradigmatic expression of divine love is the cross, which works itself out in praxis as cruciformity or Christoformity (2 Cor 5:14–15; Rom 5:6–8; 8:31–35). In announcing Philemon's already-practicing love in this letter as it is being read, the church at Colossae now turns to hear Paul's appeal for *ecclesial-shaped commitment* of Philemon to Onesimus. This appeal breaks down the Roman status system and all boundaries.

One more comment on "love": the object of this love, as in Col 1:4, is "all his holy people," traditionally translated "saints" (a good and noble term).[87] The word "saints" is commonly connected to "separation" but it is "perhaps best rendered 'dedicated', 'God's own', because it represents the O.T. conception of 'the dedicated people' whose members are 'the dedicated ones.'"[88] To define

84. Also Heb 7:22; 8:6; 9:15, 16–17, 20; 10:29; 12:24; 13:20.

85. Exod 6:2–8; Lev 26:11–12; Matt 1:23; John 1:14; John 16:1–15; Rev 21:3. See Rolf Rendtorff, *The Covenant Formula: An Exegetical and Theological Investigation*, trans. M. Kohl (Edinburgh: T&T Clark, 1998).

86. καί εἰς πάντας τοὺς ἁγίους. For love with εἰς, note 2 Thess 1:3; 2 Cor 2:8; Col 1:4; Eph 1:15; Rom 5:8.

87. See BDAG 10–11, 18–19. Paul uses the term ἅγιος often, including Rom 1:7; 12:1; 15:16, 25; 16:2, 15; 1 Cor 1:2; Eph 1:1, 4, 15, 18; 2:19, 21; 3:8; 4:12.

88. Moule, 45; *NIDNTTE* 1:124–33; also Maren Bohlen, *Sanctorum Communio: Die Christen als "Heilige" bei Paulus*, BZNW 183 (Berlin: de Gruyter, 2011). See my forthcoming study, "Saints Re-Formed: The Extension and Expansion of *Hagios* in Paul," in which I develop these ideas more completely.

holy ones/saints/holiness, then, primarily as "separation from" is only half the story; in fact, it is the second (and less important) half. A "saint" is someone dedicated to God and, *because of that dedication and consequent proximity to God's presence*, separated from common (worldly) usage. "Saints" furthermore does not refer to a special kind of Christian—the fully devoted ones versus those who are not fully devoted—but to all Christians because all Christians are indwelt by God through the Spirit.[89] The Old Testament and Jewish context for this term is that an item (grain) or a piece of furniture (lampstand) or a person (priest, levite) or the nation of Israel (Exod 19:6; Pss 16:3; 34:9; Dan 7:18)[90] or those in the Qumran community (CD XX, 2, 5, 7; 1QS I, 1; II, 25), are devoted and given over to God's presence and, because of that dedication or donation, are withdrawn from normal usage (eating and living an ordinary life). In Pauline theology, one becomes a holy person by God's saving work, the Spirit's sanctifying presence and work in Christ, and the Word's effects (Rom 15:16; 1 Cor 1:2; 6:11; Eph 5:26; 1 Thess 5:23; 2 Tim 2:21). Further, this divine work of grace is transformative and the basis for Paul's imperatives (Col 3:12).[91] In the reading of this letter before the church at Colossae, Onesimus's eye (with Paul "standing" beside him) is intently now on Philemon.

Paul thanks God constantly for Philemon's love and "faith." This occurrence of "faith" may refer to faith as a salvation-historical moment (Gal 2:15–21; 3:19–29). Yet, there is probably more at work.[92] The expression "faith in the Lord Jesus" means either personal faith or more expansively faithfulness in Jesus as Lord.[93] Because love is an ongoing practice rather than a singular moment/decision, I favor here (as at Col 1:4) the sense of "faithfulness." Too fine of a distinction collapses since faith always entails trust in Christ as the object, and thus Christology shapes the sort of response that is required. Faithfulness is trust over time and thus "faith" here means faithful trusting as well as allegiance because the one in whom they trust is none other than

89. For a good study, see David A. deSilva, *Transformation: The Heart of Paul's Gospel* (Bellingham, WA: Lexham Press, 2014).

90. Holiness is rooted in God's own and prior holiness, and if one ponders God's utter aloneness prior to all creation and that God is eternally holy, holiness cannot be reduced to separation: cf. Lev 11:44–45; 19:2; 20:7, 26.

91. In McKnight, *Colossians*, 320–24, I explore the continuity theme between Israel and the church (expanded Israel) as emerging from this term "saints."

92. On faith in Paul, see Dunn, *Theology of Paul the Apostle*, 371–85; Douglas A. Campbell, *The Quest for Paul's Gospel* (London: T&T Clark, 2005), 178–207; Dennis R. Lindsay, *Josephus and Faith:* Pistis *and* Pisteuein *as Faith Terminology in the Writings of Flavius Josephus and in the New Testament*, AGJU 19 (Leiden: Brill, 1993). See also *EDNT* 3:91–98; *NIDNTTE* 3:759–72. See too the new study of Matthew Bates, *Faith as Allegiance Alone: Rethinking Faith, Works, and the Gospel of Jesus the King* (Grand Rapids: Baker Academic, 2017).

93. ἣν ἔχεις πρὸς τὸν κύριον Ἰησοῦν.

Jesus, Messiah, Lord and Savior. Many are tempted to reduce "faith" to a single moment (i.e., the initial act of faith) and so miss out on the importance of faith over time and faith as allegiance. In v. 6 Paul speaks of a common faith that ought to be effective in Philemon's own transformation—and this, too, can be understood as faithfulness.

6 There is less of a complete break in the transition to v. 6 in the Greek NT than in the modern translations (NIV, CEB).[94] To repeat the structure proposed at v. 5:

I always thank. . .

Remember you in my prayers (v. 4)
Because I hear about your love and faith (v. 5)
[So that] your partnership in the faith (v. 6)
[By the way, to comment back on the love of v. 5,] your love (v. 7)

It is not clear how v. 6 connects to v. 5, but the general sense is clear. Paul thanks God for Philemon because of his love and faith (vv. 4–5) and now adds in v. 6 his prayer that Philemon's faith (v. 5) will result in a new understanding: "I pray[95] that your partnership with us in the faith may be effective in deepening your understanding of every good thing we share for the sake of Christ." Paul, again, seems to be working with a chiasm:

v. 5: Love (A)—faith (B)—faith (B′) in the Lord—love (A′) for his holy people
v. 6 picks up on faith (B), the second term in v. 5.
v. 7 picks up on love (A), the first term in v. 5.

Paul thanks God for Philemon's love, faith, and now faith generates perception (or understanding). This letter has a completely different agenda than does Colossians, but an emphasis on wisdom, knowledge, and understanding was found throughout Colossians (and Ephesians as well).[96]

94. The Greek conjunction (ὅπως) intends continuation from vv. 4–5 or at least v. 5 rather than a full stop. For parallels, 2 Thess 1:11; Col 1:9; Phil 1:9; Eph 1:17.

95. Most translations, consistent as they are with Jas 5:16 and Acts 8:15, add "I pray" to clarify that v. 6 is the content of the prayer in v. 4 (Lightfoot, 335; Lohse, 192; Moo, 389). Others think this is the purpose or result of Philemon's love and faith (Wolter, 254). For a full discussion, see Harald Riesenfeld, "Faith and Love Promoting Hope: An Interpretation of Philemon v. 6," in *Paul and Paulinism: Essays in Honour of C. K. Barrett*, ed. Morna D. Hooker and S. G. Wilson (London: SPCK, 1982), 251–57.

96. The themes of the thanksgiving of Phlm 4–7 make for numerous connections to the other prison letters. Cf. Col 1:3–12; Eph 1:15–23; Phil 1:3–11.

Philemon's faith(fulness) in v. 5 connects him with the apostle Paul and Timothy: "your partnership (*koinōnia*) with us in the faith."[97] The term *koinōnia* draws Philemon and the listeners into a variety of associations. Yet, the core idea is active association, mutual participation, identification with one another, relational interchange and exchange, and partnership with others. Thus, they have been drawn into fellowship with Christ (1 Cor 1:9; 10:16), the Spirit (2 Cor 13:13; Phil 2:1), the church (Gal 2:9), the gospel (Phil 1:5), and sufferings (Phil 3:10) as well as drawn out of fellowship with darkness (2 Cor 6:14). In our context, *koinōnia* refers to Philemon's fellowship in the faith, the church's mutual participation in Christ and believing (faith-based fellowship), or partnership in the ministry of the faith. What is more, "faith" could be rendered "the faith," "the act of believing," or "faithfulness." Yet, the emphasis in Philemon is on the church's and Philemon's common and reciprocating life shared because they faithfully live out the cruciform Lord Jesus. It is not a stretch to see *koinōnia* as forming the basis of the Pauline exhortation in the entire letter.[98]

Faith and faithfulness then are designed to become "effective"[99]—that is, Paul sees participation in faith as a power at work in Philemon that creates an opportunity for a new understanding. That is, faithfulness is designed to lead Philemon into "understanding." The NIV's "deepening" is an interpretation of the compound Greek term *epignōsis*, that is, not just knowledge but deep perception.[100] Among NT scholars there is disagreement as to whether or not *epi* added to *gnōsis* entails a deeper knowledge or is only a Koine Greek synonym of *gnōsis* (knowledge). The fact that this term in the NT refers only to "transcendent and moral matters"[101]—like God, sin, and mysteries—suggests the NIV's "deepening" is preferable and that in this case *epignōsis* refers to more than simple knowledge. Philemon's faith(fulness) is to work itself out into a deeper understanding of "every good thing," a subtle appeal for Onesimus.[102]

97. ἡ κοινωνία τῆς πίστεώς σου. On κοινωνία, BDAG 552–53; *EDNT* 2:303–5; *NIDNTTE* 2:706–13. For separable nuances of meaning of the term, see Fitzmyer, 97–98; Moo, 390–92; Pao, 370–71. The genitive is most likely the object (Lohse, 193–94; see discussion in Harris, 251) though some think it is subjective. The term "faith" can mean active faith or the content of faith, and it can be Philemon's or the congregation's.

98. So *EDNT* 2:304; also Lohse, 193–94; Wright, 174. Some (e.g., Bruce, 208–9; Harris, 251; Callahan, 28) prefer to understand κοινωνία as "generosity" (i.e., as gift).

99. On ἐνεργής, BDAG 335. See also 1 Cor 16:9. This term emerges from a root that expresses the efficacious nature of God's grace in the life of the Christian and the church through the power of the cross, resurrection, and ascension as well as the presence of the Holy Spirit.

100. ἐπίγνωσις, cf. BDAG 369; *NIDNTTE* 1:575–88. Callahan, 28, renders it "appreciation" and Barth and Blanke, 284, as "recognize." For discussion, esp. Moo, 393.

101. BDAG 369. Cf. Col 1:10; Rom 3:20; Col 2:2.

102. The same term at v. 14 is translated "favor."

The colorless expression "every good thing" in Phlm 6 gains some clarity in the expressions that follow. The location of "every good thing" is specified in the CEB's "among us *in Christ*" or, more colorfully, in the translation of Barth and Blanke: "which is found in your congregation."[103] How so? "Every good thing" takes place in relationships and practices under the lordship of king Jesus in fellowship with others (cf. Eph 4:12–13).[104] Thus, "good things" refers to kingdom redemption and fellowship.[105] In addition, the term has a moral edge. Thus, the Christian is to do what is *good* [106] but this *good* lies outside of human capacities and so emerges from God's transformative work[107] of accomplishing what is *good* (as in Rom 8:28). So the Christian is to strive for what is *good*. Critical here, then, is what Paul told the Galatians, "let us do good to all people" (Gal 6:10), and the Ephesians, "created in Christ Jesus to do good works" (Eph 2:10). Philemon, thus, is being summoned by Paul to let God's grace empower him to do the good, and that good will be to welcome back Onesimus and thus to be reconciled. Importantly, this is what "good thing" means in v. 14 too.

Paul has now drawn a full circle around Onesimus, Philemon, and the church at Colossae: Philemon is to see the implication of a shared faith for what life is to be in the church. Which is to say, *koinōnia* entails interchange and reciprocation of siblings and the ending of hierarchies. Paul builds from one expression to another and creates drama within the letter. These terms deserve to be listed:

103. The NIV's "for the sake of Christ" (Moo, 394) is not as preferable as the CEB's "in Christ." The Greek is παντὸς ἀγαθοῦ τοῦ ἐν ἡμῖν εἰς Χριστόν. The "every good thing" is "among us" (the church) "unto" or "in" Christ. There are five options for "unto Christ": direction, purpose, result, location ("in"), or a more general relation. If εἰς Χριστόν is not taken equivalent to "in Christ," then it may be the postponed direction/purpose/result of the ἐπίγνωσις (Lightfoot, 336). Lohse, 194, reads it almost as a suspended clause: "for the glory of Christ"; Martin, 162, sees a referent to the judgment, and Barth and Blanke, 290–91, to the coming of Christ. I see "unto Christ" as a virtual equivalent to "in Christ" (BDF §205, 206, 218; Bruce, 209; Dunn, 320), but Wright, 177–78, has more eschatology and ecclesiology to his "in": this "unto Christ" is both "in" Christ and the goal of God's work among the saints (also discussion in Thompson, 215–16). For Wright's longer treatment, see *The Climax of the Covenant*, 54, and *Paul and the Faithfulness of God*, 1:16–22. For another emphasis on eschatological hope here, see Riesenfeld, "Faith and Love," 257. For the discussion of the relation of ἐν to εἰς, Murray J. Harris, *Prepositions and Theology in the Greek New Testament: An Essential Reference Resource for Exegesis* (Grand Rapids: Zondervan, 2012), 84–88.

104. Wright, *The Climax of the Covenant*, 41–55 (here 49–55).

105. Lohse, 194. E.g., Rom 8:28. Riesenfeld sees behind this "every good thing" the third word in the triad of faith, love, and hope. See Riesenfeld, "Faith and Love," 255–56.

106. 1 Thess 5:15; 2 Cor 5:10; 9:8; Rom 2:7, 10; 12:2, 21; 2 Tim 3:17.

107. 2 Thess 2:16–17; Col 1:10; Phil 1:6; Rom 7:13, 18–19.

"Prisoner" in v. 1
"Grace and peace" in v. 3
"Thank" in v. 4
"Love" and "faith" in v. 5
"Understanding" and "good thing" in v. 6
"Love" in v. 7
"What you ought to do" in v. 8
"Love" in v. 9
"*I appeal for my son Onesimus*" in v. 10
"Formerly he was useless . . . now . . . both to you and to me" in v. 11
"My very heart" in v. 12
"I would have liked" in v. 13
"Without your consent" and "voluntary" in v. 14
"Perhaps" in v. 15
"Better than a slave, *as a dear brother*" in v. 16
"So if you consider me . . . *welcome him as you would welcome me*" in v. 17
"Charge it to me" in v. 18
"You owe me your very self" in v. 19
"Benefit" and "refresh" in v. 20
"Confident . . . you will do even more than I ask" in v. 21
"Prepare a guest room for me" in v. 22

I have put in italics words of appeal surrounded by a constant tapping on Philemon's will. The rhetorical build-up, trained or (probably) not, is masterful. Philemon is being led to "welcome him" in v. 17. This welcome is capped off with the request to get a room ready for him. If the words of the appeal are not compelling, the embodied presence of Paul in Philemon's home makes Philemon's choice inevitable.

7 Philemon 6 is a footnote on "faith" in v. 5, and Phlm 7 is now a footnote on "love," forming a chiasm with love and faith in v. 5. Hence:

I always thank

Remember you in my prayers (v. 4)
Because I hear about your ***love*** and *faith* (v. 5)
[So that] your partnership in the *faith* (v. 6)
[By the way, to comment back on v. 5's love,] your *love* (v. 7)

Philemon 7 contains one new sentence that I translate: "I have much joy and encouragement over your [Philemon's] love, and the hearts of the saints are refreshed through you [and your acts of love], brother." Paul is both preparing Philemon for The Ask and appealing to his emotions so Philemon will welcome Onesimus home (and probably send him back to Paul).

Paul's emotions are expressed first: "great joy and encouragement" (NIV).[108] The two emotions overlap but we can look at them separately. Joy (*chara*), a term cognate to grace (*charis*), speaks of God's grace at work in believers who play their part in the story of God. The term also creates a worldview that enables them to deal with suffering and hardship.[109] In this context, Paul's joy is a rhetorically-charged description of his relationship, fellowship, and hope in Philemon—both as brother and as agent of reconciliation. Encouragement (*paraklēsis*) describes the impact of another's presence on one's confidence, hope, and joy: the impact is at times to (1) comfort the troubled and at others to (2) encourage the wondering.[110] God is a God of *paraklēsis* (2 Thess 2:16; 2 Cor 1:3–7; Rom 15:5), spiritual giftedness generates *paraklēsis* (1 Cor 14:3; Phil 2:1; Rom 12:8), positive responses to the gospel and pastoral care bring *paraklēsis* to the pastor/apostle (2 Cor 7:7, 13; 8:17), Scripture brings *paraklēsis* (Rom 15:4), and the love and generosity of other Christians produces *paraklēsis* (2 Cor 7:4; 8:4). Philemon 7 belongs in the last grouping of *paraklēsis* verses in the NT: his love for others generates *paraklēsis* in the sense of encouragement for Paul.

What triggered his joy and encouragement was Philemon's love for others.[111] We do not know the specifics. Yet we can imagine quite easily that a slave-owning *paterfamilias* and pastoral leader in a house church would be called upon to evangelize, teach, pastor, distribute food and charity, and provide in a multitude of ways typical of a Roman household. The rhetoric of affirmation we find in this verse makes no sense if it does not correspond with reality,[112] and the expectation of reconciliation is best anticipated if the behaviors of Philemon are already moving in that direction.[113] One then needs to think of Philemon in terms of husband, father,

108. χαρὰν γὰρ πολλὴν ἔσχον καὶ παράκλησιν. The aorist tense is used to capture his emotions as a whole. It does not describe "when" (the past) or "how" (e.g., ingressive) but "that."

109. On χαρά, BDAG 1077; *EDNT* 3:454–55; *TLNT* 3:498–99; *NIDNTTE* 4:644–49; see Phil 1:4, 25; 2:2, 29; 3:1; 4:4–7, 10; see also Matt 5:12; Acts 2:46; Jas 1:2; 1 Pet 1:6. See W. G. Morrice, *Joy in the New Testament* (Grand Rapids: Eerdmans, 1985). Summarized in W. G. Morrice, "Joy," in *DPL* 511–12. See, too, the excursus on the joy of the apostle in Barth and Blanke, 293–95.

110. On παράκλησις, BDAG 766; *EDNT* 3:23–27; *NIDNTTE* 3:627–33.

111. On love, see Commentary at Phlm 3. The ἐπί in this instance (ἐπὶ τῇ ἀγάπῃ σου), then, means either "on the occasion of your love" or "from your love" (Harris, 253).

112. Or politeness, see Wilson, "The Politics of Politeness."

113. Many discuss Philemon's generosity: e.g., Bruce, 208–9. Generous or not, no human being is virtuous enough to possess another.

and master in the household regulations in Col 3:18–4:1. In light of Paul's affirmative rhetoric, one needs also to think of a loving leader (Phlm 5, 7, 9, 16): Philemon is to be a man who loves his wife, who refrains from harshness, who loves his children, who disciplines himself not to embitter them, who also provides what is just and equitable to his slaves because he has learned to live under the rule of the one true master, the Lord Jesus. The summons of the superordinate in the household regulations in Colossians to embody a cruciform life begins the process of Philemon reconciling with his slave Onesimus.

The emotions of the saints are expressed second: "because you, brother, have refreshed the hearts of the Lord's people."[114] Philemon shows his love and fellowship through his acts of love or through his "necessary patronage for what could have been a very mixed group, as well as hospitality to visiting believers (v. 22) and a center for religious instruction and missionary training."[115] Thereby he brings refreshment (*anapauō*) to the church of Colossae. While the nominal form of this term is connected to the Sabbath and to the eschatological rest, those need to be seen as heightened realities of the quotidian reality common to humans who love one another. In the thanksgiving of Phlm 4–7 the verbal form of "refreshed" (a perfect tense) brings this act of Philemon's to the forefront. One may intuit that his history of refreshing others forms the bridge into Paul's appeal for Onesimus in vv. 8–22.

Behind "hearts" is a common term that hides the original term, *splanchna*. This term refers to innards, bowels, and deepest seats of feeling—perhaps one's innermost feelings or one's very self.[116] The term emerges from the Old Testament's concept of God as having "bowels of compas-

114. ὅτι τὰ σπλάγχνα τῶν ἁγίων ἀναπέπαυται διὰ σοῦ, ἀδελφέ. The perfect tense depicts an action with heightened vividness, what some call a "super present" or "heightened proximity" aspect. The traditional theory where it describes a past action with present implications focuses more on time than is necessary for aspectual theory. One could perform this tense in a setting by saying, looking at Philemon, "And, you brother, *refresh* the saints." Or, "And, you brother, are one who refreshes the saints." The postponement of the vocative (ἀδελφέ) is for rhetorical impact and expresses relational warmth (Dunn, 320).

On the term ἀναπαύω, see BDAG 69; *NIDNTTE* 1:284–88; Barth and Blanke, 297–301; Andrew D. Clarke, "'Refresh the Hearts of the Saints': A Unique Pauline Context?," *TynBul* 47 (1996): 278–86. See 1 Cor 16:18; 2 Cor 7:13; with Phlm 7, 20. On the term behind "Lord's people," see the Commentary at Phlm 5; also Ryan, *Philemon*, 225–26. For a full study, note Clarke, "'Refresh the Hearts of the Saints.'" The expression is peculiar to Paul, the term refers to subjective refreshment, it is the action of others (not Paul), and it crosses established boundaries.

115. Osiek, 135.

116. On σπλάγχνον, BDAG 938; *NIDNTTE* 4:351–54. Moule, 144, thinks it means one's very self (also Moo, 396).

sion"[117] and is especially characteristic of the language and description of the ministry of Jesus (cf. Mark 1:41; 6:34; Matt 9:32–34, 36; 20:34). As such, for Philemon to be known for refreshing the *splanchna* entails three elements: a need of the saints expressed, a response of mercy by Philemon, and an action that alleviates the need.[118] Philemon is depicted here not only as a man who loves but a man of mercy who resolves the needs of the saints in his care. The three usages of *splanchna* in Philemon are worthy of attention:

> Your love has given me great joy and encouragement, because you, brother, have refreshed the **hearts** of the Lord's people (v. 7).
>
> I am sending him—who is my very **heart**—back to you (v. 12).
>
> I do wish, brother, that I may have some benefit from you in the Lord; refresh my **heart** in Christ (v. 20).

Philemon has already refreshed the hearts of the Lord's people; Onesimus is Paul's own heart; and Philemon has the opportunity to do to Paul what he has already done to the Lord's people, among whom is now Onesimus!

III. PAUL'S APPEAL FOR ONESIMUS (8–22)

There is little question what happens in this section of Philemon, but that does not mean vv. 8–22 can be schematically arranged into a rhetorical and logical flow. Rather, there is a rhetorical move toward Philemon and then a subtle backing away that creates an emotional and logical appeal. Proposals for how the passage is to be outlined vary. I offer this outline for ease of exposition.[119]

A. First Appeal in the Sketch of the Scene (vv. 8–11; appeal in v. 10)
B. Second Appeal in the Presentation of Onesimus (vv. 12–16; appeal in vv. 15–16)
C. Third Appeal in Their Partnership (vv. 17–21; appeal in vv. 17, 20–21)
D. Final Appeal in a Presence (v. 22)

Paul's movements in our passage have been called a "masterpiece of persuasion."[120] Masterpiece? Not so for some scholars; in fact, some moralists sit in

117. But see *NewDocs* 3:84, which shows the term had similar evocations in Greek.
118. McKnight, *New Vision for Israel*, 65–68.
119. For a similar structural understanding, Lohse, 198.
120. Osiek, 135.

judgment on Paul's rhetoric here, thinking he resorts to manipulation and blackmail. James D. G. Dunn rejects such a reading:

> Paul's rhetoric here, as elsewhere, should not be denigrated as manipulative and contrived. It is typical of a leader with a strong personality that he should sincerely want to encourage and leave it open to his audience to respond of their own free will, while at the same time being so convinced of the rightness of his own opinion that he naturally seeks to persuade them to share it. In the end it is Paul's courtesy and restraint which leaves the greatest impression here. Nor should we ignore the degree to which Paul's tactic reflects the social reality of his circumstances: if Philemon was a figure of social significance and power, then to press him over strongly with commands and threats might have been counterproductive in the loss of Philemon himself.[121]

Was he manipulative or not? Rhetorically compelling is not the same as manipulative. One suspects that what one brings to the text in disposition toward Paul determines what one sees in the text. I also suspect that this letter is the result of lengthy, careful, and interactive exchanges with Timothy, Onesimus, Epaphras, Tychicus, and others (Phlm 1). A student of mine suggested that in this section of Philemon Paul is embodying what he wants to see Philemon embody. That is, Paul does here—surrenders to his brother in Christ—what he wants Philemon to do to Onesimus, just as Onesimus is doing in being presented before Philemon for a decision.[122]

A. FIRST APPEAL IN THE SKETCH OF THE SCENE (VV. 8–11; APPEAL IN V. 10)

8 *Therefore, although in Christ I could be bold and order you to do what*
you ought to do,[a] 9 *yet I prefer to appeal to you on the basis of*[b] *love. It is as*
none other than Paul—an old man and now also a prisoner of Christ Jesus—
10 *that I appeal to you for my son*[c] *Onesimus, who became my son*[d] *while I was*
in chains. 11 *Formerly he was useless to you, but now he has become useful both*
to you and to me.

a. CEB has "the right thing."

b. CEB: "through."

c. CEB: "child."

121. Dunn, 323–24.

122. The student was Ben Swihart.

d. CEB: "I became his father in the faith during my time in prison." CEB is a closer rendering of ὃν ἐγέννησα ἐν τοῖς δεσμοῖς.

The first appeal proceeds smoothly into the presence of Philemon by sketching the scene, first by making it clear that the apostle Paul has dropped his status as an apostolic authority (v. 8) and second by overtly stating his moral foundation, namely love (v. 9). He furthers the appeal in v. 8 at v. 9b by fleshing out his personal status—not an apostle but an "old man and also a prisoner." Finally, Paul appeals for Onesimus potently as he describes his new relation to Paul (vv. 10–11).

8 We need to imagine our way into Philemon's household and into a first-century house church, sitting, lounging, or standing as this letter is read. We need to think, too, that the house church is not limited to Philemon's own *oikonomia* but neighbors and fellow believers and seekers who have joined in. We do not know the courier, but it is probably Tychicus or perhaps Onesimus (who may have read about himself in the third person). All eyes are on Philemon—the letter courier and reader standing there with all the authority of the apostle Paul, despite Paul's denial of his own authority in the words of the letter. We need also to realize that up until this moment only the letter courier and anyone who traveled with Onesimus from Ephesus to Colossae knew the contents of the letter. The head of the household, Philemon, a man of status and power, is about to be confronted by the apostle Paul with a request. However skilled Paul was in his rhetoric, the courier and everyone in the room understood the implications of this letter as it was read aloud to the house church. We are to imagine Philemon's will and heart being put into mode of decision and Onesimus's hands sweating in hope. Paul is in deep prayer under guard in Ephesus. The slaves in the household, as they hear the letter read, become more and more implicated in the decision Philemon is about to render.

Paul opens his appeal both claiming what he could be (and therefore do) and what he actually is: "Therefore, although in Christ I could be bold and order you to do what you ought to do."[123] Paul both "waives his authority" and at the same time indirectly concedes his authority "in Christ."[124] Both carry pow-

123. Διὸ πολλὴν ἐν Χριστῷ παρρησίαν ἔχων ἐπιτάσσειν σοι τὸ ἀνῆκον. The inferential particle (διό) assumes what Paul has said in Phlm 1–7, especially about love (retrospective; Harris, 258), and knows what he is about to argue (prospective). The word is a three-letter pivot into the appeal of the letter. The use of this particle to begin the body of a letter is unusual, but Philemon itself stands out from the other letters of Paul. On this, J. T. Sanders, "The Transition from Opening Epistolary Thanksgivings to Body in the Letters of the Pauline Corpus," *JBL* 81 (1962): 348–62.

124. Again, Paul does not anchor his authority or his commands in his *apostolic* credentials but through his connection to Christ and his fatherly, evangelistic relationship to others;

erful theological and rhetorical weight.[125] "In Christ" has both objective and subjective dimensions. As for the objective, "in Christ" believers have all that pertains to redemption in Christ (1 Cor 1:4; Rom 3:24; 6:23) including—and this is where the Onesimus-Philemon situation begins its reordering—freedom (8:2), new creation life (8:39), reconciliation (5:19), and renewed mind (Phil 2:5). As for the subjective, those "in Christ" are actually to reckon the old order dead (Rom 6:11) in decision and praxis. The claim for Paul is that all creation owes its existence to its creation "in Christ" (Col 1:16). This expression then is the inaugurated eschatological reality into which Paul, Philemon, and Onesimus are located. Paul's status "in Christ" is the apostle to the Gentiles.[126]

As one with authority Paul concedes: "I could be bold."[127] "Bold" (*parrēsia*) is a rhetorical term suggesting the freedom to speak with authority (cf. Acts 2:29; 4:13) as well as a status term (Phlm 8). The apostle could use all his status and all his skills to coerce Philemon with a "blunt order."[128] Which is to say, he could "command"[129] Philemon to "do what you ought to do."[130] We have to fill in the moment of reading this letter by taking note of how "ought

---

see Best, "Paul's Apostolic Authority–?" On "waives his authority," see Church, "Rhetorical Structure," 25.

125. On the "in Christ" theme, see esp. Dunn, *Theology of Paul the Apostle*, 390–401; Mark A. Seifrid, "In Christ" in *DPL*, 433–36; Constantine Campbell, *Paul and Union with Christ: An Exegetical and Theological Study* (Grand Rapids: Zondervan, 2012); Campbell, *Quest*; Douglas A. Campbell, *The Deliverance of God: An Apocalyptic Rereading of Justification in Paul* (Grand Rapids: Eerdmans, 2013).

126. So many, including Hübner, 32; Dunn, 325, thinks Paul levels himself with Philemon with "in Christ."

127. πολλὴν . . . παρρησίαν ἔχων. Literally, "I having much boldness." The present participle and its object are completed by the infinitive "to order" (ἐπιτάσσειν). The translation in the CEB ("enough confidence . . . to command") is more precise than the NIV ("be bold and order"). The present participle, which is concessive (Harris, 258), makes the boldness of Paul more vivid to Philemon. The adjective intensifies the noun into strong confidence/boldness. On παρρησία, BDAG 781–82; *EDNT* 3:45–47; *TLNT* 3:56–62; *NIDNTTE* 3:657–60. The translation "boldness" with the connotation of that boldness being Spirit-generated and eschatological seems best; see Wilson, 346; Witherington, 66; Moo, 401–2. For a defense of it meaning "boldness" or "frankness" and the senses of eschatology, see the studies of Willem Cornelis van Unnik, "The Christian's Freedom of Speech in the New Testament," *BJRL* 44 (1962): 466–88; Stanley B. Marrow, "*Parrhesia* and the New Testament," *CBQ* 44 (1982): 431–46.

128. Barth and Blanke, 307. Pao, 384, rightly observes that denial of this power is a claim to power.

129. On the verb ἐπιτάσσω, BDAG 383; this is the only use of this term in the Pauline corpus. That this term can evoke the highest levels of authority can be seen in some NT uses (e.g., Mark 1:27; 6:27).

130. τὸ ἀνῆκον. This neuter singular accusative present active participle indicates action done in reciprocal relation to Paul's status and relation with Philemon. Grammatically, the neuter article creates an abstraction. See BDAG 78–79.

to do" is filled in as the letter unfolds. It means that Onesimus will be "useful" instead of "useless" (v. 11); it means he will be useful "both to you and to me" (v. 11); it means Onesimus will be a help to Paul (v. 13); it means that the slave will become a fellow heir of eternal life (v. 15); it means he will no longer be a slave but a "dear brother" (v. 16); and it means welcoming Onesimus the brother-slave as Philemon would welcome the apostle Paul (v. 17). That, and surely more at the social level with reverberations and implications for the entire household of Philemon, is what it means to "do what you ought to do." All this action correlates with the relationship Philemon has to Paul. The former, Philemon, found redemption through the missionary activity of the latter. As a result, Philemon owes Paul his entire life (v. 19). That correlation or reciprocity, Paul says at the end of v. 8, should be sufficient for Philemon to send back Onesimus to Paul for the larger ministry of the *ekklēsia.*

Noticeably, inasmuch as Paul serves a cruciform Lord so he now pastors and relates to Philemon with the same cruci- or Christoformity that he wants also to be seen in Philemon (Phil 2:5–11).[131] Which means Paul will not use *parrēsia* nor will he require reciprocity on the basis of Paul's authority. Rather, Paul will pursue the "most excellent way," the way of love in the context of Christian fellowship.

9 The foundation for Paul's appeal now comes to expression: "yet I prefer to appeal to you on the basis of love."[132] Rather than coercion, Paul walks in the way of love as Jesus taught (Mark 12:28–33; Rom 13:9). No better commentary on love has ever been offered than 1 Cor 13, which emerges into four themes—a rugged commitment to presence, advocacy, and mutual growth in Christoformity (see Phlm 5). Paul's appeal here to the principle of love is not manipulative but instead the engagement of Paul with Philemon at the personal level—knowing a history of commitment to one another, a history of mutual presence, a history of advocacy for one another, and a history of mutual growth. That nexus in relationship prompts Paul to say that genuine love for one another will lead to welcoming Onesimus and sending him back to Paul for the gospel.[133]

131. Michael J. Gorman, *Cruciformity: Paul's Narrative Spirituality of the Cross* (Grand Rapids: Eerdmans, 2001); Michael J. Gorman, *Inhabiting the Cruciform God: Kenosis, Justification, and Theosis in Paul's Narrative Soteriology* (Grand Rapids: Eerdmans, 2009); Michael J. Gorman, *Becoming the Gospel: Paul, Participation, and Mission* (Grand Rapids: Eerdmans, 2015).

132. διὰ τὴν ἀγάπην μᾶλλον παρακαλῶ. The present tense does not indicate "I am appealing to you *now*" nor does it suggest "I am appealing over and over to you," but rather as a present aspect it dramatizes the act in the very presence of Philemon.

133. Hence, the love is both Philemon's love for the saints (now including Onesimus) and Paul's love for Philemon and the church in his *oikonomia*. Thus, it is love in general (Lohse, 198; Fitzmyer, 104; Moo, 402–3). Some take sides here: for Philemon's love of the saints, Callahan, 31; Barth and Blanke, 315–16.

The reader looks into the eyes of Philemon at this moment in the reading of the letter but Philemon sees Paul himself! How so? Paul's presence is expressed in the next words as he says he appeals as "none other than Paul—an old man and now also a prisoner of Christ Jesus."[134] Not only has Paul diminished his apostolic authority in v. 8, but he now deflates his very physical presence into weakness at a double layer: he's physically diminished and he is in prison (Phlm 1, 9, 10). It is that Paul whom Philemon sees in the eyes of the one reading this letter aloud. Such an image of Paul also elicits sympathy and grace for Onesimus, whose condition is similar to that of Paul.

The term behind "old man" (*presbytēs*)[135] refers to Paul's age. He is appealing to Philemon's sympathy; he is not eliciting pity even though some see in "old man" an invitation to respect the wisdom of the elder.[136] Others have argued the term does not mean "old man" but in the Greek of this period—for which the evidence is not abundant[137]—is synonymous to "am-

134. τοιοῦτος ὢν ὡς Παῦλος πρεσβύτης νυνὶ δὲ καὶ δέσμιος Χριστοῦ Ἰησοῦ. The grammar, though a bit choppy, is clear: "Because, being such a person as Paul, who is old but now one in prison because of my apostolic mission for king Jesus, I appeal to you." Discussed at Lightfoot, 337–38; Harris, 259; BDAG 1089. The present participle (ὢν)—making Paul's presence apparent in the person of the reader—is probably causal ("because I, or on the basis of being, this person . . . I appeal") but could be concessive (Moule, 144: "although I am none other than"). The opening adjective could be retrospective (referring back to the denial of apostolic status in v. 8) or prospective (looking at the words to follow, namely, his age and imprisonment). The genitive Χριστοῦ Ἰησοῦ is either objective ("I serve Christ Jesus") or more likely general reference ("I am in prison because of Christ Jesus").

135. BDAG 863. For "age," see NIV, CEB, Lohse, 199; Dunn, 327; Hübner, 33; Osiek, 135–36; Wilson, 347–49; Witherington, 67; Moo, 404–6; for "ambassador," though the lexical confusion is often exaggerated, see Lightfoot, 338–39; Moule, 144; Martin, 163; Bruce, 212; Wright, 180–81; Harris, 259–60; Callahan, 31–32; Barth and Blanke, 321–23; Stuhlmacher, 37–38; Ryan, 233–34; also Petersen, *Rediscovering Paul*, 125–28. The term means "old age" and could indicate Paul is in his 50s (Stuhlmacher, 38n76; Wolter, 260) or even older. Philo, *On Creation* 105, suggests 50–56. For a more complete defense that orients scholarship toward Greek novels connected to provincial cities, Ronald F. Hock, "A Support for His Old Age: Paul's Plea on Behalf of Onesimus," in *The Social World of the First Christians: Essays in Honor of Wayne A. Meeks*, ed. L. Michael White and O. Larry Yarbrough (Minneapolis: Fortress Press, 1995), 67–81 (esp. 78–80).

The two forms of the noun overlap in meaning at times, and here is an example of the identical term in Philemon being used for ambassador: 2 Macc 11:34, "Quintus Memmius, Titus Manius, *ambassadors* of the Romans." If "ambassador" is the preferred meaning, one might see in the clause a repetition of the concession made at Phlm 8a. Thus, the two concessive clauses would be:

Διὸ πολλὴν ἐν Χριστῷ παρρησίαν ἔχων ἐπιτάσσειν σοι τὸ ἀνῆκον. . .
τοιοῦτος ὢν ὡς Παῦλος πρεσβύτης νυνὶ δὲ καὶ δέσμιος Χριστοῦ Ἰησοῦ

136. Dunn, 327.

137. Moo, 405n26, observes that there are 45 uses of the term in the LXX that mean

bassador" (*presbeutēs*). Ephesians 6:20 is both a near parallel to our verse and uses the cognate term for ambassadorial duties. Thus, "for which I am an ambassador [*presbeuō*] in chains." If the term speaks of his ambassadorial status, Paul both exalts himself by saying he has been sent and diminishes his significance by informing Philemon that he is in prison and therefore of no status. In this case, then, vv. 8–9 both intensify Paul's qualifications and deny them at the same time. Logically it makes less sense to speak of one's apostolic sending when (1) one has just denied himself that status in the letter's salutation in v. 1 as well as in the immediate statements in v. 8, and (2) when one is seeking to earn connection to Philemon on the basis of relationship and love rather than status. A double diminishment of his power is the more cogent interpretation.[138] To speak of oneself, as Paul does, as an old man and in prison is for Paul to identify with the marginalized and powerless. Hence, Paul is standing clearly alongside Onesimus putting pressure on Philemon to reconcile.

10 Here for the first time Paul speaks the name behind the letter: "that I appeal to you for my son Onesimus."[139] Philemon 10 is the first appeal in this letter for Onesimus, and the appeal is not completely clear until v. 17's "welcome him." So what can we know about Onesimus?

First, we must speak about the one who stands by silently, namely, Onesimus.[140] This is what we know about Onesimus, whose punned name was very common in the region of Ephesus and pragmatically and demeaningly chosen for many slaves by their owners,[141] a name that means "useful."[142] He was "free" enough both to visit Paul in prison at Ephesus and to leave

---

"old man." While Moo's larger point is compelling, the near parallel in Eph 6:20–21 at least makes the case of "ambassador" reasonable.

138. Lohse, 199; Wilson, 348–49; Fitzmyer, 105; Witherington, 67; Moo, 406; Pao, 386. Also, Weima, "Paul's Persuasive Prose," 48n58.

139. The preposition περί is often taken to mean "on behalf of" as the subject rather than "about" or "for" as the object (Knox, *Philemon among the Letters of Paul*, 22–24; Winter, 303–4; but different scholars see different nuances in these English terms); see Harris, 261; Dunn, 328; also Harris, *Prepositions and Theology*, 210–11; Nordling, "Onesimus Fugitivus," 110–14. On the other hand, see Brook W. R. Pearson, "Assumptions in the Criticism and Translation of Philemon," in *Translating the Bible: Problems and Prospects*, ed. Stanley Porter and R. S. Hess, JSNTSup 173 (Sheffield: Sheffield Academic Press, 1999), 253–80 (256–63). The possessive adjective (τοῦ ἐμοῦ τέκνου) is emphatic (Harris, 261).

140. For a sketch of scholarship, Harrill, *Slaves in the New Testament*, 6–16; Tolmie, "Tendencies," 2–6. Also, Peter Arzt-Grabner, "How to Deal with Onesimus? Paul's Solution within the Frame of Ancient Legal and Documentary Sources," in Tolmie, *Philemon in Perspective*, 113–42 (esp. 120–35).

141. Varro, *Latin Language* 8.9.

142. BDAG 711. See discussion at *NewDocs* 4:179–81. Some have speculated Paul gave the man the name at his baptism.

Paul's presence to travel with the courier to return to Colossae (Col 4:7–9). There is some question *when* Onesimus did what is mentioned in Colossians: Was it perhaps in conjunction with the letter to Philemon? Or was Onesimus converted by Paul, returned to Colossae along with the letter to Philemon, released by Philemon to return to Paul and then sent back with the letter to Colossians? Either explanation works; neither is compelling. More important than the exact details of these travels by Onesimus is who he was. He was a slave. The evidence that he was a slave (and probably a runaway) who thought better of what he had done and sought out Paul[143] includes these expressions:

1. He had a common slave name, "useful" (v. 11).
2. He is being "sent back" to his master Philemon (v. 12).
3. Paul needs Philemon's permission to make use of him (v. 14).
4. Paul explains Onesimus's absence as a divine act of separation with a larger purpose in mind (v. 15).
5. Paul calls him a "slave" and "better than a slave" (v. 16).
6. Paul says his status has changed from slave to "brother" (v. 16).
7. He has apparently done something wrong, probably incurring a financial debt (v. 18).
8. Onesimus needs Paul to be his mediator.
9. Paul's delicate response could derive from his temporary harboring of a runaway.

The value of these separable items is not equal. The fifth is particularly important: he was a slave, one separated from his owner (not one sent by his owner), that is, probably a runaway. Philemon does not know his slave has been converted, Paul knows Onesimus now as a brother. Paul wants Philemon to embrace him now as a brother and no longer as a slave.

Second, Onesimus was either born into Philemon's home as the son of a slave woman or he was purchased by Philemon, and as such was part of the

143. Others think he has run to seek justice with Paul as his mediator. The argument for this has been made by Peter Lampe, "Keine 'Sklavenflucht' des Onesimus," *ZNW* 76 (1985): 135–37. Others agree: Wolter, 229–31; Hübner, 33–34; Dunn, 304–6; Fitzmyer, 17–23; Peter Arzt-Grabner, "Onesimus *erro*: Zur Vorgeschichte des Philemonbriefes," *ZNW* 95 (2004): 131–43; Arzt-Grabner, "How to Deal with Onesimus?," 134–35; Rapske, "Prisoner Paul." For the shortcomings of this theory, see *NewDocs* 8:41–43. This is a *crux interpretum* in Philemon studies: one's decision determines the concrete realities one uses to describe Onesimus, Philemon's relationship to him as slaveowner, and Paul's own appeal. It appears to me the ambiguity of the evidence can suggest a mediating view: he ran away, repented of it, and then sought out Paul for mediation. But the evidence in this letter is not clear enough to render certainty.

Roman Empire's massive slave society. If purchased, he would have been examined on a slave stand for his economic benefit to Philemon's business. Or, Onesimus (or mother) could have been acquired in a war victory, or even he could have been found after infant exposure. His most likely origin as a slave would be that he was born to a slave woman in Philemon's home, which in Latin means he belonged to the *vernae* (born slaves). As such he most likely dwelled in a cell and lived on a minimal diet—living conditions all shaped by the character of the slave owner Philemon. There is no reason to suspect Onesimus wore a slave collar.

We must now pause for two full stops, the first a reminder of definition, and the second about status. A definition of slavery:

> Slavery by definition is a means of securing and maintaining an involuntary labour force by a group in society which monopolizes political and economic power.[144]

Again, slavery describes a perceived inferior human being under the total authority of another perceived superior human being, and the reality of that perception of inferiority is established by power and authority. Which, to repeat, means slavery is about social status. Onesimus, then, is an inferior to Philemon, who is a superior. As a slave, Onesimus had no status, which is to say his "rights" were at best minimal. He experienced embodied diminishment if not a kind of social death.[145] The man was an owned man and he was an object of ownership, an "instrument of action" according to Aristotle.[146] He was owned by Philemon the slave owner. Christian though he was he remained a slave owner. There were good slave owners and bad ones, as Peter observed (1 Pet 2:18). Yet, a slave owner still is a slave owner. Which meant Onesimus owed him loyalty and obedience, and even if Onesimus showed loyalty and obedience to a good slave owner, he was a slave and Philemon was a slave owner. Location was everything in the Empire. Onesimus was located below Philemon, and when it came to public life Onesimus ranked at the bottom. Roman society was hierarchical as has recently been displayed neatly by Sondra Joshel:[147]

144. Bradley, *Slaves and Masters*, 18.

145. Orlando Patterson, *Slavery and Social Death: A Comparative Study* (Cambridge: Harvard University Press, 1982).

146. Aristotle, *Politics* 1.2.6 (Rackham, LCL).

147. Joshel, *Slavery in the Roman World*, 31, with discussion on 30–47. Also Martin Goodman, *The Roman World: 44BC–AD 180*, 2nd ed., Routledge History of the Ancient World (London: Routledge, 2012), 180–99. Women and families were part of each of the social orders by way of relation, while slaves remained at the bottom though a slave in the imperial court had more "status" than a slave of a senator, etc.

(After 27 BCE, the Emperor)

Nobles
Senators
Equestrians
Municipal Magistrates and Senators
Freeborn Roman Citizens
Freed Slave Citizens
Slaves

As a slave Onesimus learned to get along with Philemon, probably was rewarded for good behavior, punished physically (and sometimes brutally) for bad behavior, and achieved a status among other slaves within that household. That status was absolutely determined by Philemon: he could have been a treasurer, cook, or a sexual slave. In other words, he could have been a favored slave, but the evidence that he was a runaway suggests otherwise, or that he had at least fallen completely out of favor. He may have been quasi-married and may have had quasi-sons and quasi-daughters.[148] No matter his quasi-statuses, Onesimus remained a "boy."

Onesimus appears to be intelligent enough to have enjoyed fast maturation in the faith, sufficiently fast for Paul to know he wanted him to be a fellow gospel minister, perhaps a *synergos* ("fellow worker"). It is difficult to know what kind of work Onesimus performed for Philemon. It may have been a task that required great skill or a role focused on manual labor. Perhaps he was the household manager or a *paedagogus* for Philemon's son (perhaps Archippus), or perhaps an administrator or a secretary (copyist).[149] We can surmise that he was a runaway and we can also surmise he ran either because he simply wanted to escape to "freedom" or that he was in trouble with Philemon. Had he stolen something? Had he mismanaged the business? The mention of a financial debt (v. 18) may indicate that he ran because he committed some kind of offense or crime. He also ran because he knew and surely believed Philemon would bring a swift and painful punishment on him for what he had done. He would not have run had this not been the case. We also observe that Onesimus was courageous enough to risk it all on running and clever enough to get from Colossae to Ephesus without being detected.

148. Called *contubernium*.

149. On which, see Aristotle, *Politics* 1.2.23 ("steward"); Columella, *On Agriculture* 1.8 (on a manager of a farm); Quintilian, *Institutes of Oratory* 1.1.8–9. On slave work, Joshel, *Slavery in the Roman World*, 162–214.

Excursus: Performing Philemon

In light of the status of slave for Onesimus, I make a proposal about how this letter might have been performed. To be sure, there are no extant directions for performance so I propose only a model for visualizing what could make the message of this letter most potent.[150] Slaves stood above the crowd of purchasers on slave blocks when they were put on sale. Such a block was known to the church of Colossae and most especially to Onesimus and to the slaves in the church at Colossae (cf. Col 3:22–25). I propose that we put *Philemon* on a metaphorical slave block in the household as one who is now being examined. I propose further that Onesimus be given stage directions to spend his entire time not looking at the reader of Philemon, whom I suggest for performance was Tychicus, but at Philemon himself, looking so as to judge the facial responses of Philemon to the words read. I propose that when Paul mentions Onesimus, *everyone looked at Onesimus.* I further propose that the reader not only read the words but performed them by pointing to Onesimus and then giving Philemon a long look before reading the next lines. Our knowledge of public readings of letters and texts in the ancient world indicates audience participation (e.g., affirmations and questions). We are to think of this audience verbally and physically participating as this letter is read aloud.

Having stated his appeal, Paul now proceeds to describe Onesimus in three distinct expressions: (1) Onesimus became a son of Paul in v. 10, (2) as a slave he did not live up to his name "useful" but was in fact "useless" in v. 11a, and (3) his conversion now makes him fit to live up to his name "useful" both in service to Philemon and to Paul in v. 11b.

Many translations grant to Onesimus the label of "son." Yet, they may give the term more legal standing than it deserves. In Roman legal fashion, is Paul attributing to the slave Onesimus the status of a "boy" or a "child"?[151] The term Paul uses is not the Greek term for "son" (*huios*) but the term for "child" (*teknon*). I confess to disappointment at the use of this term by Paul. It may, in fact, reflect the status of a Roman slave, who could never become a man and always remained a boy. Perhaps we are seeing too much in the choice of term? A brief discussion is necessary to clarify what is meant by *teknon* (rather than *huios*). To begin with, in the well-respected classification system of Louw and Nida, whose lexicon is built on word domains, a section is labeled "Kinship Relations Involving Successive Generations." The term *teknon* acquires the meaning of "one's immediate offspring, but without reference to sex or age—'child, offspring.'"[152] All other uses

150. For an introductory text on performance, see Richard Ward and David Trobisch, *Bringing the Word to Life: Engaging the New Testament through Performing It* (Grand Rapids: Eerdmans, 2013).

151. Frilingos, "For My Child, Onesimus," 100–103.

152. L&N 1:116.

of this term in the NT they categorize as "child." The most common translation of the term in Paul's letters is "children," both biological (Eph 6:4) and metaphorical (Gal 4:19; 1 Thess 2:11; 1 Cor 4:14; Phil 2:15; Eph 5:1; Rom 8:16, 21; 9:7). At times, however, the translation "son" is preferred, as when Timothy is called "my son" (1 Cor 4:17; Phil 2:22; 1 Tim 1:18; 2 Tim 1:2; 2:1), also Titus (1:4). But in these cases one could render it "offspring" just as accurately. In fact, the term Paul uses in Phlm 10, *teknon,* has a different sense than *huios*. Thus, "child" and "offspring" are solid translations. Yet, a question remains: was he called *teknon* because he was a "boy" legally or because he was "spiritual offspring"? In light of how Paul brings to the surface the importance of spiritual new birth, not least in Philemon (cf. vv. 10–11, 15–16, 19), I believe "son" or "offspring" is most reasonable even if the first-century audience may have heard an echo of a male slave's social status as a boy. More recent study of the papyri has conclusively shown that *teknon* is not the term used for a slave as a "boy" or a slave as having non-legal manhood. Rather, when the non-legal standing of a male slave was in view the term *pais* was used.[153] Hence, the term *teknon* here describes Onesimus as a "spiritual son" or the "spiritual offspring" of Paul.[154]

Either Onesimus, as a runaway with second thoughts, found his way to Paul, or somehow Paul discovered that one of Philemon's slaves was in his circle of relations. We do not know. However, we do know that while Paul was in prison Onesimus was converted. Paul's language evokes ideas of physical birth: "who became my son."[155] He uses this term in a similar way at 1 Cor 4:15: "I became your father." One might dispute here whether Paul sees himself as father ("I procreated") or mother ("I gave birth to") because the term can describe either.[156] What seems clear is that Onesimus becomes a Christian convert under the ministry of Paul.[157]

153. Arzt-Grabner, 202–4.

154. It is possible Paul is not referring here to spiritual rebirth in "offspring" or "child" but to "fellow worker in the gospel." That is, while in prison Paul nurtured Onesimus along to become a gospel minister. This, however, is against the grain of the evidence in vv. 15–16 where former condition as "slave" is contrasted with the present condition as "brother." If the alternative interpretation of "offspring" (gospel minister) is preferred, then "brother" would have to develop the sense of "brother in the ministry." This is asking for too much from the words.

155. ὃν ἐγέννησα. The aorist does not refer to a moment but instead describes the act of regeneration or birth comprehensively (cf. Harris, 261, "summary aor.").

156. Beverly R. Gaventa, *Our Mother Saint Paul* (Louisville: Westminster John Knox, 2007), 6. She thinks fathering is in view in Phlm 10. So too Lightfoot, 339; Martin, 164; Ryan, 235; Moo, 407–8; BDAG 193–94; also Petersen, *Rediscovering Paul*, 128–31, who connects this term to "debtee" as well. Some are undecided or see the term as inclusive of both fatherhood and motherhood (Moule, 144–45; but esp. the extensive discussion in Barth and Blanke, 329–35). For more emphasis on motherhood, see Bentley, 760; Witherington, 67–68; Bird, 138.

157. Conversion to Christ tells a story of the revision of a person's autobiography as a person becomes subject to Jesus as Lord and Savior and is incorporated into a new social

Rhetorically, Paul suspends the name of the person about whom he is speaking until he has fully clarified the person's status in Christ:[158] Paul's own status is described (v. 8), the person's status is described as a "child" (one newly born and brought into the light of life and purpose by Paul), and—with the eyes of the reader Tychicus now turning to Onesimus as he enters the room and faces Philemon—Paul finally gives the person's name. Paul's overt affirmation and approval of both Philemon and Onesimus puts Philemon into a corner of will and heart, provoking this question in Philemon's mind: What shall I do with Onesimus if he is now a brother in Christ? The drama is palpable. It is at this very moment—the confrontation of Philemon and Onesimus through the apostolic presence of Paul and Timothy—that we clearly see Pauline pastoral theology.

11 Paul's second observation pertains to his pre-conversion "uselessness": "Formerly, he was useless to you."[159] How Paul knows this is not clear, but one can speculate it was from Onesimus himself in confession or perhaps from Epaphras or Tychicus though some think it is little more than typical stereotype and pun.[160] Whatever the source, Onesimus was not loyal, obedient or profitable for Philemon and was therefore disposable or had at least become disposable. One might spiritualize here and think that his former uselessness was spiritual, that is, let his present status as profitable in gospel ministry determine his pre-conversion unprofitability. But one must at least factor into this judgment about Onesi-

---

body (the church), and we have to trust Paul's word for it here in that we have nothing from Onesimus. On conversion, N. H. Taylor, "Onesimus: A Case Study of Slave Conversion in Early Christianity," *R&T* 3 (1996): 259–81; Scot McKnight, *Turning to Jesus: The Sociology of Conversion in the Gospels* (Louisville: Westminster John Knox, 2002). It remains an open, if also interesting, question why Onesimus was not a Christian in that he was a slave in the *oikonomia* of Philemon. For a discussion, Taylor, "Onesimus," 262–66. Taylor thinks Onesimus was not so much converted as reincorporated back into the fellowship of the church (267).

158. Harris, 261.

159. τόν ποτέ σοι ἄχρηστον. BDAG 160. α + χράομαι, thus, "of no use." The term pertains to labor and profit. See Lohse, 200n35. Too many today are preoccupied with this term as sexual "usefulness" (cf. Rom 1:26–27) without sufficient examination of Paul's Jewish and scriptural worlds, not to ignore what he has to say about sexual austerity in other places, and there is almost no evidence these terms are used with sexual connotations (I owe this to Glancy). For discussion of the terms in our verse, Marchal, "The Usefulness of an Onesimus," 760–68; Elliott, "'Thanks, but No Thanks'"; Alan H. Cadwallader, "Name Punning and Social Sterotyping: Re-Inscribing Slavery in the Letter to Philemon," *Australian Biblical Review* 61 (2013): 44–60. Note Jennifer A. Glancy, "The Utility of an Apostle: On Philemon 11," *Journal of Early Christian History* 5 (2015): 72–86. She proposes the term "disposable" as well as the terms arising from two registers for utility language, one from the world of slaveowners and the other from the Stoics.

160. Cadwallader, "Name Punning."

mus what we read in Phlm 18: he has done something "wrong." We know from evidence about runaways that they often filched what they would need, knowing that if they were to get caught it wouldn't matter what they took—their life could be on the line just for being a runaway. The runaway slave Sarapion, so Aurelia Sarapias informs Aurelius Protarchos, purloined "some items of clothing" before departure.[161] The term "wrong" in our verse could apply to many deeds but pilfering was boilerplate in describing runaways.

Onesimus's conversion, a story that can be told by many, turned him into loyalty, obedience, and made him fit to contribute to the church: "but now he has become useful."[162] It is an open question whether or not "now" is the eschatological/apocalyptic "now" of new creation or is simply a temporal marker of time in the story of Onesimus.[163] The term "useful" (*euchrēstos*) is found also at 2 Tim 2:21 ("useful to the Master" or "owner of the mansion" [CEB]) and 4:11, where Mark has been "useful" to Paul. The term is general, the specifics not present, but the realities easy to imagine: Onesimus could help Paul in gospel ministries in any number of ways, including evangelism, teaching, preaching, administrating, and caring for the apostle's needs. His would not be the first calling that could find a "spiritual equivalent" in the church (e.g., Mark 1:16–20). One might consider that it was Onesimus the scribe who wrote this letter.

Noticeably Paul contrasts Onesimus's former unprofitability or disposability to his present profitability and indisposability for two people: both Philemon and himself. Philemon 13 might be the best place to look for further light: "he could take your place in helping me (*diakoneō*) while I am in chains for the gospel." Again, the term is general but used often enough for gospel ministry (and not just for physical acts of service). His usefulness to Philemon is clarified in Phlm 15 and 16: Onesimus now has an eternal relation to Philemon and that relation is as a "brother" not a slave. Hence, Paul wants Philemon to see that Onesimus's value to him transcends his former unprofitability as a slave by becoming profitable in gospel ministry and ecclesial relations.

161. *NewDocs* 6:55–56.

162. νυνὶ δὲ [καὶ] σοὶ καὶ ἐμοὶ εὔχρηστον. BDAG 417. ευ + χράομαι, thus, "of good use." I do not find the pun on "Christ" (εὔχρηστον-χρὶστος) to be compelling.

163. The term νυνί can be exploited for salvation-historical or apocalyptic designs; e.g., Barth and Blanke, 346–50.

B. SECOND APPEAL IN THE PRESENTATION OF ONESIMUS (VV. 12–16; APPEAL IN VV. 15–16)

12*I am sending him—who is my very heart—back to you.*[a] 13*I would have*
liked to keep him with me so that he could take your place in helping me while
I am in chains[b] *for the gospel.* 14*But I did not want to do anything without your*
consent, so that any favor[c] *you do would not seem forced but would be volun-*
tary.[d] 15*Perhaps the reason he was separated from you for a little while was that*
*you might have him back forever—*16*no longer as a slave, but better than*[e] *a slave,*
as a dear brother.[f] *He is very dear*[g] *to me but even dearer to you,*[h] *both as a fellow*
man and as a brother in the Lord.[i]

a. The NIV's interrupted sentence, which has an unusual rhythm in Greek, is smoothed out in the CEB: "I'm sending him back to you, which is like sending you my own heart."

b. CEB: "in prison."

c. CEB: "your act of kindness.

d. CEB: "would occur willingly and not under pressure."

e. CEB: "more than."

f. CEB: "dearly loved brother."

g. CEB: "especially a dearly beloved brother."

h. CEB: "How much more can he become a brother to you."

i. CEB: "personally and spiritually in the Lord!"

Paul in consultation with Timothy continues the appeal but "screws the emotional intensity to a new pitch,"[164] this time emphasizing the embodied presence of Onesimus as well as Paul's intent to cooperate with Philemon's decision. The weight of persuasion shifts entirely to Philemon's power to decide. Paul thus prepares Philemon for what will come in the next section (vv. 17–21): to choose to reconcile with Onesimus and probably return Onesimus to Paul for gospel ministry. Perhaps most important is that in our section (vv. 12–16) Paul recognizes the legitimacy of slavery. That is the socio-moral problem (for us) this letter provokes. By *not* speaking directly of manumission or against slavery, Paul tips his cards for us to see that manumission is not the issue—reconciliation of a slave owner with his slave is (v. 17).

12 Paul reveals his sensibility about propriety and law: "I am sending him—who is my very heart—back to you."[165] In returning him to Philemon,

164. Dunn, 329.

165. ὃν ἀνέπεμψά σοι. The aorist is customarily understood to be epistolary (BDF §334). In aspectual theory, though some would connect an aorist in the indicative mood to past tense, the focus is not on *when* or *how* but *that* something occurs. Hence, instead of calling this an epistolary aorist it can be seen as a comprehensive depiction of the action of sending. Not "I am sending" or "I sent" but "I send."

The term ἀναπέμπω means to "send back" or "return"; see BDAG 70. This verb was

Paul is not violating the Old Testament law, namely Deut 23:15–16 (and Paul surely knew this law), which commanded the Israelites *not to return slaves to their masters*.[166] Not only does that command deal with a different set of conditions: either a Hebrew slave of a non-Hebrew owner or, as others contend, foreign slaves in the land of Israel. Paul does not think that law has anything to do with his situation of the runaway slave Onesimus or he would not have decided to send him back.[167] It was, whichever legal statute one considers, against the law for a slave to run away. It was contrary to Roman law to harbor a runaway.[168] Even more, whatever Torah or Roman law stipulates, Paul's principle is love—he wants to live in reconciliation with Philemon and he wants Onesimus to return to participate in the mission, so he sends the slave back *so Philemon can reconcile with him and then return Onesimus to Paul for gospel work*. One can legitimately wonder, especially if we consider Paul an *exemplum* in this letter, if Paul did not imply that Philemon could act accordingly by sending Onesimus back to Paul for support of his ministry.

Paul now expands his previous descriptions of Onesimus: who is Paul's "child" (not "son") in the faith (v. 10), who has become useful both to Paul and to Philemon (v. 11), who helps Paul (v. 13), who now has eternal life (v. 15), and who is now a brother in Christ (v. 16). To these surrounding descriptions Paul adds now that he is "my very heart."[169] This term (*splanchna*) previously described Philemon's compassion and refreshment to others (v. 7, with

---

one of the pillars of Knox's well-known theory (*Philemon among the Letters of Paul*, 25; also Winter, 304) that Paul was "sending up" the request of Onesimus to Archippus, the slave's real owner, through Philemon for legal consideration. That is, perhaps he did not return Onesimus but referred the case of Onesimus to Archippus. This theory has been all but undone by Pearson, "Assumptions," 263–65. Importantly, the word "welcome" in v. 17 indicates that Paul is sending Onesimus back.

There was some confusion over the awkwardness of the text of Phlm 12, but the only lingering option is whether or not the original text had προσλαβοῦ. I have followed the absence of this imperative in UBS and Nestle-Aland[28]. For discussion, see Roger L. Omanson, *A Textual Guide to the Greek New Testament* (Stuttgart: Deutsche Bibelgesellschaft, 2006), 450; Callahan, 36–38; Barth and Blanke, 107–8, 351.

166. See, too, for the reception of fugitives, 1 Sam 25:1–11; 30:11.

167. F. F. Bruce, *Paul: Apostle of the Heart Set Free* (Grand Rapids: Eerdmans, 1977), 399–400. For those who think the OT law is not in view, Wright, *Philemon*, 182n3. For the suggestion that it pertains to Hebrew slaves of non-Hebrews, see Davis, *Inhuman Bondage*, 38.

168. Ulpian, as recorded in Justinian, *Digest* 11.4.1: "A man who conceals a runaway is a thief" (Watson). Such a person has twenty days to return the runaway.

169. τοῦτ' ἔστιν τὰ ἐμὰ σπλάγχνα. See commentary at Phlm 7; cf. also v. 20. The personal pronoun ἐμά is emphatic ("my very heart"; Harris, 263). It is remotely possible that τὰ ἐμὰ σπλάγχνα could be translated "my dear child" or "my child" (Artemidorus, *Interpretation of Dreams* 1.44), a view mentioned by Bruce, 214, but not approved; but see Hübner, 35, who connects this term to ἐγέννησα in v. 10.

"hearts") and Paul's hope is that Philemon will do the same for Paul (v. 20's "my heart"). But in v. 12 Paul uses the same term to connect himself to Onesimus: Onesimus is Paul's own "heart" (*splanchna*)! Again, Paul has encircled Philemon with a term that will implicate Philemon in a decision in favor of Onesimus and Paul.

13 The desire of Paul that he would like to have retained Onesimus for his services could well reflect Paul's obedience of the Roman laws about the culpability of harboring or corrupting a slave. Paul may have been aware that in retaining Onesimus he could be charged with corrupting the slave to remain a runaway. Thus, from the later *Digest*:

> But is the person liable only if he has driven an honest slave to wrongdoing, or is he also liable if he has given a bad slave encouragement or shown him how he could commit an offense? The better view is that he is also liable if he has shown a bad slave how he could commit an offense. Indeed, even if the slave would have run away or committed the theft anyway, if the person gave his approval to the slave's intention, he is liable; for wickedness ought not to be increased by the approval of others. So whether one makes a good slave bad or a bad slave more so, one is held to have made him worse.[170]

However one explains Paul's choice to return Onesimus to his master, and one need not appeal to Roman law or precedent, the fact is that he returned him. Attached to Paul's announcement of his return in v. 12—and, after all, Onesimus is in the room with Philemon when the letter is being read—is another element to the story behind the letter: "I would have liked to keep him with me."[171] Why? "so that he could take your place in helping me while

170. Justinian, *Digest* 11.3.4 (Watson).

171. The use of the imperfect (ἐβουλόμην) is best translated as "I was planning/thinking" (BDAG 181; *NIDNTTE* 1:526–30). The action of an "attainable wish" (Lohse, 201n46) is depicted without consideration of either its beginning or its ending, though this does not mean the action itself was incomplete. By choosing the imperfect Paul locates his desire behind his choice of returning Onesimus. The sense of the verb can shift from wish or desire to plan or to will (BDAG 182): hence, "I was planning/thinking." This planning/thinking indicates Paul would like, instead of retaining him without permission, for Onesimus to be returned upon reconciliation and restitution.

The infinitive κατέχειν, however, probably indicates a little more than "keep" (BDAG 532) since the term normally indicates restriction of someone's actions, even to restrain or detain (Lightfoot, 341). I consider the connotation that this verb suggests "keep under protection in asylum awaiting discussion with Philemon" entirely reasonable (see Witherington, 75–76)—depending of course on how one construes Onesimus's departure from Philemon's household. Callahan, 38, has "retain" (so also Wilson, 352); for "detain," see Harrill, *Slaves in the New Testament*, 12–13.

I am in chains for the gospel."[172] The NIV translation "helping" is a deliberate indeterminate: just what that help involved is not clear, though the Greek term *diakoneō* covers a spectrum from ordinary household chores (e.g., Mark 1:31; Acts 6:1–2; 1 Cor 16:15) to gospel and church ministry (Col 1:7; 4:7; 2 Cor 11:23; 1 Tim 3:8, 12).[173] For Paul to call Onesimus both "child," which he also uses for Timothy, and to say he "serves" suggests Onesimus is doing more than "help." There is at work in this term the early Christian vocabulary for gospel ministries. As such, Paul connects Onesimus to some worthies—Timothy (v. 1), Archippus (v. 2), Epaphras (v. 23), Mark, Aristarchus, Demas, and Luke (v. 24).[174]

Onesimus's ministry is said to "take [Philemon's] place." The Greek could indicate a stricter sense of substitution (he is considered you) or only the sense of analogy (he does in Ephesus what Philemon does in Colossae). Once again, Paul's emotive tones come through as he reminds Philemon that he is in prison for the gospel[175]—as he has done in vv. 1, 9, 10, 22, 23—and to speak of being in prison for the gospel is simultaneously a claim to authentic obedience.

14 Onesimus has been with Paul, who would like to keep him. But Paul's pastoral strategy necessitates Philemon's cooperation based on choice rather than coercion or authoritative demand: "I did not want to do anything without your consent."[176] Philemon 14 shifts Paul's state of mind from thinking or planning (*boulomai*) in v. 13 to willing intention (*thelō*). What Paul wants is the "consent" of Philemon.[177]

Paul now moves one step closer to the request of v. 17: "so that any favor you would do."[178] The translation "favor" is unfortunate simply because of

172. ἵνα ὑπὲρ σοῦ μοι διακονῇ. The ἵνα-clause completes the desire clause of v. 13a: "I was thinking of keeping him so that he could serve me for you." Barth and Blanke, 377–78, render ὑπὲρ σοῦ "substituting for you."

173. With cognates, BDAG 229–31; *NIDNTTE* 1:701–5; Barth and Blanke, 372–74.

174. W.-H. Ollrog, *Paulus und seine Mitarbeiter. Untersuchungen zu Theorie und Praxis der paulinschen Mission*, WMANT 50 (Neukirchen-Vluyn: Neukirchener, 1979), 101–6. Others think the term describes quotidian matters: Moo, 414.

175. The genitive τοῦ εὐαγγελίου is probably general relation.

176. χωρὶς δὲ τῆς σῆς γνώμης οὐδὲν ἠθέλησα ποιῆσαι. Harris, 264, thinks the shift to aorist expresses a "specific past decision" (also Lightfoot, 341; Dunn, 332; Barth and Blanke, 378).

177. γνώμη. BDAG 202–3, where it is rendered "a viewpoint or way of thinking about a matter, *opinion, judgment, way of thinking*" and "without your input," or perhaps "approval." Also, *EDNT* 1:255. For "consent," see Lohse, 202; Barth and Blanke, 378–80, who also draw helpful attention to the overlap of γνώμη with συνείδησις. The term is used often in the Apostolic Fathers for "mind" (e.g., Ignatius, *Ephesians* 3.2) and "consent" (Ignatius, *Polycarp* 5.2; Shepherd of Hermas, Similitudes 55.8).

178. ἵνα μὴ ὡς κατὰ ἀνάγκην τὸ ἀγαθόν σου ᾖ ἀλλὰ κατὰ ἑκούσιον. There is no new

what this term means in English. It is far better translated as "any *good* you would do" (cf. v. 6).[179] Again a general term is all Paul provides: what "good" means will gain some clarity in (1) the welcoming of vv. 16–17,[180] (2) the releasing of Onesimus back to Paul for gospel work in v. 20, and (3) the refreshing of Paul in v. 20.[181] But specifics of the meaning of favor or good aside, the heart of v. 14 is that Paul wants Philemon to cooperate out of his own desire and not by way of necessity. Paul does not want Philemon's choice to be "forced" (*anankē*), a term that describes someone whose will is violated or coerced (1 Cor 7:37; 2 Cor 9:7) or whose will is under the control of another, e.g., God and God's call (1 Cor 9:16).[182] Correspondingly, he wants Philemon's choice to be "voluntary" (*hekousion*; cf. 1 Pet 5:2).[183] Paul's strategy here works *only because he assumes Philemon has the rights of a slave owner* and Onesimus, as a slave, *has no rights and is in the power of Philemon.*

15 The opening to Phlm 15 with "perhaps" both distances Paul from any coercion and turns the rhetoric into an invitation for Philemon to consider. In addition, that same "perhaps" in v. 15 is an example of attribution theory, namely the explanation of the course of history by attributing it to divine intentions to give an event ultimate meaning.[184] The Hebrew Bible—most especially the Deuteronomistic History and the Prophets—taught Israel to read history from a divine, omniscient perspective. Entire schools of theology have been built on ideas about God's providence and predestination. Those Scriptures also taught that what was seemingly evil can be reversed by divine redirection.[185] Hence, Paul constructs a divine angle on what Philemon might

sentence here, but it is sufficiently complete that most English translations make it a new sentence. The ἵνα-clause completes the verbal clause of v. 14a ("But I did not want") and tosses the whole into a logical contingency. The subject of the clause is τὸ ἀγαθόν σου and the verb is the present subjunctive of εἰμί.

179. Wright, 183–84; Pao, 392. Callahan, 42, understands τὸ ἀγαθόν as the "benefit" of Onesimus's ministry (also Lightfoot, 342). Such a view seems to trip over τὸ ἀγαθόν σου, although Lightfoot, 342, sees the benefit as an extension of Philemon himself. Of the many who think this term points to manumission, Bird, 140.

180. Note also 1 Thess 5:15; Rom 7:9; 12:2. Barth and Blanke, 381, analyze this into three meanings: one specific deed, a lifelong devotion to good deeds, or the performance of a good deed.

181. Dunn, 332–33.

182. For their excursus on the topic, Barth and Blanke, 384–87.

183. Again, see the excursus of Barth and Blanke, 389–92.

184. On attribution theory, see Bernard Spilka, Philip R. Shaver, and Lee A. Kirkpatrick, "A General Attribution Theory for the Psychology of Religion," *JSSR* 24 (1985): 1–20; Lynn Melby Gordon and Sandra Graham, "Attribution Theory," in *Encyclopedia of Human Development* (Thousand Oaks, CA: Sage Publications, 2005), 1:142–44.

185. Barth and Blanke, 403, point to Gen 45:5–9; 50:20; 1 Sam 2:6; Jer 1:10; Lam 3:37–38; Isa 45:6–7; 55:8–13; Acts 2:22–24; 3:13–26; 5:30–32. Note even more Phil 1:12.

learn from the experience of the runaway Onesimus. That Paul does not *know with certainty* is indicated in the opening word "perhaps."[186] A similar level of contingency is to be seen in Rom 5:7, "though for a good person someone *might possibly* [*tacha*] dare to die." The separation of Philemon and Onesimus, which in Paul's theology combined the reckless act of Onesimus with an overarching divine plan,[187] has resulted in an even fuller return.[188]

Though he may scrutinize divine plans, Paul does know that the *temporary* separation of Onesimus from Philemon has led to an *eternal* relation and fellowship.[189] The contrast is noticeable and unanticipated, but one of the central themes in Judaism as well as among the apostles was the temporary, even probationary, condition of the present life when compared with the unendingness of the age to come. Paul contrasts "little while" (CEB: "a while") with "forever."[190] The expression "little while" expresses a short period of time (in comparison with the unendingness of the kingdom), an expression found elsewhere in similar comparative and eschatological texts in the NT (John 5:35), not least the tripled "in one hour" in Rev 18:10, 17, 19. That Onesimus's return entails a "forever" is to say he is now a brother in Christ and therefore in union with the one who is life itself. There is here no devaluing of life on earth even if it is temporary; rather, there is an intensification of the present life in light of the eternal.

186. τάχα (BDAG 992). This adverb moves from uncertain to probable, which differs from classical texts in both the use of the indicative rather than the optative as well as in the absence of ἄν (cf. BDF §385.1).

187. Hence, the divine passive (Bruce, 216; Wright, 184–85; Harris, 265; Fitzmyer, 112–13; Moo, 419; Pao, 393–94): ἐχωρίσθη. The aorist depicts the act, not from its outset, iterations, travel or result, but as a whole. Callahan, 43, reads it as a deponent and translates "he (de)parted"; so too Arzt-Grabner, "How to Deal with Onesimus?," 123–24. Weima finds more evidence of Paul's appeal in divine providence; see Weima, "Paul's Persuasive Prose," 50.

188. The verb ἀπέχῃς, a present subjunctive, can mean "paid in full, receive in full" and thus may see the entire event in terms of a financial transaction or relational restitution (Lightfoot, 342); or it can be softened into "have him back" (NIV, CEB) or "hold him properly" in the assumption that Philemon's behavior was not entirely above board in the past (Barth and Blanke, 395–97); see BDAG 102; *EDNT* 1:120–21. The term is in contrast to κατέχειν in v. 13, thus giving the two the senses of "hold, release" and "return, retain, restitution."

189. For the meaning "forever," Lightfoot, 342; Bruce, 216–17; Barth and Blanke, 397–402; Ryan, 245; Moo, 420–21; Pao, 394. Some take αἰώνιον as an adverb meaning "permanently" (Moule, 146–49; Harris, 266–67; Wilson, 355; Fitzmyer, 113), a meaning that could imply that Onesimus would remain a permanent slave-brother in Philemon's household (cf. Exod 21:6; Lev 25:46; Deut 15:17; Job 41:4). Dunn, 333–34, thinks both meanings could be in view, while Wright has recently emphasized reconciliation in the new creation family of Christ (Wright, *Paul and the Faithfulness of God*, 1:13–15).

190. πρὸς ὥραν vs. αἰώνιον. Sometimes πρὸς ὥραν describes not so much "temporal life on earth" but, as in Phlm 15, a short period of time (e.g., Gal 2:5; 1 Thess 2:17; 2 Cor 7:8).

16 The theological weight and social manifestations of this letter rest on the revolution that occurs to the Roman household found in Phlm 16–17. The final words of v. 15, "have him back forever," now gain their full clarity with dramatic implications for the ecclesial fellowship in that Philemon is to see Onesimus, Paul's new offspring and fellow gospel minister, "no longer as a slave, but better than a slave, as a dear brother."[191] Slavery, to repeat, is about status.[192] As noted above, Aristotle put into words how the ancient world perceived slaves: "some [tools in the *oikonomia*] are lifeless and others living,"[193] and "the slave is an assistant in the class of instruments of action."[194] Slavery, too, is not in the first instance about race, intelligence, appearance, vocation, capacity, skill, or strength, even if the elites of Rome thought of other nations as born for such a status (cf. Cicero, *On Consular Provinces* 10).

These observations about that status of slaves are on full display the moment the letter from Paul is carried into Philemon's presence. Philemon 16 envisions local churches where status and worth would look for a new way (Gal 3:28; Col 3:11). The "neither slave nor free" seems not to be the same as "neither slave nor citizen." Rather, the binary deals with the various statuses of slaves who have been manumitted but may well still be under the dominant eye of the masters (one class of which was called Junians). At the level of status and term, the charter of Gal 3:28, where we first read from Paul the binary "neither slave nor free," means here in Philemon "no longer as a slave . . . but a dear brother." The language elevates a slave from the margins of the family to the family table. New conditions have been created in a sibling-shaped rather than status-shaped community, as Mary Ann Getty observes:

> A common Baptism changes the basis for relationships among persons. Christians define themselves and their relationships on new familial and ministerial grounds distinct from those recognized in an alien society. Former class distinctions are transformed. Former debts are abolished.

191. Harris, 267, states that οὐκέτι ὡς δοῦλον differs from οὐκέτι δοῦλον, the latter indicating manumission and the former indicating that Onesimus would remain a slave. Callahan, 44–50, builds a weak case that Paul here means Onesimus was a "servant of God" not a slave; this trips over the contrast between "slave" and "brother" (οὐκέτι ὡς δοῦλον ἀλλὰ ὑπὲρ δοῦλον, ἀδελφὸν ἀγαπητόν). The second item "more than a slave" must transcend the first ("slave") and thus make "brother" the higher category. On ὡς δοῦλον expressing "just as" or "as if," see Barth and Blanke, 419, pointing to 2 Thess 3:15; 1 Cor 7:25, 29–31; Eph 6:5–6; 2 Cor 6:4, 8–10. Moo counters this (421n92; cf. 2 Thess 3:15 where ὡς refers to a factual condition).

192. See the Introduction, 12–15.

193. Aristotle, *Politics* 1.2.4 (Rackham, LCL).

194. Aristotle, *Politics* 1.2.6.

> Forgiveness is not a purely personal option. Retaliation is precluded. A new form of justice is required.[195]

Or as another observed, "the man baptized by Paul is no longer the man that was owned by Philemon."[196]

"No longer" expresses the eschatological shift from the world into the *ekklēsia* and reminds Bible readers of "no longer two, but one flesh" (Matt 19:6), but also perhaps "no longer let them do anything for their father or mother" (Mark 7:12) or the transfiguration's "they no longer saw anyone with them except Jesus" (9:8) or the Last Supper's "I will [no longer] drink again from the fruit of the vine" (14:25), or the later text in John 6:66 ("and no longer followed him") or 14:19 ("the world will not see me anymore [no longer]"; also 16:16, 25; 17:11).[197] The "no longer" of Phlm 16 reverses the prodigal son's confession: "I am no longer worthy to be called your son" (Luke 15:21), and echoes John 15:15: "I no longer call you servants . . . I have called you friends." Paul's own theology comes to expression in "no longer" statements, as in Rom 6:9: "death no longer has mastery over him" (cf. 7:17, 20; 11:6; also Gal 3:18, 25), and so do his ethics: "If your brother or sister is distressed because of what you eat, you are no longer acting in love" (Rom 14:15). But perhaps the two most poignant parallels at the theological level are Gal 4:7 ("So you are no longer a slave, but God's child ['son' translating *huios*]") and 2 Cor 5:16 ("So from now on we regard no one from a worldly point of view. Though we once regarded Christ in this way, we do so no longer"; cf. Gal 2:20 [Jewishness]; Eph 2:19 [Gentileness]). This musical percolation of "no longers" in the NT indicates both a salvation-historical theme of fulfillment and a revolutionary new way of life at the social and ecclesial level. New creation theology means a slave like Onesimus is now a "brother," which is to say far "better than a slave."[198] The language of "better than" is about hierarchy in Roman society. One could translate it as "higher than a slave."

Does "better than a slave" mean that Onesimus is to be manumitted? Or does it mean that he is now received into the family of Philemon on the basis of his Christian status, although he remains a slave or a freedman? Many have thought "better than a slave" means to transcend traditional statuses of Roman society.[199] Others think Paul is pleading here—albeit indirectly—for

195. Getty, "The Theology of Philemon," 506.

196. David Daube, "Onesimos," *HTR* 79 (1986): 40–43 (esp. 40).

197. Norman R. Petersen, *Rediscovering Paul: Philemon and the Sociology of Paul's Narrative World* (Philadelphia: Fortress Press, 1985), 93–124.

198. ὑπὲρ δοῦλον. For the common use of this preposition as comparative, BDAG 1031.

199. Martin, 166; Harris, 267–68; Pao, 395–96. Martin, 166, connects Paul here with the Stoic approach to slavery: "In that way Paul has put a new face on slavery by regarding the human condition as unimportant in contrast with a person's desire to fulfill his Christian

not free → brother

his manumission. Or is the language sufficiently unclear that we cannot tell?[200] We perhaps need to be reminded of a rugged first-century reality, namely, that siblingship language did not necessarily alter social realities: "The use of fictive-kinship language by slave owners did not transform the slave's social reality."[201] As I have already indicated in a number of places, there is no evidence in this letter that Paul was thinking in terms of manumission. One might say he thought in terms of liberation in the context of the household and church, but to think Paul is moving into the categories of legal manumission is both to impose modern sensibilities on Paul and to avoid what Paul does emphasize: reconciliation in Christ. The new label is not "free" or "citizen"; rather, the new label for Onesimus is "brother."

Onesimus, in fact, is not just a brother but a "dear brother" or "a brother who is loved,"[202] the only time in all of Paul's letters a slave is called a brother (or a sister). The language derives from the social relationship of siblings, with notes of love, honor, and unity.[203] This expression combs its way through the entire system of classification in the Roman Empire, leaving no hair untouched, and then connects this runaway slave with some of the most notable coworkers of Paul: all those in Christ are *beloved* brothers and sisters (1 Cor 4:14; 15:58; Rom 1:7; 12:19; Eph 5:1), including folks like Timothy (1 Cor 4:17), Epaphras (Col 1:7), Tychicus (Col 4:7; Eph 6:21), and the woman Persis (Rom 16:12). In Colossians Paul also calls Onesimus "our faithful and dear brother" (4:9). Most dramatically, this is what Paul calls Philemon himself in Phlm 1: "To Philemon our dear [*beloved*] friend and fellow worker." Paul assumes (and desires) that Philemon will respond in forgiveness and reconciliation, that is, that he will create a complete alteration of his status in the *oikos*.[204] The current Roman system of social classification is "no longer" for Paul and he presses Philemon to embody that system's termination.

Onesimus's new status as a "dear brother" describes his relation both

---

vocation." De Vos thinks Paul has in mind a "significant change in the quality of their relationship"; see de Vos, "Once a Slave, Always a Slave?, " 102.

200. Dunn, 335.

201. Mitzi J. Smith, "Utility, Fraternity, and Reconciliation: Ancient Slavery as a Context for the Return of Onesimus," in *Onesimus Our Brother: Reading Religion, Race, and Culture in Philemon*, ed. Matthew V. Johnson, James A. Noel, and Demetrius K. Williams, Paul in Critical Contexts (Minneapolis: Fortress Press, 2012), 54. See also Taylor, "Onesimus, " 270–71.

202. For an extensive study of "brother," Barth and Blanke, 423–46; briefer, Thompson, 219–20.

203. On Philemon's sibling language, Thompson, 233–37; Reidar Aasgaard, *"My Beloved Brothers and Sisters!" Christian Siblingship in Paul*, JSNTSup 265 (London: T&T Clark, 2004), 237–60.

204. Kumitz speaks of the new creation reality in these terms: "eine irreversible qualitative Veränderung zum Guten"; see Kumitz, *Der Brief als Medium*, 216.

(and especially)[205] to Paul and to Philemon, drawing Philemon into Paul's circles where he will find Onesimus's status changed and challenging Philemon to embody the same. What made Onesimus especially important to Paul is not stated specifically, but the general impression is clear enough: he enhanced Paul's gospel work even in prison.

Though he was comparatively "useless" as a slave he is now to be loved by Philemon both "in flesh" and "in the Lord." The "in flesh" and "in the Lord" could describe Onesimus as a slave and as a (Christian) brother,[206] either in the sense of remaining a slave as an obedient Christian (Col 3:22–25) with a just relation with Philemon (4:1) or, with emphasis on conversion, his former status as a slave contrasted with his present (manumitted) status as a brother in the household of Philemon. Alternatively, "in flesh" and "in the Lord" could refer to his new embodied state in the household as a "freedman" and family member or brother and not a slave as well as his new relation to all "in the Lord."[207] Another option: the terms could refer to Onesimus as a human in a body[208] or even his "fleshly existence in the world" and in the spiritual reality of being "in the Lord."[209] One's overall interpretation of this letter determines how one interprets these two expressions. I believe Onesimus remained a slave. However, in the household of Philemon that status was no longer determinative; he had become family in the kingdom. Therefore, in the house of his master he was family and therefore no longer a slave *deprived of status and power*. I do not know the specifics of what this looked like at the level of life in the household.[210]

205. The NIV's translation ("very dear to me") does not bring out the nuance of μάλιστα ἐμοί that is found in the CEB's rendering ("especially"). On the elative μάλιστα (from μᾶλλον), BDAG 613; Harris, 267 (elative, not superlative since it is followed by πόσῳ δὲ μᾶλλον σοὶ). Barth and Blanke, 447, retain μάλιστα as a superlative and take πόσῳ δὲ μᾶλλον as "Loved most of all by me, yet how much more by you!"

206. Martin, 166; Witherington, 80, emphasizes transformation of the flesh condition by being "in the Lord."

207. Evidently Bruce, 217–18; Wolter, 271–72; Fitzmyer, 115–16; Moo, 424–25. Hence, ἐν κυρίῳ is the same as ἐν Χριστῷ (Barth and Blanke, 451–53).

208. The term σάρξ at this period in Paul's ministry often means "body" or "physical" or "personal presence" (cf. Col 1:22, 24; 2:1, 5, 23; 3:22) or "fleshly existence" apart from the Spirit (Col 2:11, 13, 18). Barth and Blanke, 450: "as the person he is." For a history of interpretation of flesh here, Barth and Blanke, 455–61, with 461–71. Callahan, 50, considers "in flesh" evidence that Onesimus was a blood brother to Philemon.

209. Moule, 148; Hübner, 37; Wilson, 357; Fitzmyer, 115–16; Ryan, 246–47. From a different angle, Petersen, *Rediscovering Paul*, 95–102. But the issue of "equality," a term that is so resonant with modernity and post-modernity (not to say politics of our day), is intrusive. The issue for Paul is not equality as we render it but siblingship as he renders it, and what he renders is innovative and revolutionary in his day. Siblings are not necessarily equals but are governed instead by love; see Aasgaard, *My Beloved Brothers and Sisters!*

210. An emphasis of Barclay, "Dilemma of Christian Slave-Ownership," 161–86.

We need to step back now because the moment of decision for Philemon is imminent. What are his options?

(1) Philemon could exact justice by way of punishment for what Onesimus has done, or
(2) Philemon could welcome him back as
  (2a) a slave to serve Philemon permanently or
  (2b) manumit him into either
  (2c) a freedman's status or into
  (2d) total freedom, with the latter suggesting
  (2e) that Onesimus would return to serve Paul on his own.[211]
  Or, (2f) Onesimus would be reconciled with Philemon, remain a slave in Philemon's household but be commissioned by Philemon to serve with Paul.

C. THIRD APPEAL IN THEIR PARTNERSHIP (VV. 17–21; APPEAL IN VV. 17, 20–21)

Although Paul has already stated that Philemon can receive Onesimus as a "child" and "no longer as a slave," it is only at Phlm 17 that he uses a term that clarifies what he expects: "welcome." He prefaces the appeal with some buttery language—"If you consider me a partner." Philemon is not an abstract or philosophical letter, nor is it a professional piece of rhetoric. Hence, Paul moves from his more direct appeal in v. 17 to welcome Onesimus back into supplementary, personal themes: a promise to cover any expenses incurred (vv. 18–19a) with an argument from personal, spiritual indebtedness (v. 19b). But this leads back to another example of welcoming Onesimus by way of indirection in the terms "benefit" and "refresh" (v. 20). His appeal is then propped up when Paul expresses his confidence in Philemon's "obedience" (v. 21). Noticeable in this third appeal is the face-to-face type of juxtapositions in the first and second person, as seen in "if *you* consider *me*" or "*you* owe *me your* very self."[212] Once again Paul touches upon the nature of giving and reciprocation: Philemon is in Paul's debt because of the gift of redemption Paul has given to Philemon.

Many think Paul here is indirectly asking for the manumission of Onesimus.[213] My contention is that Paul was a man who spoke his mind. So I repeat: *the rhetoric of Philemon is not so much an example of professional and hand-*

211. Slight variations on Bird, 141.

212. Harris, 278–79.

213. For one discussion, Barth and Blanke, 412–15.

book rhetoric as it is an example of clear and compelling communication. That is, *what Paul wants is for Philemon to welcome Onesimus back in the church as a brother and to establish in the house church of Philemon a kingdom reality not seen in the Roman Empire.* Paul is summoning Philemon not to manumit Onesimus in a legal ceremony but to *liberate Onesimus in the church.*[214] How would this work out? Would it mean additional privileges? Some funds to save for his manumission? Better food, clothing, and housing? More responsibility? Higher status opportunities? We do not know, but one can assume that liberation in the household involved such matters and others in the elevation of Onesimus's status. To be clear, this is not a proposal for the Stoic theories that contend what happens in the body pertains only to the material and less important reality. Rather, "in the Lord" new creation realities are breaking into the present orders of the Empire. It is also important to be clear about a corollary: Paul knows that God has broken into the Empire "in Christ" and that "in Christ" reality is *supra-imperial* and therefore the truest and most complete social reality known to the Empire. Hence, though Paul's, Philemon's, and the church's puny status in the Empire rendered a social-legal revolution for widespread manumission impossible, that social revolution was being established nonetheless in the house church of Philemon. The revolution Paul has in mind is to be seen in the three imperatives, each in bold.

17 *So if you consider me a partner,* ***welcome*** *him*[a] *as you would welcome*
me. 18 *If he has done you any wrong*[b] *or owes you anything,*[c] ***charge*** *it to me.* 19 *I,*
Paul, am writing this with my own hand. I will pay it back—not to mention that
you owe me your very self.[d] 20 *I do wish, brother, that I may have some benefit*[e]
from you in the Lord; ***refresh*** *my heart in Christ.* 21 *Confident of your obedience,*
I write to you, knowing that you will do even more than I ask.

a. CEB: "Onesimus."
b. CEB: "harmed."
c. CEB: "owes you money."
d. CEB: "life" instead of NIV's "self."
e. CEB: "this favor."

17 Paul's appeal to receive Onesimus back is based upon a dynamic ecclesial reality that runs right through Paul's entire ministry but which became especially important during Paul's prison experiences and ministries: "So if you consider me a *partner*."[215] The conditional phrase ("If . . .") is not an ex-

214. Aasgaard, *My Beloved Brothers and Sisters!*, 254–57.

215. Εἰ οὖν με ἔχεις κοινωνόν. The particle is resumptive (Lohse, 203n64). The present tense (ἔχεις) with the double accusative depicts Philemon's "consider" more vividly. The performance of the letter then would entail looking at Philemon and perhaps even motioning to

pression of doubt but an *assumption* Paul uses to get to his appeal: Philemon and he are "partners."[216] "Partners" is surrounded by a cloud of connections in Philemon: Philemon is a "dear friend and fellow worker" (v. 1), the church meets in his home (v. 2), God is their Father and Jesus is their Lord (vv. 3, 5), Philemon loves God's new people in Christ (v. 5), he is a "partner" (or they fellowship) in the faith" (v. 6), this partnership/fellowship expands his mind theologically in wisdom (v. 6), Philemon is a man of love that leads to the refreshing of the Lord's people (vv. 7, 9), God's plans for Onesimus transcend ordinary experienced realities (v. 15), Philemon is to love Onesimus and know that he is now a "brother" (v. 16), Philemon can accept restitution through Paul (vv. 18–19a), Philemon can bring a "benefit" in this matter with Onesimus (v. 20), Philemon is generous (v. 21), Philemon is hospitable and will host Paul (v. 22), *and most especially he has a special relationship to Paul "in Christ" shaped by God's grace and their love for one another that respects one another's freedom* (vv. 1b, 9, 11, 13, 14, 16, 17–21). All of this, with nothing omitted, is involved when Paul says, "If you consider me a *partner*." To be a "partner" (*koinōnos*) then is neither a commonplace of friendship nor standard rhetoric. They are more than partners in a cause. This is the core of Paul's entire appeal: *as fellow believers and as those who share life "in Christ" in the ecclesial body of Christ,* they now have opportunities and obligations to one another that form a new socio-ecclesial reality, the new creation kingdom of God, most especially so because they are *koinōnoi* in ministry in Christ.[217] In Philemon, Paul concentrates on mutually reciprocating life under the cruciform Lord Jesus, life established by *reconciliation.* It is not a stretch to see the term *koinōnos*/ partner as forming the core of Pauline theology and ethics. This observation should inform contemporary discussions of Christian ethics. Unfortunately, love, fellowship, and reconciliation are often overlooked in favor of personal spiritual formation. Paul's ethics are radically shaped toward ecclesial forma-

Philemon with a hand upturned in petition. On the verb, see the similar use at Matt 14:5. For discussion of the first class conditional, Brook W. R. Pearson, "Assumptions in the Criticism and Translation of Philemon," in *Translating the Bible: Problems and Prospects*, ed. Stanley Porter and R. S. Hess, JSNTSup 173 (Sheffield: Sheffield Academic Press, 1999), 268–74.

216. On the term κοινωνός, see the comments on v. 6 and also 2 Cor 8:23, but see also BDAG 553–54; *EDNT* 2:303–5; Dunn, *Theology of Paul the Apostle*, 533–64; N. T. Wright, *Paul and the Faithfulness of God*, vol. 4 of *Christian Origins and the Question of God* (Minneapolis: Fortress, 2013), 2:1473–519. Some see "business partner" (Barth and Blanke, 474–75). Note also Arzt-Grabner, "How to Deal with Onesimus?," 135–39, who provides ample evidence from the papyri. His argument is that Paul urges, in v. 17 albeit indirectly, to make Onesimus a business partner. How one constructs the story behind this letter will shape what one sees in "partner" here.

217. Dunn, 337 (with emphasis on being a "fellow worker" in ministry), Hübner, 37; Moo, 426 (partners in faith, as in v. 6). Petersen sees the term "partner" nearly synonymous with "fellow worker" in the mission; see Petersen, *Rediscovering Paul*, 104–6.

tion, and only within that ecclesial context does the individual Christian find personal formation.[218]

The appeal is direct, clear, and the climax of the entire performance of the letter in Philemon's presence: "welcome him as you would welcome me." The "as you would welcome me" repeats in new terms "if you consider me a partner." The mutual and reciprocal exchange of gifts as hospitality is surely in mind, but behind the "as you would welcome me" could be the words of Jesus (Luke 10:16; Matt 10:40–42; 25:35, 40). Not to be pedantic, the term here (*proslambanō*) is not the term in the Gospels (*dechomai*), even if they are synonymous at times and the principle is the same. Emissaries represent the sender. The classic text affirming this is m. Ber. 5:5 ("a man's agent is like [the man] himself"). Paul puts his relationship to Philemon on the line: positively, to receive Onesimus is to receive Paul;[219] negatively, to reject Onesimus *is to reject Paul himself.* To "welcome"[220] Onesimus is to receive the man into the household as forgiven, as a brother, as one "in Christ," as one who like Paul is a partner in the gospel ministries of the apostle, and this "welcome" implies reconciliation, restoration, restitution, and reinstatement. As Priscilla and Aquila welcomed Apollos (Acts 18:26), as the "barbarians" of Malta built a fire and welcomed the shipmates of Paul (28:2), and as the apostle Paul will tell the Romans that the strong and the weak are to receive one another in the fellowship of "differents" because God has received both (Rom 14:1, 3; 15:7), so Philemon is to welcome Onesimus. To give the term social purchase, we might imagine Philemon washing the feet of Onesimus.

It is not without merit to see Paul here as the agent of reconciliation, as one embodying the grand statements of 2 Cor 5:17–21: new creation has arrived, God has reconciled us to himself through Christ, and Paul knows he is now an agent of reconciliation between God and humans and between humans and humans in the *ekklēsia*.[221] Here Paul pleads with Philemon to be

218. Scholars tend to gravitate toward extremes in these matters; see Ben C. Dunson, "The Individual and the Community in Twentieth- and Twenty-First-Century Pauline Scholarship," *CurBR* 9 (2010): 63–97.

219. The ὡς ἐμέ could indicate "just as you receive me" or "as if he were me." Witherington, 83n5. On envoys, Callahan, 55; MacDonald, "New Testament Envoys," 641–62.

220. On προσλαμβάνω, BDAG 883 [4], a term that suggests Onesimus could be the envoy (1 Cor 16:10–11; Phil 2:29; Rom 16:1–2).

221. There is much discussion about reconciliation, but not enough about reconciliation between those in the churches. One can begin with these for the larger perspectives: Ralph P. Martin, *Reconciliation: A Study of Paul's Theology*, New Foundations Theological Library (Atlanta: John Knox Press, 1981); Stanley Porter, *Καταλλάσσω in Ancient Greek Literature, with Reference to the Pauline Writings*, EFN 5 (Córdoba: Ediciones el Almendro, 1994); Stanley Porter, "Paul's Concept of Reconciliation, Twice More," in *Paul and His Theology*, ed. Stanley Porter, Pauline Studies 3 (Leiden: Brill, 2006), 131–52; Stanley Porter, "Reconciliation as the Heart of Paul's Missionary Theology," in *Paul as Missionary: Identity,*

reconciled to Onesimus just as both are reconciled with God.[222] Thompson has expressed this theme most explicitly:

> It is exactly this reconciling work of Christ of which Paul understands himself to be the agent, not only in calling people to be reconciled to God, not only in bringing Jew and Gentile together, but also in bringing two friends, two Christian brothers, together into a new relationship within the household of God. Paul carries out his role as Christ's ambassador of reconciliation by identifying himself first with Philemon as beloved friend, coworker, partner, and brother, thus establishing their mutuality and collegiality in the Lord. Paul next identifies Onesimus as his child and his heart. By means of his identification with Philemon as a peer and fellow worker, Paul can call on Philemon to act graciously and to extend the welcome and forgiveness to Onesimus that he could command but prefers not to. By means of his identification with Onesimus, Paul puts himself in the slave's place, showing the lengths to which Christian love will go and demonstrating the full extent of Christian brotherly love.[223]

There is no better summary statement of the theology of Paul at work in this letter.[224]

18–19a Paul turns here to another *if* clause: "If he has done you any wrong or owes you anything."[225] There is much speculation about why Paul brings this up, and most think the topic is raised only because a wrong has occurred.[226] What that injustice might have been is not defined. The language

---

Activity, Theology, and Practice, ed. Brian S. Rosner and Trevor J. Burke, LNTS 420 (London: Bloomsbury T&T Clark, 2011), 169–79.

222. This theme is at the heart of a number of publications by Wright. See, for example, Wright, 194, where he said most poignantly "God is in Paul reconciling Philemon and Onesimus."

223. Thompson, 225.

224. In the performance of this letter a variety of social realities would come into play. For example, the most common means of acquiring a slave was through the birth of a child from a female domestic slave. Let us assume this to be the case. *If so*, perhaps Onesimus's mother was watching the performance of the letter. *If so*, she would have heard Paul's words that her "boy" was now a "son"; she would have heard the plea for her runaway son to be forgiven, to be reconciled, and to be reinstated in the family. And, most importantly, *If so*, she would have begun to wonder what siblingship was to mean for her and for all the slaves in the *oikonomia* of Philemon. Given that slaves most commonly resulted from slave births we can say that such a situation is at least possible.

225. εἰ δέ τι ἠδίκησέν σε ἢ ὀφείλει. The change from the aorist indicative to the present is a shift in depiction not in the time when something occurred or occurs. The wrong action is depicted as a whole while the indebtedness is more vivid and expansive to the mind of Philemon. Philemon might be thinking, "The man owes me many things!"

226. E.g., Lightfoot, 343; Stuhlmacher, 49; Bruce, 219–20; Wright, 187–88; Wither-

of debt ("owes") leads many to suggest the kind of injustice entailed a financial injustice; at the very least, the term suggests Onesimus did something to cause Philemon financial loss.[227] The commercial or financial terms at work in vv. 18–19 ("owes," "charge," and "pay it back") as well as Paul's emphatic promise to be a guarantor for Onesimus make it more than likely that Onesimus has somehow incurred a financial debt.

How so? The proposals are multiple: (1) theft to finance travel,[228] (2) abandoning of his post, (3) prior to running away Onesimus had done something costly and knew he would be punished and therefore ran away, (4) he somehow did something that was costly; instead of simply running away he sought to secure Paul as his mediator or, (5) much less likely, Onesimus abandoned his contract to work off his debt in a debtor's slave arrangement.[229] Whatever the specific detail of the injustice and the indebtedness (each of the above fits into what we know of slaves, masters, and runaways), we are left only with inferences. Surely what Onesimus had done was the greatest hurdle in the reconciliation Paul was seeking.

In a rare moment when the *real voice* breaks through the *narrator's voice*—earlier than in other letters[230]—Paul says, "I, Paul, am writing this with my own hand. I will pay it back" (v. 19a).[231] The first sentence assures Philemon and the second repeats the previous verse's "charge it to me."[232] Four times (in addition to our text) in the Pauline correspondence Paul's voice comes through with regard to his writing:

> See what large letters I use as I write to you with my own hand! (Gal 6:11).
>
> I, Paul, write this greeting in my own hand, which is the distinguishing mark in all my letters. This is how I write (2 Thess 3:17).

---

ington, 84. Some think this is merely an inference (e.g., Martin, 167) or even a hypothetical (Felder, 899), but one must ask why Paul continues as he does in the rest of vv. 18 and 19 if no wrong had been done.

227. See John G. Nordling, "Onesimus Fugitivus: A Defense of the Runaway Slave Hypothesis in Philemon," *JSNT* 41 (1991): 104–5.

228. E.g., *NewDocs* 8:12–13.

229. On the debtor slave theory, Barth and Blanke, 480–82.

230. E. Randolph Richards, *Paul and First-Century Letter Writing: Secretaries, Composition and Collection* (Downers Grove, IL: InterVarsity Press, 2004), 171–75.

231. That vv. 19–20 are so tied to vv. 17–18 makes dividing the letter at vv. 19–25 into the letter closing more difficult; *pace* Weima, "Paul's Persuasive Prose," 51–58, esp. 53–54. Yet, Weima's observation is supported because these autograph lines do seem to be part of the letter closings in other instances. Rhetoric, content, and epistolary conventions do not always form parallel lines. Witherington, 91, divides the letter closing at v. 23 while Moo, 433–34, at v. 21.

232. ἐγὼ ἀποτίσω. Future of ἀποτίνω (BDAG 124).

I, Paul, write this greeting in my own hand (1 Cor 16:21).

I, Paul, write this greeting in my own hand. Remember my chains. Grace be with you (Col 4:18).

The line in 2 Thessalonians indicates Paul may write with his own hand in each of his letters. Here, Paul assures Philemon that he can be relied upon to pay any debt of Onesimus.

Paul assumes the debt upon himself—forming a promissory note: "charge it to me."[233] In Col 2:14 Paul used his now well-known image of the *cheirographon*, a certificate of indebtedness, and now this verse—and this letter by extension—is precisely that at the personal level.[234] While "charge it to me" could again be metaphor, more likely some kind of restitution at the financial level is in mind. The language of "pay it back" occurs often in the Greco-Roman sources for financial compensation.[235] How Paul the prisoner had the funds for such a promise we do not know. Additionally, if this is looked at through the lens of reciprocal benevolence in the Roman world then Paul is putting Philemon under obligation by assuming the debt that Philemon would otherwise have to suffer.

19b Paul appends what could be taken as a shaming device: "not to mention that you owe me your very self." As Harris has observed, this verse contains a paralipsis (instead of "passing over" the author mentions what he does not want to mention).[236] In what sense does Philemon "owe" Paul his "very self"?[237] Most interpreters think Paul refers to Philemon's own conversion and eternal life in Christ through the gospel ministry of the apostle, not unlike the two sides of debt and obligation in Rom 15:27: "They were pleased to do it, and indeed they *owe* it to them. For if the Gentiles have shared in the Jews' *spiritual blessings*, they *owe* it to the Jews to share with them their *material blessings*."[238] Indeed, such may be true but it may also be true that Paul somehow engineered an escape for Philemon (who may have been converted through Epaphras[239]) from some life-threatening situation. However we read the line in specific detail, the rhetoric is sharp: "I could mention that you owe

233. ἐμοὶ ἐλλόγα. On the verb, see BDAG 319.

234. So Martin, 167; Wright, 188; Harris, 273; Barth and Blanke, 482–83; Fitzmyer, 118.

235. Lohse, 204n70, has some good examples. Callahan, 62, suggests what will be owed will be travel expenses back to Colossae, but this is harder to square with the "wrong" of v. 18.

236. Harris, 274.

237. ὅτι καὶ σεαυτόν μοι προσοφείλεις. The verb indicates "owe besides, still owe" and "you owe me even your very self (besides)" (BDAG 883–84). The present is for the sake of a vivid depiction as the letter is read.

238. Lohse, 204–5; Bruce, 220; Wright, 188; Barth and Blanke, 484 (less confidently); Fitzmyer, 119; Moo, 430–31.

239. For discussion of a slightly more distant relationship of Paul to Philemon (only perhaps through Epaphras), see Dunn, 340.

me your life, and I won't, but I have gone ahead and said it. Now I would like you to factor this into your decision in welcoming back Onesimus." One needs also to see in Paul's language of v. 19b the very common *obligation* that a *gift* imposes on the one who has received the gift *to respond in kind, in gratitude, and in reciprocal benevolence.*[240]

20 From his order to Philemon to charge any debts to him and some strong assurances that he will pay off any debt, Paul subtly shifts the appeal to two hopes: (1) "I do wish, brother,[241] that I may have some benefit from you in the Lord" and (2) "refresh my heart in Christ." Two terms rise to the surface for discussion: *benefit* and *refresh.* The first term—which in Greek (*oninēmi*) evokes a sense of joy more than the blander English term "benefit"[242]—is in the optative mood, the mood of wish.[243] The optative creates the atmosphere of hope, of contingency, and of a shift of responsibility onto the decision of Philemon. The second hope shifts into the imperative mood: "I wish" becomes the mild imperative "refresh." Noticeably, Paul says refresh "my heart," the same term he used in v. 7 ("because you, brother, have refreshed *the hearts* of the Lord's people") and v. 12 ("I am sending him—who is *my very heart*"), and as noted in both verses the term is not the typical word for "heart" (*kardia*) but *splanchna.* That is, the term often refers to one's inner organs where emotions and deep compassion and love are experienced. Inasmuch as Paul has now brought Onesimus into the family of God and inasmuch as Philemon has been in the business of refreshing the hearts of the people of God, Paul tells Philemon that he wants his heart refreshed by how Philemon welcomes Onesimus. Paul has drawn a circle around himself and Philemon and now exhorts the slave owner to welcome the slave into the circle with them, something Paul has already done![244]

240. Esp. Gillian Feeley-Harnik, "Is Historical Anthropology Possible?," in *Humanizing America's Iconic Book: Society of Biblical Literature Centennial Addresses 1980*, ed. Gene M. Tucker and Douglas A. Knight, Biblical Scholarship in North America 6 (Chico, CA: Scholars Press, 1982), 95–126; Barclay, *Paul and the Gift*, 24–51.

241. The expression is vocative: ναὶ ἀδελφέ, "Indeed brother," which is emphatic (Harris, 275).

242. Ignatius, *Ephesians* 2.2; *Polycarp* 6.2, which can be read as "May I always have joy in you" (Holmes). See Lohse, 205.

243. ἐγώ σου ὀναίμην ἐν κυρίῳ. The aorist of ὀνίνημι does not indicate a one-time benefit but it sums up the benefit(s) into a bundle. BDAG (71) translate "let me have some benefit from you in the Lord." Some see in the verb a possible play on the name of Onesimus (e.g., Lightfoot, 345; Bruce, 221; Wright, 188–89; Dunn, 341; Callahan, 63; Osiek, 141; Barth and Blanke, 486; Witherington, 85; Moo, 432; see discussion in Lohse, 81), and hence translate the verb with "profit."

244. The rhetoric trades in the commerce of honor and reputation for Philemon's generosity, as can be seen in David A. deSilva, *Honor, Patronage, Kinship & Purity: Unlocking New Testament Culture* (Downers Grove, IL: InterVarsity Press, 2000), 124–25.

The location of these emotions and reciprocal blessings is "in the Lord" and "in Christ." Each makes clear that joy and refreshment only come in their ecclesial fellowship in Christ. Even more importantly, these expressions walk us straight up the letter to v. 17's "If you consider me a *partner*." Thus, "in the Lord" and "in Christ" are where all this fellowship and the new creation kingdom reality are to be found. Paul is a prisoner of Christ (vv. 1, 9), grace and peace derive from Christ (vv. 3, 25), the partnership in the faith occurs in the wisdom found in Christ (v. 6), and in Phlm 20 he wants to find joy and to be refreshed in that same fellowship circle. All of which is to say that for Paul "benefit" and "refresh" require Philemon to respond as Paul hopes: welcoming back Onesimus, forgiving him, reconciling with him (restitution assumed), and the further sending of him back to serve with Paul in gospel work.

21 Now comes a simple, plain and direct appeal in v. 21: "Confident of your obedience, I write to you, knowing that you will do even more than I ask." Paul expects Philemon's "obedience."[245] What is this obedience? From this letter we are to think of welcome (v. 17), benefit (v. 20), and refresh (v. 20). But why does he call what he wants to be by choice "obedience"? In Phlm 8–9 Paul explicitly denied an appeal to his authority. Perhaps then "obedience" in v. 21 refers to a general sense of the will of God (notice vv. 6–7) or a life of obedience to the gospel (Rom 1:5; 2 Cor 10:5).[246] But obedience is just that and it requires command/imperative and authority at some level.[247] Perhaps one could argue the terms develop: from not commanding in v. 8 to appealing in vv. 9–10 to seeking Philemon's willing consent in v. 14 to the rather surprisingly abrupt obedience in v. 21.[248] Philemon's obedience, then, at least means welcoming Onesimus into the household.

Paul is "confident" of Philemon's proposed response. The Greek expression could be translated "I, confident as I am in your obedience, write to you."[249] Affirmations like these work three ways: they can be a bolstering

245. BDAG 1028–29; *EDNT* 3:394–95; Barth and Blanke, 487–88; Pao, 418–19. Harris, 278, translates "compliance." For obedience, Lohse, 206; Martin, 168; Pao, 418–19. For a softer sense of obedience, Bruce, 222; Wright, 189.

246. Wright, 189; Dunn, 344; Moo, 434–35.

247. There is no tension in the Jewish world between freedom and obedience; cf. Barth and Blanke, 488–91.

248. See discussion in Petersen, *Rediscovering Paul*, 131–51. Petersen notes, "Paul's rhetorical style serves to mediate the paradox that the egalitarian social structure [siblingship] of Paul's churches is complemented by a hierarchical axis" (133, all in italics).

249. Πεποιθὼς τῇ ὑπακοῇ σου ἔγραψά σοι. The participle—the perfect active participle of πείθω (BDAG 791–92)—is more adjectival (with implied "I" as the subject of the verb "to write") than adverbial. The tense—perfect tense as present or stative—makes Paul's confidence especially vivid to Philemon, revealing the rhetorical moment Paul has created. The aorist (ἔγραψά) is taken by most interpreters as an epistolary aorist (cf. v. 19; e.g., Harris,

moment for the author, they can be a motivating tool to persuade Philemon, and they can be a transparent window onto the very mind of Paul. Those who love Paul are persuaded of the third, probably the second, and think the first is unnecessary. Those less persuaded of him lock onto the first or the second. I stand with those who love Paul.

A confident apostle believes that Philemon "will do even more than I ask."[250] What is this "more" that Philemon "will do"? Philemon 16 has already told us: "no longer as a slave, but *better than* a slave." The same kind of expression is found here: the "better than" and the "more than" open the door for Philemon to treat Onesimus as a brother, to welcome him home, to forgive, to reconcile, and to reshape the household on the basis of the kingdom of God's new creation realities that there is "no longer a slave" but rather a grand encompassing unity in Christ (Gal 3:28; 1 Cor 12:13; Col 3:11). Even more is the return of Onesimus back to Paul for ministry.[251]

One last time, is "even more than I ask" the language for manumission?[252] Again, Paul does not strike me as the kind of person who was afraid to speak his mind or to use bold language. While indirection plays an important role in rhetorical handbooks, I doubt this is an example of thinking one thing (manumission) but saying another ("more than I ask"). Rather, this is an example of saying the very thing he means. Paul *only hopes* Philemon will do more but everything is in Philemon's court now—and manumission could be one choice Philemon could make but that is not Paul's desire. Nor should we elevate manumission to the highest level of moral insight in order to understand the apostle Paul in his context. He wants Philemon to welcome the man back, forgive him and restore him and be reconciled and then, because Philemon has the keys, to open the door for Onesimus to return to Paul for ministry. This letter is an

---

278), but the aorist tense depicts action as a whole and had Paul wanted it to be "I am writing" or "I write" he could use the present (as he does with λέγω in this verse).

250. εἰδὼς ὅτι καὶ ὑπὲρ ἃ λέγω ποιήσεις. The perfect participle (εἰδὼς) sums up the basis for Paul's writing with confidence. The future (ποιήσεις) sketches imperfective aspect in the temporal future (to Paul and at that moment to Philemon). The present tense (λέγω) makes vivid the speech of Paul to Philemon in this letter's performance in his presence.

251. Hübner, 38; seemingly Barth and Blanke, 492–93; Iralu, 1707; also Pao, 420.

252. For those who think this means manumission, Harris, 278–79; Wright, 189; Witherington, 86; Soungalo, 1488; Moo, 436; also Wessels, "The Letter to Philemon in the Context of Slavery in Early Christianity," 164–68; Isak J. du Plessis, "How Christians Can Survive in a Hostile Social-Economic Environment: Paul's Mind Concerning Difficult Social Conditions in the Letter to Philemon," in *Identity, Ethics, and Ethos in the New Testament*, BZNW 141 (Berlin: de Gruyter, 2006), 387–413 (esp. 401–8). For those who do not, e.g., Lohse, *Philemon*, 206; Michael Wolter, "The Letter to Philemon as Ethical Counterpart of Paul's Doctrine of Justification," in Tolmie, *Philemon in Perspective*, 174–76.

exercise in shifting responsibility to Philemon.[253] We should speak here of *ecclesial liberation* rather than manumission. The "more" might mean the latter two terms but if Paul wanted that to happen he would have said that. He did not.

D. FINAL APPEAL IN A PRESENCE (V. 22)

A personal theme now rises to the surface, namely, Paul's request to prepare a guest room (v. 22). Philemon 22 may sound more like an addition or a tangent than a continuation of the appeal, but the request to prepare a guest room in v. 22 heightens the sense of Paul's presence in the performance of the letter. Lohse recognizes the rhetorical impact of Paul's arrival: "By announcing his visit, the Apostle lends a certain emphasis to his intercession for Onesimus. For he will come and see for himself how things have gone."[254] Thus, I read v. 22 as the final appeal.

22*And one thing more: Prepare a guest room for me, because I hope to be restored to you*[a] *in answer to your prayers.*

---

a. CEB: "released from prison to be with you."

22 Before Paul can move into his characteristic and community-informing farewells he has "one more thing," or perhaps more precisely, "now alongside" the appeal to welcome Onesimus.[255] His additional request is that Philemon—who has a sizable home (four centuries later, Christians claimed to know its location[256]) "prepare a guest room." Hospitality is shown to non-family members in a household and was central to earliest Christian travel and fellowship. The common term "guest room" (*xenia*) appears only twice in the New Testament (Acts 28:23; Phlm 22).[257] The term takes on the sense of "hospitality" and the provision of a room, which Paul was in need of in many of his visits to his churches (cf. 1 Cor 4:18–21; 2 Cor 12:14; 13:1). To ask

253. Lewis, 443; Barclay, "Dilemma of Christian Slave-Ownership," 175.

254. Lohse, 206–7.

255. ἅμα δὲ καί. The adverb ἅμα indicates simultaneity (BDF §425.2), while δὲ καί indicate conjunction with adjunction: "Now at time same time also." See Harris, 279.

256. Bruce, 222n100, referring to Theodoret, bishop of Cyrrhus.

257. See the exceptional study rooted in ancient novels by Andrew Arterbury, *Entertaining Angels: Early Christian Hospitality in Its Mediterranean Setting*, New Testament Monographs 8 (Sheffield: Sheffield Phoenix Press, 2005). In addition, Christine D. Pohl, *Making Room: Recovering Hospitailty as a Christian Tradition* (Grand Rapids: Eerdmans, 1999); Amy G. Oden, ed., *And You Welcomed Me: A Sourcebook on Hospitality in Early Christianity* (Nashville: Abingdon, 2001).

for (or expect, or demand) hospitality is to ask as well for reception of his appeal in this letter.

The reason for Paul's request anchors both the request and the entire plea for Onesimus in Christian fellowship (*koinōnia*): "because I hope to be restored to you in answer to your [plural] prayers."[258] Paul's mention of his imprisonment (cf. vv. 1, 9) again reminds the hearer or reader of Paul's social proximity to Onesimus. Paul, like Onesimus, is in need of the powerful's decision on his behalf. Paul is laying before Philemon the opportunity to liberate a brother in Christ. Paul is confident that he will be released from prison[259] and he believes his release is the result of the prayers of the church ("your" is plural) at Colossae, but the term for his return indicates less than might at first be seen in the NIV's "restored." The term is *charizomai*, a word that often means "giving/gift" or "forgiving/forgiveness." However, in our context—as at Acts 3:14—it probably means "released" in the sense of being granted a pardon from a legal accusation. Hence, the NIV's "restored" suggests that Paul has fallen out of favor with Philemon or the church at Colossae, when nothing of the kind is suggested. Rather, the term is better translated "released" as in the CEB. This translation magnifies the importance of both intercessory and communal prayers in the early church, and we are drawn immediately to Peter's imprisonment and release through prayers (Acts 12:5–17). Intercession is a constant element in Paul's own life (e.g., 1 Cor 1:4–9; Col 1:9–11; Eph 1:15–19) as are the intercessions of others for him (1 Thess 5:25; 2 Thess 3:1; 2 Cor 1:11; Rom 15:30; Phil 1:19).

This verse figures into configurations of Paul's life and his location when writing. That Paul anticipates progressing on to Spain after Rome (Rom 15:24) makes any imminent visit to Colossae far less likely, and thus an imprisonment in Ephesus more likely.[260]

258. ἐλπίζω γὰρ ὅτι διὰ τῶν προσευχῶν ὑμῶν χαρισθήσομαι ὑμῖν. The present tense again places Paul in the presence of Philemon; the future passive χαρισθήσομαι is probably a divine passive (Wilson, 366). The hope expressed here can be confident or more tentative (Dunn, 346). The plural "your" prayers deserves emphasis; see Michael A. G. Haykin, "Praying Together: A Note on Philemon 22," *EvQ* 66 (1994): 331–35.

259. Prison, again, is not a punishment but the holding of someone suspected or charged until a judicial court renders a decision in the case. On Roman imprisonment, see Rapske, *The Book of Acts and Paul in Roman Custody*, 9–70, 177–182, 195–422. For his own shorter version, see Rapske, "Prison, Prisoner," *DNTB*, 827–30.

260. A change in plans then would be necessary between Romans and the writing of Colossians-Philemon, not to mention a later date for the Lycus Valley letters, and this change of plans can be seen in Bruce, 222–23; Moo, 438, diminishes the distance from Rome to Colossae. For an Ephesian imprisonment explanation, Wright, 165, 190–91; Hübner, 38; Wilson, 326–27 (with hesitations); Bird, 134. Also, see *NewDocs* 8:44–45; Bartchy, 5:309; Hans-Josef Klauck, *Ancient Letters and the New Testament: A Guide to Content and Exegesis* (Waco, TX: Baylor University Press, 2006), 329; Arzt-Grabner, "How to Deal with Onesi-

IV. CONCLUSION (PHLM 23–25)

The quotidian nature of Paul's conclusion illustrates the reality out of which they emerged more than the unimportance of the mundane. The Christian movement was enveloped in normal, loving, and, at times, fractious relationships. The reading of these conclusions garnered the kind of attention readers today give to the Preface or Foreword to a book.

[23]*Epaphras, my fellow prisoner in Christ Jesus, sends you greetings.* [24]*And so do Mark, Aristarchus, Demas and Luke, my fellow workers.* [25]*The grace of the Lord Jesus Christ be with your spirit.*

23 One of Paul's coworkers was Epaphras.[261] In Colossians he is called a "dear fellow servant," "faithful minister of Christ," a "servant of Christ Jesus" and mighty in prayer and, most importantly, Epaphras was both "one of you," that is a Colossian, and the founding evangelist/pastor of the church in Colossae (Col 1:7–8; 4:12). In Philemon he is a "fellow prisoner in Christ Jesus" and, while this might be taken as a metaphor for serving Christ,[262] in this letter Paul's own imprisonment is emphasized (vv. 1, 9, 13, 22) so the term[263] indicates custody alongside Paul.[264]

Epaphras, a fellow Colossian and perhaps a part of Philemon's house

mus?," 134–35n92. For a full study of Paul and Ephesus, see the exceptional analysis and cautious conclusions of Paul Trebilco, *The Early Christians in Ephesus from Paul to Ignatius* (Grand Rapids: Eerdmans, 2007), 53–196. Trebilco makes a cautious case for an Ephesian imprisonment but does not think an Ephesian origin for the prison letters is as demonstrable. Against Trebilco, one might counter with the following argument: it is clear that Philemon is written from prison. Which of Paul's imprisonments? Since Paul was imprisoned in Ephesus (per Trebilco), one can suggest that, say Philemon, is just as likely (or more likely) to have been written from a prison in Ephesus than from one in Rome (or Caesarea). On these matters, of course, we should avoid dogmatism and even more building theology on the ordering of Paul's letters, as is done in Garwood P. Anderson, *Paul's New Perspective: Charting a Soteriological Journey* (Downers Grove, IL: InterVarsity Press, 2016).

261. Dunn, 348, thinks Epaphras and Aristarchus became substitutionary prisoners for Paul and Epaphras in prison while in Col 4 Aristarchus is in prison.

262. Moule, 136–37.

263. ὁ συναιχμάλωτός μου. On this term, BDAG 964; L&N 1:551–52. See also at Col 4:10; Rom 16:7.

264. Lohse, 207; Martin, 169; Wright, 191; Hübner, 38; Barth and Blanke, 496; Moo, 439–40. On Epaphras, see M. Trainor, "Excavating Epaphras of Colossae," in *Colossae in Space and Time: Linking to an Ancient City*, ed. Alan H. Cadwallader and Michael Trainor, NTOA 94 (Göttingen: Vandenhoeck & Ruprecht, 2011), 232–46; Michael Trainor, *Epaphras: Paul's Educator at Colossae,* Paul's Social Network: Brothers and Sisters in Faith (Collegeville, MN: Liturgical Press, 2008).

church and potential source of the information assumed in this letter, sends his "greetings" to Philemon (the "you" is singular).[265] The inclusion of Epaphras strengthens Paul's appeal. Epaphras was the founder of the church at Colossae, spiritual agent behind the house church of Philemon, and *someone on Paul's side in the sending of this letter*. The naming of Epaphras puts even more pressure on Philemon to respond affirmatively to the appeal to welcome Onesimus back.

24 The names of Phlm 24 are simply continuations of the subject of the verb "sends you his greetings"[266] in v. 23. The four names are then defined as "my fellow workers." First, the four names:[267] Mark is common enough in the Roman world, although many think it is John Mark,[268] author of the Gospel of Mark and a one-time travel companion of Paul in his missionary work. In fact, we learn from the records that Paul and Barnabas fell out of agreement over the character and faithfulness of Barnabas's relative Mark and also that Mark was evidently restored to become a fellow worker with Paul (cf. Acts 12:12, 25; 15:36–41; Col 4:10; 2 Tim 4:11; cf. too 1 Pet 5:13 a "son" of Peter). Mark evidently visited Colossae (Col 4:10).

Aristarchus, a travel companion of Paul's from Macedonia at Thessalonica—who was (perhaps willingly) imprisoned for the gospel[269]—appears in the New Testament at Acts 19:29; 20:4; 27:2 and Col 4:10, while Demas appears at Col 4:14 and 2 Tim 4:10. The latter text is notable for describing his apparent apostasy as one who "loved this world, has deserted me and gone to Thessalonica."

Luke—Paul's companion, doctor, and "dear friend"—is traditionally considered the author of the Gospel of Luke and the Acts of the Apostles (cf. Col 4:14 and 2 Tim 4:11).[270]

All four are "my fellow workers," though in Demas's case that ministry was not to last.[271] The circle around Paul enclosed a large group of those who

265. The present tense of the verb (ἀσπάζεται) virtually brings Epaphras into the room.

266. The verb is singular, concentrating as it did in v. 23 on Epaphras, but the singular is extended to include the four persons in v. 24 (Harris, 206, 280). Also, Bruce, *The Pauline Circle*, 73–80.

267. The only name not mentioned here that is found in Col 4:10, 14 is Jesus Justus and, in spite of the ingenuity in thinking we ought to see Jesus Justus in v 23, now rendered "in Christ. Jesu[s Justus]," it appears Paul simply does not mention the man (for the emendation, see Lohse, 175–77; most disagree: Bruce, 224; Wright, 191–92; Fitzmyer, 124: "highly arbitrary").

268. E.g., Barth and Blanke, 496–97.

269. See McKnight, *Colossians*, 389, at Col 4:10a.

270. Karl Allen Kuhn, *Luke: The Elite Evangelist*, Paul's Social Network: Brothers and Sisters in Faith (Collegeville, MN: Glazier, 2010); Bruce, *The Pauline Circle*, 35–43.

271. On Paul's coworkers and fellow ministers, see Dunn, *Beginning from Jerusalem*, 566–72; Bruce, *The Pauline Circle*, 81–90; Kathy Ehrensperger, *Paul and the Dynamics of*

worked alongside and with Paul to spread the gospel and establish churches throughout the Mediterranean. That circle of "fellow workers" included not only these four *and Philemon* (Phlm 1), but also Jesus called Justus (Col 4:11), Epaphroditus (Phil 2:25), Clement (4:3), Titus (2 Cor 8:23), Priscilla and Aquila (Rom 16:3), Urbanus (16:9), and not least Timothy (16:21; 1 Tim 1:2). Paul, it must be emphasized for many pastors, was not a lone ranger but a deeply embedded and widely connected apostle and missional church planter. He led some of these to Christ, he catechized them into the faith, he mentored them into their gifts, and he expanded gospel work by sending them out and supporting their ministries. Their love, companionship, and fellowship sustained Paul as well. Not least of such persons was Epaphras of Colossae and, so it seems, Onesimus was next—if Philemon responds as Paul thinks he will.

25 The letter—as with others (Gal 6:18; 1 Thess 5:28; 2 Thess 3:18; 1 Cor 16:23–24; Col 4:18; Eph 6:23–24; Phil 4:23; 2 Cor 13:13; 1 Tim 6:21; 2 Tim 4:22)—ends (as it began in Phlm 3) on Paul's characteristic note of grace extended to the entire church ("your" is plural) at Colossae: "The grace of the Lord Jesus Christ be with your spirit." The term "grace" here is both a customary greeting for a Jew but also at least echoes the characteristic theology of grace in Paul.[272] The echo is made certain since the grace is "of the Lord Jesus Christ." This expresses the source (*from* the Lord Jesus Christ), possession (the Lord Jesus Christ's grace), or, less likely, an attribute of the grace (a Lord Jesus Christ kind of grace). He blesses the church at Colossae with a Jesus-originated grace and, as he does elsewhere (Gal 6:18; Phil 4:23; 2 Tim 4:22), directs the grace at their "spirit,"[273] revealing an anthropology in which humans can relate to God who is Spirit,[274] while also being a variant on the common "with you" (1 Thess 5:28; 1 Cor 16:23; Phil 4:23).

THE AFTERMATH?

One cannot but wonder and speculate about the response of Philemon. The majority of scholars agree that this letter survived only because it was successful in convincing Philemon to forgive, receive, and probably return

---

Power: Communication and Interaction in the Early Christ-Movement, LNTS 325 (London: T&T Clark, 2007), 35–62.

272. Again, Barclay, *Paul and the Gift*, 183–88.

273. The singular (τοῦ πνεύματος) is distributive; thus, "the spirits of all" or "your spirits" (Harris, 281). See also Gordon Fee, *God's Empowering Presence: The Holy Spirit in the Letters of Paul* (Peabody, MA: Hendrickson, 1994), 635–36.

274. Dunn, 349; also see John R. Levison, *Filled with the Spirit* (Grand Rapids: Eerdmans, 2009); John R. Levison, *Inspired: The Holy Spirit and the Mind of Faith* (Grand Rapids: Eerdmans, 2013).

Onesimus to Paul.[275] Norman R. Petersen, for instance, thinks Philemon "responded affirmatively to Paul's appeal, and that if he did not he was excommunicated"![276] Some more cautious heads admit that we do not know.[277] We are not so sanguine that this Onesimus became the bishop of Ephesus. Although Ignatius continues to fuel the imagination of exegete and homiletician alike:

> Since, therefore, I have received in God's name your whole congregation in the person of Onesimus, a man of inexpressible love who is also your earthly bishop, I pray that you will love him in accordance with the standard set by Jesus Christ and that all of you will be like him. For blessed is the one who has graciously allowed you, worthy as you are, to have such a bishop. (*Ephesians* 1.3)

I hope that is true.

275. E.g., Bruce, 200; Witherington, 86.
276. Petersen, *Rediscovering Paul*, 287.
277. Barclay, 113–19 (esp. 118–19).

Index of Subjects

Index of Authors

Index of Authors

Index of Scripture and Other Ancient Texts

EARLY CHRISTIAN TEXTS

OTHER ANCIENT TEXTS